MADE OF PEN & INK:
FLEISCHER Studios

THE NEW YORK YEARS

BY
G. MICHAEL DOBBS

inkwell productions™

inkwell productions ™

Published by
Inkwell Productions
Office of Publication:
17 Spruce Street
Springfield, MA 01105 USA

In association with
Not Dog Books

Second Edition: Revised August 2024
ISBN 978-1-7330144-4-1

Made of Pen & Ink: Fleischer Studios.
©2022 G. Michael Dobbs.
All prominently featured characters are trademarks G. Michael Dobbs.
All rights reserved. No text or artwork from or any part
of this book may be reproduced or transmitted in any form or by any means,
electronic or mechanical, including photocopying, recording, or by an
information storage and retrieval system without permission in writing from the publisher.
All rights reserved. Any similarity to persons living or dead is purely coincidental.
For more information or comments, e-mail us at gmdobbs@comcast.net

Book & cover design ©2022 Mark Masztal.

This book is dedicated to the late Myron Waldman
whose support was so important to me.

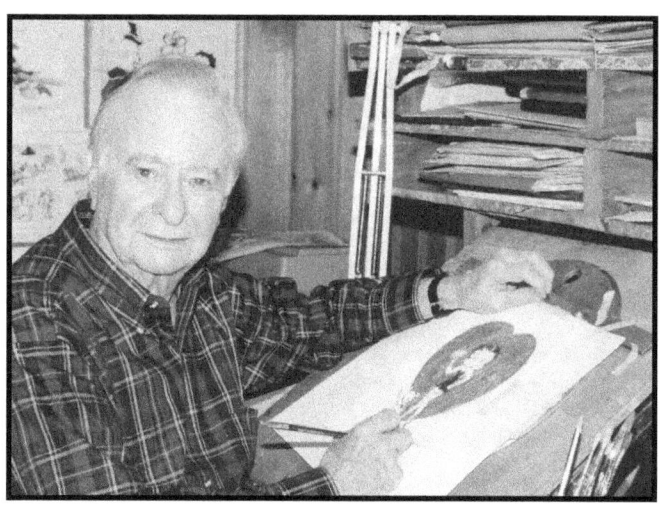

G. MICHAEL DOBBS

G. MICHAEL DOBBS

Introduction
Made of Pen and Ink: The Fleischer Studio Cartoons

Are you old enough to remember a time when someone could actually repair a television and these technicians actually came to your house to do so? Believe it or not in the 1950s and '60s that actually happened.

Our TV repairman went by the nickname of "Smiley" and he came to our house in Springfield, MA, often enough to notice something: I liked Popeye cartoons a lot. So much in fact he dubbed me "Popeye."

Your childhood does mark you.

I wound up being an animation nut. So much so that I edited and published two magazines – "Animato" and "Animation Planet" on the subject and started researching the life and career of animator and inventor Max Fleischer for a book that has proven to be my Holy Grail.

This is how this project came about.

The innocence of youth

While I was in college (University of Massachusetts, class of 1976) my love for the classic Fleischer cartoons re-asserted itself when I attended a screening of a compilation film released by a company named Crystal Pictures in 1975. The Fleischer Popeyes and Superman cartoons played a prominent role in my childhood memories.

Little had been written about the Fleischers and I decided to undertake a book on them. Ah, the innocence of youth!

I had sent a letter to Dave Fleischer in June of 1976 and in August I found an address for Max's widow and wrote her how I would like her permission to write a book on her husband and his brother Dave.

Dave replied first saying he was too busy to speak with me about a project as he was preparing a new animated feature based on the myth of Pandora's Box.

I also wrote to Max's son Richard, the successful movie director, but his son, Mark, wrote back on Sept. 5, 1976, giving me a green light and I was elated. Mark suggested that I contact Vera Coleman, his grandfather's long-time secretary, as his grandmother had not been feeling well.

"She also feels that she doesn't remember enough about the business and sequence of events to be of much help," he wrote.

I forwarded an outline that I had assembled based on my knowledge up until that point to Coleman.

However, a letter that came to me on March 1, 1977 that at first caught me off guard:

"Dear Mr. Dobbs,

"Your letter to Mrs. Vera Coleman has just been turned over to me. I'm sorry for the delay in answering but I have been in England until just a few days ago and Mrs. Coleman was waiting for my return.

"As you probably realize we receive many requests for the kind of cooperation you are seeking from people interested in writing a book about the Fleischer family. We have never cooperated for several reasons, the main one being in all cases the lack of professional writing ability. A perfect example of this is the Leslie Carbaga book…The unfortunate outcome, however, was that Carbaga went ahead with his book but without the cooperation of the Max Fleischer family, which is ninety percent of the story, the book turned out to be a completely distorted and lopsided affair full of inaccuracies and slanted so as to denigrate my father. It is interesting to note that Carbaga has subsequently realized his error and wishes he could rewrite the book.

"Another reason we have not cooperated thus far has always been the idea that either my sister [Ruth Kneitel] or myself would one day write the story. More and more this seems increasingly remote and we have just about given up that idea.

"I have read over your material and your outline carefully and I feel that perhaps you are the most qualified person I've heard from to take on this assignment. I would be able to make available to you a vast amount of material that has never been seen or utilized in any biographical study. However, I think it would be proper that if a book such as you contemplate writing with our cooperation should be published there should be a profit participation for us.

"Please let me know how and if you wish to proceed."

Max's son, Richard Fleischer, signed it.

Needless to say, I was over the moon. It looked as if I was given the green light by a guy whose work I admired – I'm still of the opinion that Richard Fleischer is a very under-rated director – on a dream project.

The nitty gritty

Still there were details to discuss and in a letter dated April 20, 1977, Richard made it clear that the project he would authorize would be a biography of his father and not a book that would present Max and Dave as equals. He also wanted a fifty-fifty split on the profits from the project.

I wrote back that my intent was to feature Max and that the split was fine. I was in no position to bargain and again, it was his family's story, not mine.

On May 10, 1977, Richard wrote back saying he was "much relieved" by the contents of my letter and answered some questions I had posed about the whereabouts about various people who had worked at the studio.

He also sent a "to whom it might concern" letter stating that I was authorized by the Max Fleischer family to write a biography.

I subsequently made an appointment with Ruth Kneitel who lived in New York. She was very gracious and talked about her father and showed me a wide variety of artifacts, which she allowed me to photograph. She also gave me information about animator Myron Waldman and how I should contact him.

After our meeting, Ruth looked over my outline and made some factual corrections.

I take the plunge

I was working in a department store at the time by day and writing freelance articles at night – a full-time journalism job hadn't come my way as yet. However, I chased down people as best I could for telephone interviews and spoke with animator Grim Natwick in April 1977. I interviewed composer Sammy Timburg during this early period as well as singer Lanny Ross who provided the singing voice for the prince in the Fleischer's first feature film "Gulliver's Travels."

I wrote British director Richard Williams about the Fleischer Raggedy Ann short. Williams had finished his own feature on the classic children's story and wrote back in a letter dated Jan. 20, 1977:

"When we started 'Raggedy Ann,' we bought a print of the Fleischer colour short from 1940 and ran it at our first animation conference with Art Babbitt, Emery Hawkins, Tissa David, John Kimball and Corneilius Cole. We were appalled and although we may not have been altogether successful in getting Raggedy Ann, as we wanted her, I hope to God we did better than they did! I must say I do like a lot of Fleischer's work but he really missed on Ann. Here's hoping we don't."

I took my slides of Ruth's memorabilia and put together a presentation that made its debut at the late Phil Seuling's – the father of all comic book conventions – Tenth Annual Comic Art Convention in July of 1977 in Philadelphia. The reception was excellent and I felt that I was on my way. I organized several screenings of Fleischer films and spoke about my research.

When the chance came to work for a company that provided reading teachers for private schools, I took it, thinking this was a way to be closer to the New York area. I exploited the locations of my three assignments in New York City, Baltimore, and Annapolis in the period of Oct. 1977 through April 1978 as best I could.

During this time, I interviewed Popeye's voice Jack Mercer, long-time Fleischer employee Edith Vernick, animator John "Wally" Walworth, and director Myron Waldman. I went to the Library of Congress, while in Maryland and the Lincoln Center library when in New York.

To a person, everyone was pleased to speak with me. The fact that Richard has given me his blessing opened many doors.

Fifty ways to say "no"

I started sending out my outline and quickly found that publishers in the late 1970s and early '80s could care less about Max Fleischer and his role in animation history. And I knew that I needed to do serious interviews with Richard and Ruth.

Ruth replied to my request in April of 1979 and stated that she didn't give interviews any longer, and although I pleaded with Richard – I still have a Western Union "Mailgram" from the summer of 1979 I sent to him – there was no interview forthcoming from him.

I got the impression that until I got a serious bite from a publisher Richard wasn't going to give me the time I needed. Although irksome, I rationalized it as a by-product of dealing with a guy who was jetting around the world making movies.

So, I continued on with interviews with people such as Hal Seeger who worked at the studio as a teen, to Alden Getz, who played a role in the bitter strike at the studio. I also met with animators Shamus Culhane and Joe Oriolo and spoke on the phone with Al Eugster.

And I kept sending out the outline, which I would revise periodically for the next nine years. Interestingly enough, one recurring theme in the rejection notices was that editors wanted a book on Popeye and Betty Boop and not on Max.

There were also several false starts from smaller publishing companies that initially accepted the book and then backed out.

The end...or not?

My career had taken an interesting course. After the teaching job, I sold ads for a local daily newspaper and then landed a reporter's job at another daily. That led to an editor's job at another newspaper. I then spent five years on local talk radio as an evening drive time host. A gig as the program supervisor for a historic house museum followed. When the city cut the funding for the job, I was hired as the manager of a new independent first-run theater in our area.

I continued to write freelance articles and columns on my Fleischer research.

Through 1988 I carried on with my research. I had stopped communicating with Richard, as I didn't see the point unless I had good news. In September of 1988 I learned that Richard was working with Layla Productions on a book. The book packaging company was seeking a writer and I wrote a long letter to Richard asking for the chance to work on the project.

"You certainly have been tenacious about the Max Fleischer book and I certainly commend you for that. But I'm sure you will understand when I tell you that ten years without attracting a publisher doesn't exactly instill confidence in the future of your project," he wrote back on Sept, 12, 1988.

But he did give me another chance. Lori Stein, president of Layla Productions wrote me on Oct. 13, 1988, that Attorney Stanley Handman had given her my letter to Richard and that she was interested in collaborating with me. I set up an appointment to see her in New York.

She had worked on a book on the Warner Brothers cartoons and wanted to do something similar for the Betty Boop cartoons. She had a very impressive mock-up of some laid out pages, but I dropped a bomb that she hadn't considered. She wanted to do an opulent full-color book and I told her only one Betty Boop cartoon had been in color.

The book never went forward.

My last efforts were an exchange with a publisher in 1989 as well as a meeting with a literary agent who wanted me to write the book in a narrative style. At that time, I was tired of rejection, tired of people asking me when the book was coming out and tired of people wondering who was Max Fleischer.

So, I gave up. I never wrote Richard Fleischer. I'm sure he figured it out.

When my former business partner and I bought "Animato" – a magazine devoted to animation – in 1992, I thought that this would be the vehicle for sharing some of my research. As I said before, the articles I wrote were well received and that was quite gratifying.

When I ceased publication on my second animation magazine in 1997 "Animation Planet" – because of the dwindling ad base and increasingly unfavorable distribution deals – I had planned another lengthy Fleischer piece.

A book on the rise of adult animation I had planned with a writing partner almost got a contract at St. Martin's in 2000. A change in editors doomed that project. It would have had substantial material on the Fleischer shorts.

For more 20 years, I've been the managing editor of a group of weekly newspapers serving more than 200,000 readers in the Springfield, MA, area. I write about animation every chance I get – I did a lengthy interview piece with Joe Dante on his "Loony Tunes Back in Action" feature, an interview with cartoon voice legend and Springfield native June Foray and another on Academy Award nominated independent animator Bill Plympton, among others.

Much of what I've written about animation was collected and revised for my book, "Escape: Animation went Mainstream in the 1990s" (Bear Manor Media, 2007).

Richard Fleischer finally wrote a book about his father himself. "Out of the Inkwell: Max Fleischer and the Animation Revolution," was an unabashed love letter to his father. Although it offered many insights, it also contained a number of errors – especially about the creation of Betty Boop. Richard died in 2006, a year after the publication of his book and five years after the passing of his sister Ruth.

With the advent of the Internet, I decided to place some of the material on a blog dedicated to the book. It received much positive reaction and so I was encouraged once again to seek a publisher.

With the subsequent revolution in publishing technology I decided to self-publish.

The Fleischer material still called to me and after over many years the cartoons produced by the studio are still influencing new generations of animators and finding new audiences. How many times do you see an image of Betty Boop somewhere – on clothing, on bumper stickers, purses and dolls? The enduring popularity of that character alone says something about the legacy of the Fleischer Studio.

It would be easy enough to reduce a discussion of the Fleischer Studio cartoons – the studio that brought Ko-Ko the Clown, Popeye the Sailor, Betty Boop and Superman to movie screens – and the men and women who made them to simply either an exercise of nostalgia or a timeline of technical achievements.

It would also be simple to paint the Fleischer story in dark colors – how the personal differences between two brothers in business together ultimately cost each of them their careers and how their dependence on a corporate partner doomed them.

The story of the Fleischer Studio is all of the above and much more. It is a story of artists creating an ephemeral product that turned out to be enduring and influential.

Don't take my word for it. Just look around. The Fleischers come up as inspirations with a lot of contemporary animators such as Academy Award nominated animator Bill Plympton and "Ren and Stimpy" creator John Kricfalusi. Frank Miller – the comic book artist responsible for "Sin City" and "300" – credited Max and Dave Fleischer in his seminal "Dark Knight" comic book series that revived and re-defined Batman. Warner Bros. Animation turned to the design of the Fleischer Superman cartoons as inspiration for its first "Batman" cartoon series. That circle construction and rubber-limbed look that the Fleischers did the best remains a favorite of art directors. And the Japanese love of Betty Boop was the basis of that big-eyed look prevalent in many manga and anime.

The Fleischer's "Follow the Bouncing Ball" is a pop culture icon that is still used today. It's simply part of the American landscape.

Max's invention of the Rotoscope has remained one of the standard tools in special effects. I doubt, though, that the critics who lavished praise of the 2006 release of "A Scanner Darkly" understood that the device that made the execution of the film possible was developed before the First World War.

The Fleischer cartoons still loom very large on the animation horizon.

The focus of this book

Something I've come to realize is there is a generation of animation fans who know something of the legacy of the Fleischer Studio but may not have had the opportunity of seeing as many of the cartoons they would like to see.

Unlike my generation, which saw many of these cartoons on television and then revisited them through home video, the availability of many of these shorts has been limited to watching material on YouTube and the release of several vital collections on DVD/Blu Ray.

Readers will see that I have noted where to see featured cartoons – yes, some of them are on YouTube – in current collections.

My goal is to give new animation fans information on how these cartoons were made and why they are worth watching. This is not a formal biography of either Max or Dave Fleischer, but a story of a different scope.

And yes, the second volume is in the works.

Many thanks

This book could not have been made possible without the help of many, many people.

First and foremost is my wife Mary who has supported my interest almost since she first met me for more than 40 years ago. Thank you for everything.

My late mother Sue and father Gordon may have been mystified at times by my interests, but they never discouraged me.

Rosalie Waldman and her late husband Myron became very important friends and mentors to my wife and me.

Although things did not work out as they had hoped, I sincerely thank the late Richard Fleischer and Ruth Kneitel for their initial approval and help.

The men and the women of the Fleischer Studio who took their time to tell their stories to me were uniformly kind and generous. They included Jack Mercer, Mae Questel, John Walworth, Seymour Reit, Joe Oriolo, James "Shamus" Culhane, Edith Vernick, Al Eugster, Grim Natwick, Sammy Timberg, Alden Getz, Hal Seeger and Hi Neigher.

Other people who provided invaluable opinion and information were JJ Sedelmaier, David Gerstein, Len Kohl, Stephen Worth, Ray Pointer, Karl Cohen, Mark Langer, Patricia Timberg, Jackson Beck, Bill Melendez, George Evelyn, Ron Magliozzi and Dan Dalton.

Donald Crafton's essential book "Before Mickey" was an inspiration, as was Leonard Maltin's "Of Mice and Magic." Thank you to both authors.

Others that deserve a tip of Ko-Ko's hat include the late Richard Gordon, Stephen R. Bissette, Joseph Citro, Patrick Dobbs, as well as Kyle Macabee, the late David Mruz, Jerry Beck and the late Michael Sporn for their good will and help.

My friend, the talented artist Mark Masztal, designed this book and I deeply appreciate his help.

G. Michael Dobbs
2022

Foreword
By J.J. Sedelmaier

I was thrilled when Mike told me that he was embarking on a set of books about the Fleischer Studios! I knew it would be handled with both enthusiasm and affection. This project of Mike's has been in the works for decades, and the fact that he was able to meet and talk to so many of the important artists and Fleischer personalities while they were still with us, sets his work on a terrifically solid foundation. I value too, his choice to try and put some of the previously written histories in context.

The history of the Fleischer Studios isn't simply the story of an immigrant family or even the animation industry. It's the epitome of the traditional American tale of opportunity coming to those willing to dedicate themselves to hard work. Through the generosity and encouragement of the descendants of brother Lou and Joe Fleischer, I recently became somewhat of a Fleischer Family Archivist. I have scanned, transferred, and restored thousands of photographs, films and other pieces of family ephemera from all aspects of the entire family. There's no better way to become acquainted with any family than continuously looking into the eyes of the family members throughout their lives. I feel I know these folks intimately. Mike's book made me feel even closer to all the Fleischers!

The other aspect of Mike's work in this volume that I was so pleased to experience was the feel for what it must've been like to watch the early animation industry evolve in New York City. The work of the Fleischers often reflected and took inspiration from their New York roots and presence. Sometimes it was the music, sometimes it was their urban themes and scenarios, and it always had a gritty, edgy quality. The animation industry started in the NYC area. It grew up along side the motion picture itself. Pioneers like the Fleischers, Bray, McCay, and J. Stuart Blackton, all carved out their careers – and their fledgling industry, in New York City.

Through the years, most of the focus on Fleischer Studios seemed to center around their cartoons starring Ko-Ko the Clown, Betty Boop and Popeye. But thanks to some recent publications, as well as efforts on the part of film restorers and archivists, and now the book you hold in your hands (as well as the volume following), we're getting the whole picture. The family, the artists, the inventions, and the struggles – both external and from within. Much of what caused the demise of their studio and the Paramount takeover stemmed from internal familial conflict. Volume 2 will explain in detail.

Finally, I should tell you all that the work of the Fleischer Studios was what made me say, "That! I wanna do THAT!"

Once I discovered their "Superman" series of the early 1940s, it was the first time that my interest in an art career had a more defined mission.

Thanks to television "Kiddie Shows," I'd always been a fan of everything from the hilarious

Warner Brothers cartoons, to the beautiful (but never hilarious) Disney fare, but I'd never seen anything like the Fleischers' cartoons depicting the "Man Of Steel"! I have felt so fortunate these past 40 years, to have come up through the ranks along side journeypeople in the New York animation community. And so many of them had their roots in the Fleischer/Famous Studio legacy. A legacy that not only helped create and define New York animation, but an industry as a whole.

J.J. and Patrice Sedelmaier founded J.J. Sedelmaier Productions, Inc. (JJSP) in 1990 and since then the animation and design studio has been recognized with more than 600 awards of recognition from films and print competitions in 25 countries.

Among the studio's many credits is being exclusive animation house for the first three seasons of the SNL "Funhouse" films, designing characters and animating such memorable series as "The X-Presidents," "Fun with Real Audio," "Animated Outtakes" and "The Ambiguously Gay Duo" (originally designed by J. J. Sedelmaier himself, and created by JJSP and Robert Smigel for the short-lived "Dana Carvey Show"). JJSP developed the pilot episode of "Harvey Birdman Attorney at Law," with Cartoon Network, that helped initiate the Network's Adult Swim block of cartoons. JJSP was also the studio entrusted by MTV to animate the first season of MTV's "Beavis & Butt-Head."

The cast of characters

There were two advantages I had in starting this project in the late 1970s. The first was the fact that Richard Fleischer approved of my involvement at least initially and therefore allowed his sister Ruth Kneitel to speak with me.

Ruth welcomed me into her New York City apartment, and was very supportive. She allowed me to photograph memorabilia of her father's and she opened doors for me by telling former studio personnel that I was worth their interview time.

The other advantage was the fact that in that time period there were still many people alive who had worked for the studio. With the exception of Dave Fleischer, who declined an interview because of lack of time due to his work on an animated feature based on the myth of Pandora's Box and Lou Fleischer who simply sent me a note starting he did not wish to speak about the subject, everyone else I approached was candid and receptive.

This book contains interviews from the following people:

Myron Waldman

Of all of the interviews I conducted the one with Myron meant the most as it blossomed into a friendship that lasted until his death in 2006. He was my mentor.

Myron was not only a skilled animator; he was also an independent at the Fleischer Studio, a guy who earned respect from Max and Dave for being willing to speak his mind.

He didn't care for productions with supernatural themes, horror or violence and became known for his mastery of sentiment. He called them "ooh, ah" pictures. He directed more Betty Boop cartoons than anyone else and created Betty's dog, Pudgy.

I first met Myron in a studio in mid-town Manhattan where he was still working at a time when most of his colleagues had retired. He and his wife Rosalie became friends and mentors. He didn't believe in full retirement and continued to draw to the time of his death at the age of 97.

Jack Mercer

The man who was the voice of Popeye from 1935 to his death in 1984 invited me into his home in the Woodside section of New York City for an interview. A modest, soft-spoken gentleman, Jack had never received any screen credit as Popeye's voice until the Robert Altman/Robin Williams "Popeye" feature in 1980. The thought of that injustice continues to anger me.

Mercer worked as a story man at Fleischer and then at Famous Studios, which provided him screen credit. The lack of credit for the voice of Popeye created confusion with claims from other voice actors who tried to claim the body of work as their own. I wish Jack had lived long enough to have attended pop culture conventions at which he would have seen how his work was revered by animation fans. Talk to voice actors today – as I have – and they express their admiration for his talent.

Mae Questel

The actress who was most closely associated with Betty Boop and Olive Oyl and I never formally had a chance for a formal interview, although there were letters exchanged and I spent an evening with her at a Sons of the Desert meeting in Connecticut – the Stan Laurel and Oliver Hardy fan club – where we talked. Unlike Mercer, Questel pursued an acting career in front of the camera that included in her later years a stint on Scott paper towel commercials as "Aunt Bluebell" and a final performance as Betty Boop in "Who Framed Roger Rabbit" in 1988.

Lanny Ross

Lanny was the first person I interviewed about his involvement with the studio. A very popular singer on radio, in the 1930s, Lanny provided the singing voice for Prince David in "Gulliver's Travels." He also appeared in several other musicals for Paramount.

His appearance, along with singer Jessica Dragonette, marked the first time an animated feature used celebrity voices.

A Yale graduate and former attorney before his success in show business, Lanny and I met at his private club, The University Club in New York City. He was dapper, charming and answered my every question.

Still active as a performer when I spoke to him, Lanny had an ad in Variety that read, "I've not forgotten you. Don't forget me." He passed in 1982.

Grim Natwick

Another early interview was a telephone call to Grim Natwick, a seminal figure in animation history whose involvement in the art started in 1919. Grim was the designer of Betty Boop and later returned to the studio to work on "Gulliver's Travels."

He provided an interesting comparison between the Disney and Fleischer Studios for me.

Natwick lived to 100 and his last animation work was in the Richard Williams film "The Thief and the Cobbler."

Shamus Culhane

James "Shamus" Culhane was a fascinating figure in animation who got his start the Fleischer Studio. When a number of skilled animators left for another studio Culhane was suddenly elevated into the position and did so well he left for the West Coast and stints at Ub Iwerks and Walt Disney Studios. He came back to Fleischer to work on "Gulliver's Travels" and then went to the Walter Lantz Studio.

Talking to me in his New York City home, Shamus was highly opinionated. We started off with a warm relationship, but that later soured when I wrote a critical review of his memoir "Talking Animals of Other People." I last saw him at an animation conference in Ottawa, Canada in the mid 1990s and heard him ask someone, "Hey is that the guy who didn't like my book?"

He passed in 1996.

Al Eugster

Shamus Culhane gave me the phone number for Al Eugster, the veteran animator and his friend. Al provided me with great observations on the earliest days of the Fleischer Studio after its rebirth from the bankruptcy of the Red Seal operation. Like Shamus Culhane and Grim Natwick, he worked on both "Snow White" and "Gulliver's Travels." He died in 1997.

Edith Vernick

Starting an as office employee in the 1920s, Vernick later became the supervisor of the In Between Department. She was given a try-out as an animator on the "The Fresh Vegetable Mystery" and while her animation was good, animator Myron Waldman told me she was too slow.

I interviewed her in her retirement home at Atlantic City, NJ, in the late 1970s. I had been warned she was quite a character and she lived up to the description by regaling me with stories of her time with the Fleischers as well as working for others in animation.

At one point she worked for Larry Harmon, the owner of the Bozo the Clown character and the producer of the "Bozo" cartoons as well as a series of cartoons based on the screen characters of Stan Laurel and Oliver Hardy.

"Larry Harmon is a schmuck. Do you know what schmuck is, Michael? It's a penis. Larry Harmon is a penis," she said flatly and definitely.

Joe Oriolo

I met the veteran Fleischer animator in his New York City office. Although he worked on both of the Fleischer features as well as the "Raggedy Ann" Christmas two-reeler, Joe was best known for his series of "Felix the Cat" cartoons he produced for television, as well as his series "The Mighty Hercules."

He claimed he had created "Casper the Friendly Ghost" to me, which was not true, as Seymour Reit, the writer behind the character, told me.

Joe was eventually able to obtain to the full rights to the Felix the Cat, which is now controlled by his son Don.

Joe told me a wild story about animator Nick Tafuri and him. He said that he would bug Tafuri about Tafuri's brother who was a soldier in combat in Europe, Tafuri became tired of Joe's insistence for war stories – according to Joe – and rigged the drawer in his desk so he could slip his penis into it and then into a small box. When Joe next came over to him, Tafuri said to the effect, "You want to see what my brother took off a German soldier" and showed him the box. Joe was so startled that he dropped his cigar on Tafuri's penis.

He died in 1985.

John Walworth

An animator at Fleischers, "Wally" was a gracious host to me in his home in Delaware. He had stayed on with the studio when it made its transition to Famous Studios and had designed the model sheet for the first "Casper the Friendly Ghost" cartoons. Before coming to Fleischers he had worked for animation producer Ted Espaugh.

Many of the models sheets in this book came from his collection.

His career after animation was successful. He became a designer for toy giveaways from Cracker Jacks and other companies. He told me at that time – the late 1970s – that Cracker Jacks was cutting back on the budget for its iconic "prize inside," which made his work more difficult.

Alden Getz

Getz, who was a member of the animation staff, invited me into his Park Avenue home and fed me lunch – a nice surprise – before our interview which centered on the labor strike at the studio prior to the studio's move to Miami, FL. He had been involved in the talks with Max Fleischer about establishing a union. After animation, he worked in advertising.

Hal Seeger

Seeger got his start at the Fleischer Studio at a young age as an office boy, but later got the opportunity to do some animation work. Perhaps his most significant contribution to the story of this book is how he revived the Koko the Clown character with a series of TV cartoons in the early 1960s. Seeger recalled that many of the people who had worked for Max wanted the rights to the character but Max was resistant. Apparently though he liked Seeger's presentation and Seeger filmed a pilot with Max playing himself as he had in the 1920s. Myron Waldman was the director of the pilot and he told me that Max dyed his hair for the filming. Seeger lived until 2005.

Hi Neigher

I was surprised to learn that a Fleischer Studio alumnus lived near me in Longmeadow, MA, but Neigher, a writer, artist and advertising man, did and we became friendly. He lent me items from his collection that have found their way into this book. He reached the age of 100 by the time he died in 2015.

Sammy Timberg

Composer and performer Sammy was an important part of Fleischer cartoons as he wrote many original and memorable songs for both Betty Boop and Popeye. His impressive compositions for the studio's Superman cartoons showed the breath of his talent. A show-biz veteran, I interviewed him by phone in 1977. At the time he was retired and living in Scranton, PA. Later I met and spoke with his daughter Patricia who produced a CD of new recordings of some of her father's songs. He passed in 1992.

Jackson Beck

Beck worked with both Mae Questel and Jack Mercer on the Famous Studios Popeye cartoons – he played Bluto – and provided insights about each performer. His voice perhaps was one of most heard in this country with a lengthy career in radio followed by years of work in television commercials and voice acting for animation. He appeared on camera in the 1986 film "Power." He died in 2004.

Pauline Comaner

The artist who was hired to appear on behalf of the Fleischer Studio to make promotional appearances was interviewed when she appeared near my home to publicize a children's book featuring her character "Chunky Monkey." She died in 2005.

Dan Dalton, Bill Melendez, George Evelyn

These three men were involved in different efforts to revive the Betty Boop character. Dalton produced the feature "Hurray for Betty Boop," which recycled original footage, now colorized, with a new soundtrack. Melendez made half-hour TV special "The Romance of Betty Boop," while Evelyn made "Betty Boop's Hollywood Mystery," definitely the most successful in presenting the spirit of the original cartoons.

Gordon Sheehan and David Tendlar

Interviews with veteran Fleischer and Famous animators Sheehan and Tendlar were conducted by film historian Leonard J. Kohl, who graciously supplied them for this project.

A word about these cartoons:

This book is about an animation studio active from just after World War I through the spring of 1942. This was a time in American popular culture when ethnic humor and stereotypes were every day elements of vaudeville, movies, radio shows, comic strip and novels.

This was an era in which one of the most popular radio shows in the nation starred two white men portraying stereotypical and racist depictions of African-Americans. It was a time the sound movie that was credited with ending the silent period had sequences of its star in black face. It was also a time one of the most highly visible and highly paid African-American actors in film portrayed a character that was slow, lazy and dim-witted. The most popular Asian-American character in movies was played by a succession of white actors and Native American characters in film and radio were almost always played by white actors as well.

Although the Fleischer Studios did not have on-going characters that were negative stereotypes – unlike other studios – there are moments of ethnic humor that are not positive, especially when viewed today. There are Asian and Black stereotypes in some of these cartoons and especially through the early 1930s, there are gags revolving around Jewish elements, often a reflection of the ethnic backgrounds of some of the Fleischer staff members.

I don't agree with the use of ethnic stereotypes in pop culture, but I have to acknowledge their existence and the pain they can cause today.

When examining any element of popular culture, context is essential and discussion is important. The Fleischer Studio made many wonderful and groundbreaking cartoons that are still influencing animation today. It should be celebrated for that accomplishment without ignoring moments that no longer justifiable.

Chapter One
Art and mechanics: a strange combination

Will there ever be a technology married to an art form that will have as much impact on modern society as motion pictures?

It is difficult to truly imagine how the first motion picture audiences must have felt when they gathered to see the works of the Lumiere Brothers at the end of the 19th century. There are reports that sophisticated French audiences gasped and moved out of the way when they saw footage of a train arriving into a station in a Dec. 28, 1895 showing.

Consider for a moment that the experience of seeing moving photography on a large screen basically had no precedent for these early audiences. While the Internet has changed our lives today, its form and function were not shocking to us.

The literal reproduction of everyday life was indeed startling and when early filmmakers began to realize that motion pictures could be used for telling stories that normally would have been considered for the stage, new horizons were discovered.

Like the development of the linotype and wood pulp paper, which made the mass production of books and newspapers possible, motion picture technology created a way for people to share drama, humor, and fact with breathtaking immediacy.

When French stage magician and theatrical producer George Melies discovered through an accident that a wagon was transformed into a hearse on street scene footage he was filming, the reputation of cinema changed from being a medium that mirrors reality to one that could create a reality. Melies became one of the most celebrated filmmakers of this earliest era by producing hundreds of short "trick" films that exploited the strengths of the new medium.

It was in this heady time of pioneers that two men emerged who changed the face of motion pictures forever.

Film scholars credit Emile Cohl and J. Stuart Blackton as the fathers of cartoon animation. Blackton, a cartoonist turned film producer, was one of the partners in the Vitagraph Company. He used a chalkboard to create crude animation in 1905. Blackton had come from a rich stage tradition known as the "lightning artist." These artists, who were a staple of vaudeville, would create humorous drawings in a matter of moments. Blackton used many of the non-animated tricks developed by Melies, in his 1906 "Humorous Phases of Funny Faces," but also began to actually animate as well.

A French caricaturist and avant-garde artist, Cohl took Blackton's idea and went further. His film, "Fantasmagorie" in 1908, established much of the format of what we know now as animated cartoons.

It was made of sequential drawings – 700 of them – and had a central character that appeared in other Cohl films. It also originated connecting the action on the screen with an artist by showing the artist's hand at work creating the drawings.

Motion pictures were quickly becoming one of the most collaborative artistic mediums. Cohl's inclusion of his hand was a reminder that there was a single person behind these moving drawings – a convention adapted by many subsequent artists even when a studio of artists and technicians produced the film.

Cohl was a live-action filmmaker as well and he integrated animated sequences into his live action comedies. In his 1909 film, "Les Joyeaux Microbes," a doctor invites a patient to take a look into a microscope. There he sees a series of gags in which microorganisms transform themselves into human faces.

In 1909, Cohl was the first to combine animation and live action through the use of matte photography in the film "Clair de Lune Espagnol."

"Le Peintre néo-impressionniste," made the next year, had the animated sequences as canvases presented by an artist to a potential client. Although "Les Joyeaux Microbes," used pen and ink on paper as the animated medium, this film featured hinged cut-out paper figures that were introduced by a vaudeville "lightning" sketch.

"Bewitched Matches," showed what happened when a father shooed away a "witch" about to tell his daughter's fortunes. She manages to put a spell on his matches, which move in a variety of ways, terrifying the father.

Another Cohl accomplishment was his producing the first animated series. He made 13 shorts based on the George McManus comic strip "The Newlyweds" from 1912-13.

Cohl's films were highly popular and influential on both sides of the Atlantic. However, the First World War essentially halted Cohl's career in animation. His last live-action motion pictures were made in 1921. And he faded from sight and memory for many years. He died in France in near obscurity in 1938.

By today's standards the stick figure drawings are crude, but Cohl – and to a lesser extent Blackton – deserve their credit as the men who developed the rudiments of animation. In many ways, Cohl was the D.W. Griffith of animation. He developed techniques and conventions that others would follow. There would be many innovations made, but they were always built on the foundation laid by Cohl.

***

It was another artist out of vaudeville who brought animation up to a new level: Winsor McCay. Still celebrated today for his incredible imagination and draftsmanship in his comic strips such as "Little Nemo in Slumberland" and "Dreams of a Rarebit Fiend," McCay was also an accomplished stage performer who was a vaudeville star as early as 1906.

McCay has been often described – sometimes by himself – as "the father of animation." He wasn't, of course. As a seasoned vaudeville performer and newspaper artist, McCay understood the necessity of hyperbole to sell himself in show business.

What McCay did do was to elevate the art of the animated film. He took his time to create films with the kind of detailed art one saw in his comic strips. This attention to detail was timely and costly, but since McCay was producing the films himself, he apparently didn't care what it took to achieve his artistic goal.

In 1911, McCay had begun using his first film, one based on "Little Nemo," as part of his vaudeville act. His next film, though, became the one for which he is still known today, "Gertie the Dinosaur."

Gertie is the first "character driven" film. The humor comes naturally out of the personality McCay established rather than through a succession of gags. Gertie, although looking like a brontosaurus, is just a pet – an occasionally willful one – but a pet none-the-less.

McCay broke new ground in animation again in 1918 with the release of "The Sinking of the Lusitania." For the first time, animation was being used to portray a real event and to make an overt political statement.

2-page Trade Ad for Winsor McCay's dramatic use of animation "The Sinking of the Lusitania." Author's collection.

McCay's films were the product of one artist, with the help of an assistant. For the busy cartoonist and illustrator, they were a sideline to his career, though. McCay made only six films that were released to theaters, plus three more that were never completed, from 1911 to 1921.

McCay's films edged closer to fine art, reflecting his superior draftsmanship, than any other animated film seen in theaters during that time. They were like boutique cartoons, charming and breath-taking single works.

For those who didn't share McCay's vision of animation reflecting in motion what artists could accomplish in print, animation presented a bruising reality. No matter how much audiences might enjoy it, it was expensive to produce.

The problem remained on how to make animation cost efficient.

***

It was the combined vision of two men who made commercial animation possible. John R. Bray and Earl Hurd were both artists and animators who sought a way to conquer the crushing costs and time needed to produce animation.

Hurd's 1914 invention of using transparent cels instead of paper as the medium for animation drawings was the key to affordable animation. Up until then, artists had to re-draw everything in the scene over and over, including backgrounds. The clear acetate cels meant the illustrative elements that comprised sequences could be broken down and only those elements that actually moved needed to be re-drawn.

Artists could draw a background one time and use it over and over for a sequence. For instance, McCay and his assistant re-drew the background mountains in "Gertie" on every rice paper drawing.

A character could be drawn on one cel and only those parts of his body that moved needed to be drawn again on other cels.

Bray's contribution was borrowing the division of labor from manufacturing. Bray understood that one artist could not produce an animated film like they would a comic strip. For this he was called "the Henry Ford of animation."

Cels enabled producers to establish an assembly line to produce animation in a cost-effective manner and Bray and Hurd's collective patents made them the industry leaders.

Taking a page out of Thomas Edison's playbook – who tried to control the film industry by making producers take out licenses on cameras and other equipment – Bray and Hurd then enforced their patents, making other animation companies buy a license from them if they wanted to use the techniques they developed.

What Bray and Hurd did was to wrestle the medium of animation away from individual artists and make it commercially feasible. One person could guide an animation studio, but one person couldn't do all of the artistic chores.

In Edison's motion picture career, while he made money through patent enforcement, his films were soon artistically eclipsed. The same in many ways happened to Hurd and Bray. Although Bray's "Col. Heeza Lair" was a staple in the early silent era, Pat Sullivan's Felix and the Cat and Max Fleischer's Ko-Ko the Clown shorts surpassed it in popularity.

In animation, it was the people who used the technology more effectively than those who developed it who are remembered.

***

Max Fleischer was one of the second generation of cartoon animators, artists who followed pioneers such as McCay, Cohl and Blackton. Max was just a teenager when Blackton produced his first animated films that used a chalkboard instead of paper and pen.

Max's "class" included Paul Terry of Terrytoons and Mighty Mouse fame and Walter Lantz, the father of Woody Woodpecker, both of whom had long and successful careers. Unlike Terry and Lantz, though, Max was something more than just an artist. He was an inventor and innovator.

It's no wonder that Max was attracted to animation and its combination of art and science.

Born July 19, 1883, Max immigrated with his family to the United States from Krakow, Poland when he was four or five years old. Max's father, William, was a tailor, specializing in riding outfits for the upper classes. The family settled in New York City and had a shop at 69 West 46th Street in Manhattan.

Courtesy of JJ Sedelmaier.

Max was the second eldest child in a family of four other boys and one girl. The talents of his brothers and his relationship as the leader of the Fleischer siblings would later prove to be an asset to Max's adult career.

Lou, (left) Joe, (right) and in the front, Dave Fleischer.
Both photos are dated 1897.
Courtesy of JJ Sedelmaier.

Max described the roles his siblings played at the Fleischer Studio in a 1939 autobiographic essay.

"I have four brothers. Dave is the director. Joe is the electrician. Lou is in the music department. Charlie is the machinist. I have one sister – Ethel – whose job is being married."

In a 1980 interview conducted by animator Ray Pointer, Lou Fleischer said that his father's business was successful until ready-to-wear garments became popular. Despite an effort by the elder Fleischer to enlarge his operation so he could sell to wholesalers, his business failed and the family moved from Manhattan to Brooklyn.

A label designed to be sewn into the custom-made garments shows the address of 69 West 46th St, New York City. The location is now a retail store.

There was an additional Fleischer brother, Sol, whom Lou said died at age two of typhoid fever.

In photos supplied to this author through courtesy of Sedelmaier, taken in 1897, Louis and Joe are seen with younger brother Dave, who is dressed in a gown. In another photo, Max is standing on a bike next to Charles.

Max's daughter, the late Ruth Kneitel, showed this writer yellowing notebooks that attested to Max's childhood love of drawing. Max attended the public schools of New York, the Art Student's League, Cooper Institute, The Mechanics and Trademen's School and the New York Evening High.

Surviving comic strips from Max's days at the "Brooklyn Eagle" at the turn-of-the-century show an interest in humor. Fleischer started as a copy boy at the newspaper and eventually became a staff artist, a position he left to go to "Popular Science Magazine" as its art editor. At his new position, Fleischer produced many two-color illustrations of engines and other machines.

At age 21, Max married Ethel (Essie) Gold and subsequently had a family of two children; his eldest was Ruth who eventually married Fleischer Studio artist Seymour Kneitel, and the youngest was Richard who became a prominent and successful film director.

Charles and Max Fleischer are seen on with a bike – Max is riding it.

Max wrote in his 1939 autobiography, "I worked with cartoons ever since I can remember – even when I went to school. My first job was with the 'Brooklyn Daily Eagle' in the art department. Got $2 a week running errands. I was willing to pay them $2 a week to let me in.

I was advanced and became a cartoonist on the 'Eagle.' Then I went into the photoengraving business and stayed in that business for a number of years. I became art editor of the 'Popular Science Monthly' and while I was in their employ, I realized I was not only artistically inclined, but had a very keen and instinctive sense for mechanics. I liked them both. A strange combination. To me, machinery was an art, also. I still see great art in machinery."

Ruth Kneitel had originals of Max's artwork when I met her in 1977. She had a pen and ink original of a comic strip Max did when at the "Brooklyn Eagle" and several paintings of various machines he did for "Popular Science." The paintings are small masterpieces of the use of gray tones to portray the shine of metal surfaces.

This fascination with machinery became a recurring theme in Fleischer cartoons. Perhaps the most famous is "A Dream Walking," in which Popeye tries to rescue a sleep walking Olive Oyl as she passes through a construction site narrowly making missteps on moving girders.

***

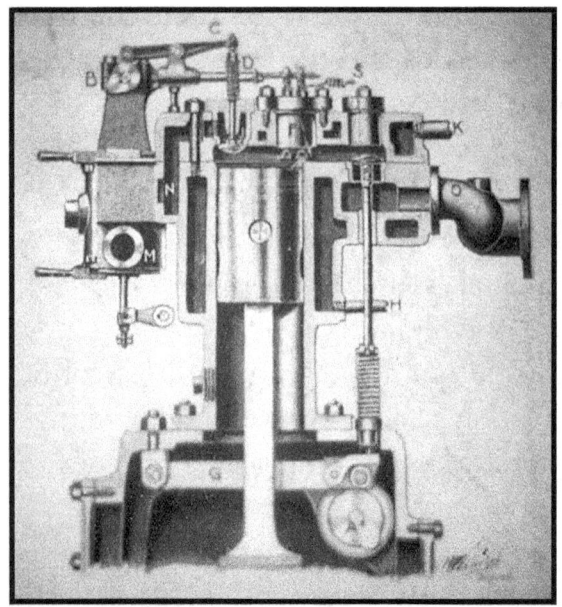
Max's mastery of black, white and gray tones can be seen in this painting he did for Popular Science. Courtesy of Ruth Kneitel.

In the new medium of animation, finding the artists who could imagine movement in their minds and then construct the sequence of drawings to convey that movement to the screen was not easy. Undoubtedly the cost of labor was one of the most significant expenses in the industry.

Perhaps that's why Bray was intrigued by Max's invention of the Rotoscope.

The Rotoscope was designed to produce life-like movements by tracing over individual frames of live-action footage. The skills of the artists did not have to be as developed when working with the Rotoscope and yet the results were very life-like.

"While working with the 'Popular Science Monthly,' I had an opportunity to write technical articles on the latest inventions and I began to wonder whether it wouldn't be possible for me to apply cartoons to the mechanics and make it a practical thing for producing motion picture cartoons by machinery," Max wrote in his 1939 essay.

The first rotoscoped film was begun in 1915, the year after "Gertie the Dinosaur's" debut. The youngest Fleischer brother, Dave, had always shown an interest in show business, and he was photographed on the roof of Max's Brooklyn apartment building cavorting in his clown suit. The live-action footage was then projected one frame at a time onto a frosted glass plate that was part of a drawing board. The animator could then trace the movements of the live action, frame by frame onto paper or cels. The completed drawings were then photographed, and the first rotoscoped cartoon was made. The Fleischer brothers, which also included Joe, worked at night in Max's apartment with improvised equipment, and the production took two years to complete.

Max patented the Rotoscope in 1915. It is still a basic tool in the special effects field more than 100 years after Max developed it.

It should be noted that within the family there were disputes that lingered for decades about the extent each brother – Dave and Joe – contributed to the development of the Rotoscope. A letter from Dave to Joe in the 1970s reflected Dave's long concern about receiving the proper credit for the Rotoscope for both him and Joe.

Max recalled an anecdote that described the origins of the name "Out of the Inkwell," which was ultimately the name of Max's studio and his first cartoon series. Max wrote of an accident during the production of the first rotoscoped cartoon. Late one evening in 1917, Max and his brothers Dave and Joe knew they were in serious trouble. They had been testing the patience of Max's wife Essie by working nightly in her parlor on Max's animated cartoon, but now they were worried. A bottle of India ink had fallen off their worktable and had left an indelible stain on her prized carpet. No amount of soaking or scrubbing could lift the blot, so, quietly they re-arranged the furniture to hide it.

"At the time I was making these experiments, I explained the idea to my brother Dave. Told him I had applied for a patent. I used up every cent I had on the machine with which I was experimenting – about $100. I explained the system I intended to use and he was fascinated by it. He couldn't sleep any more. We built the machine but we had nowhere to work it, so our [sic] missus said we could use the living room, if we didn't upset it too much. But we wanted a place that no one could disturb during the day because I was working at 'Popular Science.' We would meet at night and work after hours, from seven in the evening until three or four every morning. We would close the doors and ask our missus not to disturb us. We did make the room look very bad, I guess. We had electric wires from the chandeliers, motors, etc. But we didn't want anyone to go in there until we were through, for the slightest disturbance would upset our work," he wrote.

The first production took the Fleischer brothers almost a year to make and ran only 100 feet – about a minute's worth of footage.

Max made the rounds of the New York studios with his test reel with initially no luck and recalled in 1939, "I took the film to a distributor and in the blink of the eye it was run off. He said, 'That's very nice. What are you going to do with it?' I said, 'I don't know. I just thought it was something. That's all.' He said, 'Could you make one of these every week?' I laughed. 'Why no, it's a physical impossibility.' 'How long did it take you to make this thing?' he asked. 'It took a year.' 'My dear fellow, go home and make something practical. If you had something, we could offer for sale every week or every month, you'd have something, but once a year – Nix.'"

He finally found some interest at Famous Players where a colleague from the "Brooklyn Eagle" was in charge of short subjects, J.R. Bray.

Bray realized Fleischer's film had beautiful fluid movement and was impressed enough to hire Max and Dave Fleischer. World War One interrupted Bray's plans to use the Fleischer product as part of the "Paramount Screen Magazine," a weekly short subject that had both cartoon and newsreel elements.

The existence of theatrical cartoons and other short subjects has much to do with the legacy of vaudeville and the initial form of all movies. Unlike today, individuals or local companies owned theaters –both vaudeville and motion pictures. Because competition for discretionary money was so fierce, the owners of these theaters worked hard to develop an audience. The best way to bring back customers was to make sure they would see a great show time after time.

With vaudeville, that meant developing a program of acts that would complement one another. The earliest movies were five minutes or less and exhibitors learned they could also be grouped for the best competitive advantage.

Early movie trade publications are filled with ads designed to convince exhibitors to try their product and carried testimonials from other theater owners about audience acceptance.

Motion picture theater owners coming from the vaudeville tradition were looking for the blend of elements that would serve them best. Especially with the development of feature-length films, studios began offering theaters short subjects to complete a bill.

"The Paramount Screen Magazine" was one of the weekly collections of short elements theaters could book. After the First World War, the newsreels and cartoons that had been grouped together were eventually sold as standalone items to exhibitors.

The concept of building a program – using productions such as cartoons, news reels, comedy and dramatic shorts, and serials – was junked in the 1950s when television was presenting this kind of material for "free" to eager audiences. The production costs of short subjects quickly became almost impossible to recoup.

While serving in the Army, Max made some of the first training films used by the U.S. military. "In 1917, I joined the general staff of the U.S. Army under [General John] Pershing. I went to Fort Sill, Oklahoma, with the U.S. Army and produced a series of education motion pictures for the rapid training of troops. The pictures were very successful. They were practically all drawn by hand and it was estimated that the films cut training time down by ten percent. Prints of these pictures were sent to all army camps and are still in use [in 1939]. They were designed to show men what went on inside their rifles as there was no other way of showing them," he wrote.

This instrument that looks so much like a wooden giraffe is a carriage for the camera which travels from the ground up to where you now see it. It is stopped automatically and shoots at the snake-like looking affair underneath, which in reality represents a mountain.

Max in the army during WWI preparing a model to be used in a training film Aug. 1925 edition of Film Fun magazine. Max is at the top of the rigging smoking a pipe. Author's Collection.

Some of the films Max worked on included "How to Read an Army Map," "How to Fire a Rifle Grenade," and "Methods of Harnessing Artillery Horses."

An account published on June 21, 1919 in the Motion Picture News speaks of the Bray Studio's efforts to expand its operations with additional filmmaking services for educational clients. The article was initially published in the Educational Film Magazine by Charles Fredrick Carter.

The article noted that after a screening at West Point of a series of educational shorts, the "head of Bray's technical department" J.F. Leventhal was commissioned a lieutenant and sent to Fort Sill to produce training films. Leventhal took Max with him into the Army.

Carter wrote, "Take some simple thing as map-reading. Under military sharps, long on science but short on psychology, map-reading is far from simple."

He continued the training film approach was successful.

"Here is the way it was done. To teach the reading of contour lines, the hardest less of all for the average man, Mr. Fleischer, with the aid of a sculptor, built a miniature clay mountain seven inches high around which cords were laid to represent contour lines ten feet apart. A vertical semicircular arch on which a camera was mounted panned the mountain. The first picture showed the mountain as seen from its base level, making it clear the fact that the con-

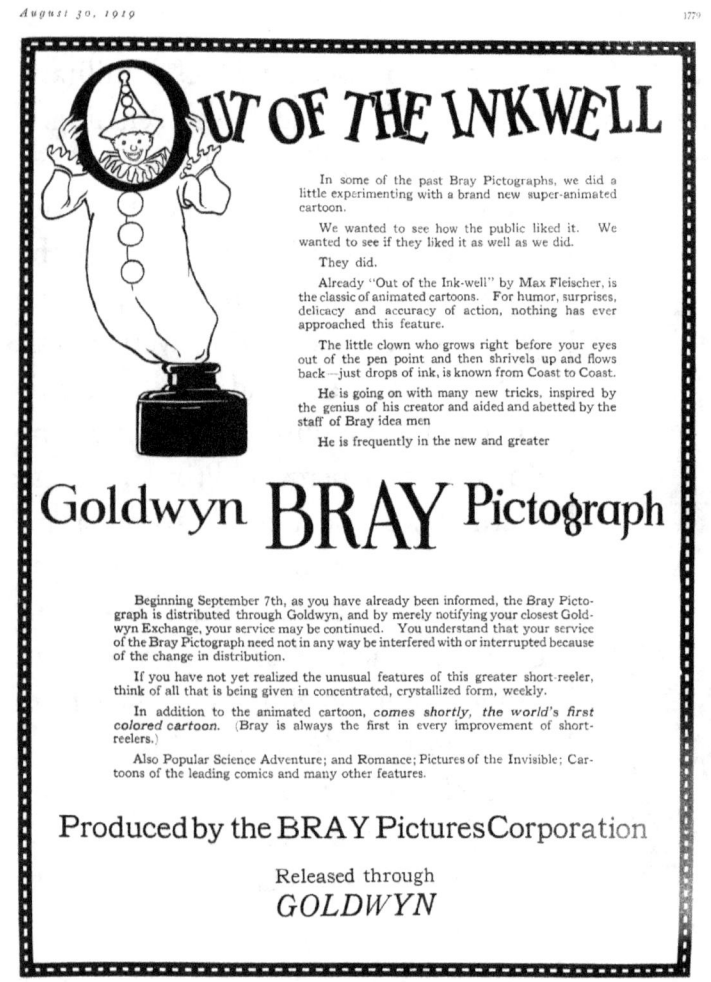

A trade ad from 1919 publicizing the first appearances of the "Inkwell Clown," later to be known as Ko-Ko.

tour lines were parallel and equidistant, vertically. The camera slowly traversed the arch, showing the progressive changes in the appearance of the contour lines until it was vertical, looking straight down on the top of the mountain, which showed the contour lines as the eyes see them on the map. By the time the camera had completed its journey the students had learned that contour lines were far apart when the slope was gradual and close together when it was steep. No one who saw the animated diagram ever had any difficulties with contour lines thereafter."

***

Out of the army, Max rejoined Bray and Max's cartoon creation began his career there. Slowly but surely, a star in the shape of a cartoon clown named Ko-Ko was born.

Initially known as simply the Inkwell Clown, Ko-Ko the Clown was undoubtedly inspired by Dave Fleischer's cavorting in a clown suit in the earliest experiments, but the character soon developed into a classic 19th century "bad boy" in the tradition of Tom Sawyer. Although he was the creation of the on-screen cartoonist played by Max, Ko-Ko held little respect for him, and delighted in making as much mischief as possible.

"I selected the character 'Ko-Ko the Clown' because he would be universally understood in pantomime. A clown doesn't have to say very much because his action tells the story. The title 'Out of the Inkwell' was used for want of a better name. The pictures were done in pen and ink. In addition, there are so many things which can come out of an inkwell," Max wrote.

The early Fleischer cartoons were part of the Goldwyn-Bray Pictograph, an omnibus sort of short subject reel that also included educational footage. Bray had not been wrong about the Fleischer short. Trade publications soon took notice.

Moving Picture World noted in its June 22, 1918 edition the following: "One of the most remarkable evidences of what the animated drawing has to offer in the way of realism is demonstrated in a simple bit of pen work by Max Fleischer in the Paramount-Bray Pictograph No. 123. This work is entitled 'Out of the Inkwell' and is nothing more than a pen drawing of a clown performing some funny stunts; but the animation of said drawing is so remarkable that the movement of the figure are as smooth and easy as those if the human body. In a fade-out, which finishes the cartoon, the clown continues to wave his farewell until only the tips of his fingers are visible.

"We would judge that one of the secrets of the realism of this work is a matter of a greater number of drawings to the foot of film than usual. After witnessing such an exhibition of artist ingenuity, it is hard to predict just what splendid future is in store for the animated drawing."

This may have been the first review Fleischer received.

Less than a year later New York Times expressed its admiration for the misadventures of the Fleischer clown.

"One's first reflection," wrote an anonymous critic in "New York Times" on April 21, 1919, "after seeing this bit of work is 'why doesn't Mr. Fleischer do more?' After a deluge of pen and ink 'comedies' in which the figures move with mechanical jerks with little or no wit to guide them it is a treat to watch the smooth motion of Mr. Fleischer's figure and enjoy the cleverness that animates it."

The Moving Picture World featured Fleischer in a story in its June 7, 1919 edition, which painted him as a man of mystery of sorts.

"There is not surer proof of the fact that genius does not grow on trees than a close examination of cause and effect in technical art. Max Fleischer, inventor of the mystery process of lifelike action in the animated cartoon, is a living example of what can be accomplished by hard work and concentration. Most of us marveled when Max's clown from the inkwell made his appearance at the Strand Theatre a couple of months ago. We laughed at the grotesque star of 'Out of the Inkwell' as he confided to the public his likes and dislikes or yowled with rage when his creator's pen point showed too strong an affection for his trouser leg."

The article continued, "A visit to the Bray studios brings one easily face to face with the creator of 'Out of the Inkwell,' but not with his dark secret, the shaping of which covered one and half years. He tells you, if you have the nerve to ask him, that it takes 1,800 drawings to make 300 feet of film and then shuts up like a clam. So, we have to be satisfied to let the thing remain as an illusion for the present."

The story concluded, "Mr. Fleischer is now devoting considerable time to applying his method to the technical field, where the possibilities are large. These lifelike animated drawings form the Fleischer pen will appear from time to time in the Bray Pictograph."

***

Another un-credited "New York Times" reporter wrote the following in the Feb. 22, 1920 edition: "The neat appearance and movements of the clown and his defiance of the laws of pen-paper-and-ink, led an investigator to Mr. Fleischer at the Bray studios where the little fellow is made. It was learned first, that whereas most animated drawings are made with four or five separate pictures for each foot of film, there are 15 to 16 drawings of the clown in each foot of film. This means of course that his arm, say, is going from a horizontal to a vertical position, does not make the complete movement in one or two jumps and so appear to move jerkily, but is pictured at four or more points of its progress and seems to make the whole movement without interruption. Patience and pains, therefore, account for much of the clown's naturalness. But not all. There is another reason.

"Mr. Fleischer explained that many pen and ink drawings were made from the imagination. An artist, for example, will simply sit down and with a certain character in mind, draw the figures that are to be animated. If he wants an arm to move, he will draw the figure several times with arm in the positions necessary to give it motion on the screen. The probability is that the resulting movement will be mechanical, unnatural, because the whole positions of the figure's body will not correspond to that which a human body would take making the same motion. With only the aid of his imagination an artist cannot, as a rule, get the perspective and related motions of reality.

"Mr. Fleischer does not draw his clown from imagination. He draws him from life. A real man dressed as a clown poses for him in the principal positions to be assumed by the animated figure.

"But how about his climbing and running all over the room? Some think that in scenes with obviously real backgrounds, a cutout figure or doll is substituted for the drawing, but neither is the case. The figure who slides down the table legs and climbs into chairs is drawn, just as he is when he remains on his sheet of paper. Mr. Fleischer prefers not to make public the full explanation of how the trick is done, but it may be said that a certain method of superimposing the drawings of the clown upon photographs of the real background is employed. Spectators may be assured, therefore, that no dummy substitutes for the clown when he takes his hazardous journey around a room."

The story also noted that 300 feet of finished film could be made in three weeks "by the combined work of four or five men."

The story concluded, "It may be seen that this somewhat tedious and expensive process still precedes each emergence of the clown from the inkwell, but those at the Bray studios feel he is worth while in more ways than one and they promise that he or some creditable successor will continue to appear from time to time."

Max's "strange combination" was beginning to pay off.

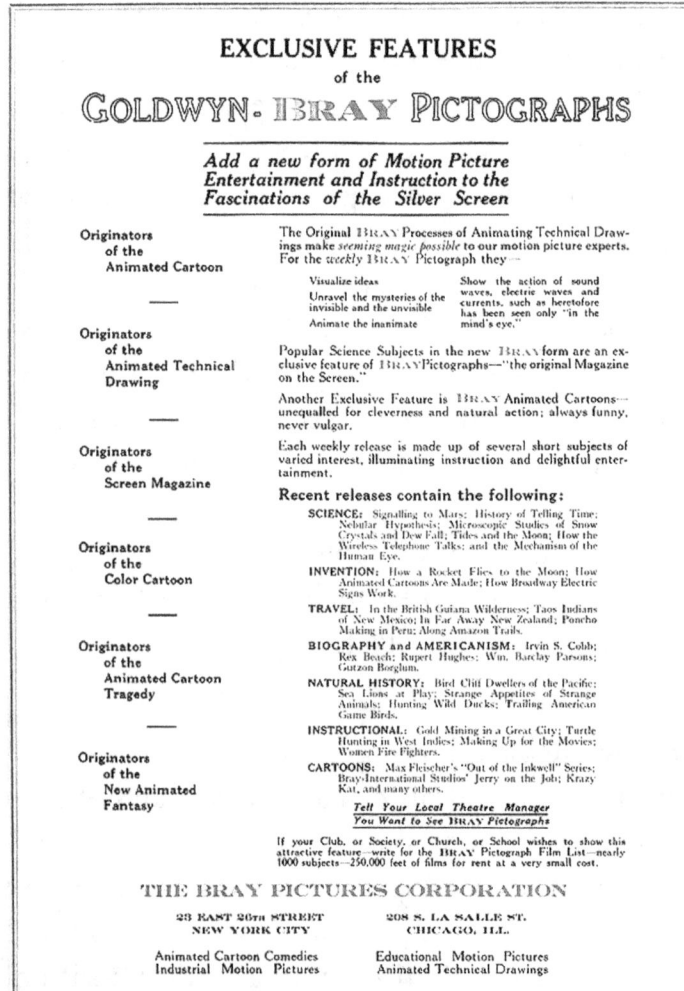

This trade ad may be a bit hyperbolic but shows the features of the Bray screen magazine in 1920.

The early Fleischer cartoons showed a willingness to push the conventions of the animated cartoon at that point. Although the interaction between the animator and the creation were not new – Winsor McCay did that with Gertie the Dinosaur – nor was the device of seeing an animated hand of the artist draw the on-screen characters, the Fleischers seemed to be willing to do things other animators had not.

"The Clown's Pup" (1919) started as many of the cartoons did with Max drawing Ko-Ko, who starts to argue with Max once he is done drawing him. Ko-Ko says. That's pretty fair." Max responded, "What do you mean pretty fair?" Ko-Ko pulls up his pants legs to show his own skinny legs and says, "You don't mean to say that this is high art?"

Max attempts to pull down the pants legs but instead pulls down the pants to reveal a frilly set of underwear. Ko-Ko goes to pull them up and Max covers the drawing with his hand. Ko-Ko says, "Alright, censor."

Even in his early short, the format of the cartoons is set. The action is frequently based on the adversarial relationship between Max and the clown. They are in many ways father and son or Dr. Frankenstein and his creation.

In "Tantalizing the Fly," (1919) Max is drawing Ko-Ko but is distracted by a housefly. The fly is not cartoon animated but rather a three-dimensional model that is animated in sequence with the drawing. Max borrows a fly swatter, which knocks Ko-Ko out. The fly is still there and Ko-Ko borrows Max's pen. His effort to hit the fly results in spraying ink around the room and onto Max. Ko-Ko then draws a little bald man sitting asleep in a chair – "a fly trap." Koko waits for the fly to land the man's bald head and then wallops him. Thinking he has taken care of the problem he leaps through the paper and Max "pours" him back into the inkwell. The fly is still alive.

It's a simple story on which to hang some gags, but this cartoon is impressive with its use of live action.

***

"The Ouija Board" (1920) firmly established the concept the drawing board is a place from which Ko-Ko can easily escape. In this short, Ko-Ko sees Max, another artist (Roland "Doc" Crandall) and the studio janitor are debating about a Ouija board. Without them noticing, he dives off the paper – to escape cartoons ghosts – and hides under the board planchette making it move.

The antics of the unseen Ko-Ko terrify all three men.

In this frame enlargement from "The Ouija Board," we see the human cast's reaction to Ko-Ko's efforts to frighten them. The actor playing the janitor is not identified, but Max is seen with Roland "Doc" Crandall, a very important and longtime Fleischer animator. Courtesy of JJ Sedelmaier.

In this short, we have traditional cartoon animation, live action, Ko-Ko appearing in that live action and stop motion animation. The cartoon is marred by some unnecessary ethnic humor, but it is an example of how the Fleischers were willing to experiment beyond just cartoon animation.

1920's "The Chinaman" opens with an artist whose specialty is portraits applies for a job with Max. Max hires him and one of the drawings the new artist has is that a caricature of a Chinese man. Ko-Ko jumps out of the inkwell and while the new hire is doing a drawing of Max, Ko-Ko jumps into the drawing of the Chinese man and starts pulling his hair. A fight ensures – complete with the Chinese character brandishing a cleaver – and Ko-Ko loses. Slinking back to the inkwell, he changes his appearance to pass as Asian and attacks the other character. The new artist sees the fight and rushes over, leaving his drawing of Max, which Ko-Ko amends. The new artist is attacked by Ko-Ko who effectively drives him out of the office. When Ko-Ko "escapes" into a painting on the wall, Max uses an eyedropper to suck Ko-Ko out of the painting and deposit him back into the inkwell.

The cartoon is problematic for its depiction of a racist caricature, but it very effectively done. When Ko-Ko is traveling down the new artist's leg the moving bulge of the clown is animated by the changes in the pants. It is a slight additional detail that adds to the overall illusion.

***

Max did more than just the Inkwell cartoons while at Bray. On the cover of the July 1919 edition of Reel and Slide Magazine is an astonishing image. A gigantic mirror is depicted with an inset illustration showing it reflecting light to Mars. The caption reads, "Huge mirror to reflect sun's rays to Mars. From 'Hello Mars – This is Earth,' by Max Fleischer of the Bray Studios. (Suggestion of Prof. Pickering of Harvard for communication with the planet Mars which we are to be nearest in August 1924)."

An ad in a January 1920 edition of Moving Picture World, described "The Mysteries of Snow." The ad described the short as "a wonder story, scientifically accurate in detail of the frozen rain of winter. In the series of enlarged animated microscopic drawings, no two snowflakes are seen to be alike."

The ad continues, "The unfathomed possibilities of these animated enlargements of the marvels of the microscope are developed by Mr. Bray in connection with his assistants Max Fleischer, his production manager and E. Dean Parmelee, who is head of the technical department."

Another publication mentions the scientific side of Max's work at Bray. The Feb. 22, 1920 edition of Wid's Daily noted, "Considerable discussion has been aroused recently by several scientists who for a living are planning various ways of butting in on the residents of some other planet, which may or may not be very pleasant. In this Bray Pictograph the first part is called 'All Aboard for the Moon,' a diagram study animated by Max Fleischer. It is one of the best bits of educational film ever made. The clearness with which each point is illustrated and the manner in which it has been screened is such as to hold the attention of those scientifically inclined as well as other."

A trade ad for the short proclaimed, "Science has made the trip theoretically possible. This unusual Bray Pictograph by Max Fleischer, edited by Popular Science Monthly, has made it a visual reality."

A trade ad for Bray in the Moving Picture Reel and Slide magazine in June 1920 emphasized the scientific and educational side of the studio's output as well as making some bold claims. The ad boasted the studio was the "originators of the animated cartoon, "originators of the animated technical drawing," "originators of the screen magazine," "originators of the animated cartoon tragedy" and "originators of the new animated fantasy."

Max's "Out of the Inkwell" cartoon are mentioned on the bottom of the ad along with "Jerry on the Job" and "Krazy Kat" cartoons, which Bray produced with the Hearst animation studio.

Brothers

Max worked for Bray for several years and then established his own studio – Out of the Inkwell Films, Inc. – in 1921. He brought along his youngest brother Dave and the two provided a contrast in personalities and styles.

No discussion of the Fleischer cartoons could or should omit his brother Dave. The two were joined at the hip professionally for the height of their careers. Reportedly, as early as the late 1920s, Dave had wanted to strike out on his own. Max's parents, though, wanted the brothers together, and an uneasy alliance continued.

Max Fleischer as he appeared in the 1930s. Courtesy of Ruth Kneitel.

In an article published on Dec. 10, 1939 in This Week Magazine of the New York Herald Tribune, writer Frederick James Smith described the two brothers as follows:

"Dave sees things in terms of laughter. Max in terms of fantasy. Max is shy and retiring, avoiding publicity. Dave, on the other hand, will enter a restaurant and start clowning with the orchestra leader."

Smith wrote, "[Max] Fleischer likes to explain why he made 'Gulliver's Travels.' 'Every adult is still a child at heart,' he says. 'They are sorry they have been told there is no Santa Claus and they would like to say 'You're wrong, there is a Santa Claus – and there are elves and witches and fairies.' People want believe in fantasy because it is an escape from the hard realism of the world.'"

Max repeated to Smith a statement he made in his 1939 autobiographical essay: "I must have been born with my moustache." Whether Max was making a joke at his own expense about his age or rather it was an expression of the responsibilities he had, as the family leader, is open to interpretation.

To understand the Fleischer studio and its cartoons, one must understand the Fleischers and their family dynamic.

***

Eventually, aside from his sister, Max eventually employed all of his siblings. His paternal outlook was well known at the studio. Jack Mercer, the voice of Popeye for almost 50 years, told this writer that Max was like "the godfather … If you had a problem with something, you went to him."

"Everyone in this organization can come right into my office and air their grievances and their troubles and speak directly to me," Max wrote in his 1939 autobiography. "Everyone in the organization calls me 'Max.' Not merely as a convenience, but I feel I have actually earned this salutation."

Edith Vernick, who started at the studio as an office assistant in the 1920s, told this writer, "I don't remember anyone saying anything bad about Dave or for that matter, Max." Vernick may have forgotten to consider the bitter strike in 1937, which divided the studio.

James "Shamus" Culhane worked at the Fleischer Studio twice. He got his break as an animator at the studio but left in 1932 and eventually worked for Walt Disney. In 1937, Culhane returned to the Fleischer studio.

In a 1978 interview with this writer, Culhane noted that both men – Max and Disney – were good employers but had one personality flaw in common.

"I found him an extremely nice man, but like so many people, like Walt, who I considered a very good employer – I guess you know about Walt and his idea of giving you a bonus that was unheard of. Now both of these guys had the same problem, they got great satisfaction out of paternalism, enormous. They didn't know that but that's really what they were… paternalistic and tyrannical in it. Otherwise, very nice, but if you scratched a guy like that, you find underneath a very tough egg. Very tough."

He added, "Max fought the union [the studio went through a strike in 1937] tooth and nail and so did Walt. They both destroyed the morale of the company. That move down to Florida [the studio relocated to Miami in 1939] cost Max a mint and he could have paid people a little more and saved money. It's not logical, it's neurotic ae hell. So any kind of reason wouldn't enter into at all."

Despite the paternalism, Culhane said, "Max was a benevolent employer, I think. For example, one day I never had so much money as $100 a week. It was really a fortune. And I was only 19 or something like that. Making $100 a week then is like $800 a week now. And it came so easy, it seemed to go so easy.

"So, one day I went to Max to borrow a week's salary. Max sat me down and gave me a big talk how I should not waste my money. Obviously, I was spending more than I was earning and that was a bad idea and that I should put away some money. I was young. I should start. Of course, I never did. But he was interested."

Speaking of the difference between working for Max and Disney, Culhane noted, "There was an elite socializing with Walt. Not many of us were involved in that, including Grim [Natwick] and me. We never bothered with that stuff. It was a very close circle."

Myron "Grim" Natwick was another animator who worked at both the Disney and Fleischer studios. He was an animation veteran by the time he arrived at the Fleischer studio in 1930. Natwick created a female dog character for a cartoon titled "Dizzy Dishes" who would became Betty Boop.

"Max did something so very different [than Disney]. They were two different people. Disney was Yankee, coming from several generations of Americans. I believe Fleischer was probably the first generation. I don't know," Natwick said in a 1977 conversation with this writer.

"And [the Fleischers] were Americans in every sense of the word. Disney had this in-bred thing that he didn't have to think about doing something, but the Fleischers did. They accepted exactly as it was the society in which they lived. And they grew up in the Jazz Age and their cartoons are jazz cartoons."

"When I worked with the Fleischers, it was very much like a big family – a very close association between every one. Every Saturday, Max and Dave would get together with animators, story men, cameramen and others and drink beer and bowl. During the semi-pro boxing season, they had an arena out on Long Island and we used to go out and see these semi-pro boxers. They had loads of energy and loads of interest in everything that was happening and they liked company. They were a bunch of people who were working together. You never actually felt that was at Disney," Natwick said.

He continued, "Disney had an aristocratic studio. Actually, at Fleischer's I never had a room of my own. There were one or two or three big rooms with one desk sitting behind another. But at Disney, we had private rooms and they had a little buffet service. If you wanted a drink of pop or something to eat you could phone the girl downstairs and it would be brought up by an errand boy.

"They [Disney and Max] were two different characters. I never got the impression that Walt thought he was better than anyone. And you certainly never got that from Max and Dave. They were two fine fellows who seemed to enjoy life."

Culhane spoke of the differences working at the Fleischer and Disney studios. "Max had this approach; let me give you the other side. At Walt's no one cared how much work you did in a day. I mean you could work all day and at the end of the day, look at your work and throw it in the wastepaper basket. The whole goddamn thing and do it over again. And over again. But when you put it in for Walt to look at it, it better be damned good. If it wasn't, if you made a mistake of putting in something inferior, you were in trouble. I mean serious trouble. If you did it often enough, you got thrown out without any recourse.

"At Max's, things were different, My education at Max's was in fact wrong for working at Walt's because we just worked according to the mood on a picture we cooked up or started from someone else's ideas. In my own case, I was very much an in and outer. One day I felt I was doing very good animation and I did. The next day it wasn't good at all but it was used. Everything was used. Nothing was ever thrown out."

***

In December of 1934, Fleischer studio employees launched a monthly newsletter called "Fleischer Animated News." Written by the employees, the newsletter featured profiles of studio personnel. In its first issue, it profiled Max and Dave. The uncredited writer wrote of Max, "He is kind and considerate, with always time to listen to the personal problems of his employees and offer his advice, which is always sincere and beneficial.

"Loves hot dogs and chocolate éclairs. Always grubs cigarettes from his secretary. His favorite sport is bowling (and he thinks he's good.) His favorite color is red. (Must be the Spanish in him.) All in all, he's swell guy and we all think the world of him – fat belly and all.

"As Max (we all call him Max) walks through the studios from one department to another greeting the boys and girls of our organization, his democratic and unassuming manner makes it hard to believe that he is a figure of international fame – a real celebrity."

Smith's 1939 profile in the New York Herald Tribune added this description of Max: "Away from his studio and his inventions, Max Fleischer seems a little lost...Fleischer dislikes riding in a car unless he drives himself. He considers himself the perfect driver. 'Nobody thinks of the gas or the oil or the gears,' he explains, 'except me.'

Dave Fleischer in a publicity shot during the making of "Mr. Bug Goes to Town," showing the 3-D set that was seen in the opening of the movie.

"He admits one general enemy – doctors; and he loves to put things over on them. Recently physicians have been demanding that he rest. He says yes and gets to the studio next day at eight, staying on to five in the afternoon.

"The doctors insist that he put something into his stomach every three hours. He has a habit of forgetting to eat when he starts working out an idea. So, his secretary pursues him about the studio with a watch and a glass of buttermilk.

"The fantastic Fleischer touch is as apparent in his home as in his studio. Located on Meridian Avenue in Miami Beach, his house is a seven-room Spanish air-conditioned bungalow. The place is illuminated at night by blue floodlights. Maybe that is his touch of whimsy. Fleischer's own study, small and cozy, is crowded with books of fairy tales.

"Fleischer is also very fond of music. On social evenings at home, he gets together with several old friends who play the piano and violin, shyly plays the mandolin or guitar himself, and makes records of the results. Later he sits by himself for hours, listening to the records.

"Max has been happily married for some 30 years. 'Happily married?' we asked. He seemed puzzled. 'Isn't that what marriage is for – happiness?' he asked."

In his 1939 autobiographical essay, Max wrote, "Hobbies: Bowling. My average is about 165 which is very low for me. I should bowl better than that. I have bowled as high as 289, 11 points below a perfect score. That was an accident, I guess. I have been bowling for about 18 years. That's why I'm ashamed of my average score. I was at one time near the top of our studio bowling club, but now I'm near the bottom. That's the only sport I engage in."

Max also wrote about his management style. "We have quite a few people who have been with us for 20 years. At least 25 of them have been with us for 12 years. About 40 of them have been here for eight years. I am a firm believer that you should strive for as much power and authority as you can attain in business. Then, don't us it. Every time we advance a man from a minor position to the head of a department, I always give him my policy. Get as much power and authority as you possibly can and the more you get, the less you use. Use authority in self-defense only. Don't use it for anything else. Work for the people in your department.

Don't make them work for you. Make them work for themselves – that's my policy."

***

Although Max was by most accounts an approachable and humble man, he was one of the few people in animation who had achieved name recognition among the general public. During the 1920s, Max acted in many of the studios silent Ko-Ko the Clown cartoons. He was the front man for his company.

He was an inventor whose work did affect the animation industry. Besides the Rotoscope, Max developed a means of combining three-dimensional models with two-dimensional cel animation for some striking results. It is described in a later chapter.

His daughter Ruth told me that her father invented rear projection – a staple special effects tool in the film industry, although I've yet to confirm that.

Max anticipated the advent of photocopying an animator's pencil drawing directly onto a cel – photocopying became an industry standard in the 1960s – with a device that was described like an old-fashioned printing press. Animator Myron Waldman said that Max wanted the studio to use it during the production of its first feature film, "Gulliver's Travels," but wasn't because the process couldn't reproduce fine lines.

Max's status as an inventor was noted in the April 1927 issue of "Scientific American" as part of the magazine's series of inventors who have achieved commercial success. The magazine article described Max's success with his way of avoiding using cels by cutting pieces of paper and overlaying them.

"It was Fleischer's idea – which he patented – to cut out the stationary parts with a pair of scissors, laying the changed part on top in various positions. Each part could thus be used for many successive exposures," Milton Wright wrote.

This Week Magazine of the New York Herald Tribune writer Frederick James Smith noted that even with his many successes, Max was still an inventor.

"Fleischer's pictures have made box-office millions. But he always does his personal shopping on the installment plan – says he can't save money, even though he never bets on the horses. He spends it all working out eccentric ideas, such as a mechanical ashtray or a trick inkwell. And any scheme to improve cartoon comedies interests him vitally."

Smith reported that Max designed the studio the brothers built in Miami, Fla. in the late 1930s.

"Fleischer worked out every detail of the studio himself. The whole plant is air-conditioned and there is indirect lighting throughout. Fleischer's own office looks like a drugstore. That's because he is eternally experimenting with the effects of various chemical on celluloid, ink and film 'In my spare time,' he puts it."

In his 1939 autobiographical sketch, Max wrote, "My wife has been very patient with my so-called crazy ideas. But it's a funny thing – most of the crazy ideas did amount to something. You must realize that when you're working on an idea and struggling with it – at the time you don't know whether the thing is going to fade out into nothing or not. While you're doing it, the outlook is black. Usually, an inventor can't possibly see what will become of his inventions and it takes a lot of patience on the part of those around him to let him go on.

"Then she has been very patient with a lot of disturbances within the house. At times our rooms looked like a chemical laboratory. At other times a machine shop."

***

Working with his older brother certainly had an impact on Dave (1894-1979). He told historian Joe Adamson in an interview conducted in 1968 that "Max's name was always first. Under that it said: 'Directed by Dave Fleischer.' I suggested that he have his name on it. He was my older brother and I never thought we'd separate or anything. It didn't matter; it was in the family."

Dave explained to Adamson, though, that later in the 1920's, he did attempt to begin his own business, only to have his family insist that he reunite with Max.

In his discussions with Adamson, Dave insisted that he had developed the famous Bouncing Ball and that Max had patented several of Dave's inventions in his name. Dave also claimed that the Rotoscope was at least partially his idea.

Dave's remarks have to be taken at face value, however. In the same series of interviews, Dave insisted to Adamson that he had made the original Casper the Friendly Ghost cartoon, which actually had been produced years after Paramount had forced Dave and Max out of their studio. He also said that the technique that used models to add three dimensions to the Fleischer cartoons had not been used in the Popeye series, although it had to great effect.

The "he said-she said" quality of the interviews reflected the long-standing resentment Dave had towards his brother and that his efforts should have been given the recognition he believed he deserved. Dave told Adamson at length about his various inventions, which ranged from an artificial sweetener to a penny arcade scale.

By the mid-Twenties, Max became less involved with the animation of the shorts, although he would still appear on-camera, and concentrated on the management side of the business. Creative control of the cartoons was passed to Dave. Depending upon who was talking Dave has been described as either one of the industry's greatest gagmen or a relatively talent-less man who should not have taken credit for screen direction.

Here's how the first issue of the "Fleischer Animated News" described Dave: "Dave Fleischer is the youngest of six children. After he was born his parents decided to quit.

"Soon after birth, Dave received public recognition as the most beautiful baby in Brooklyn. He quickly outgrew this handicap.

"During boyhood he divided his time between amateur nights in the local theater and school. He filled his schoolbooks with caricatures and the theater with customers, His teacher gave him a diploma when he handed over the sketches and the theater gave him 'walking papers' when he tried out a new act.

"Equipped with a sense of humor and optimism, Dave joined a theatrical company. The company went broke and Dave went to work.

"Associating with his brother Max in developing the 'Inkwell comedies,' Dave played the part of the clown. From the role of clown, he rapidly advanced to the clown's director.

"During the World War, Dave enlisted and was stationed in Washington, D.C. While he was in the nation's capital, women were given the right to vote, the Armistice was signed and the country was swept by a wave of prosperity.

"Retiring from public life, he seriously returned to comedy. Under his direction Betty Boop has advanced from a hard-working 'extra' to stardom while Popeye the Sailor has packed the theaters and saved the country from the 'big bad wolf.'

"Dave's philosophy is to look at life from the proper viewpoint. Consequently, he stands on his head to write a scenario and walks around on his hands.

"His personal characteristics are a penchant for honesty, a scrawlly [sic] handwriting and dislike of details. His hobbies are bowling, fishing, chocolate ice cream and striped shirts."

An anecdote from Lou Fleischer as told to animator Ray Pointer illustrated Dave's early interest in gags. As a child, "Dave went occasionally to Lipman's grocery to do the marketing. Not yet able to write he would draw symbols representing whatever article was needed, amount, weight, etc. In one instance 'peas' were needed. This was represented by a boy urinating. Mr. Lipman kept some of these lists to show customers."

From the late Twenties through the demise of the studio in 1942, nearly every Fleischer cartoon carried a Dave Fleischer direction credit.

"Well, that's a sore point with me," recalled Shamus Culhane in an interview with this writer.

"I believe that everybody should get credit for the actual work they did. Now, Dave, although he may have thought himself something else, was a gagman and he was a good one, too. But we usually wrote our own stories. We did for a long time until Bill Turner and Bill Stoltz became regular story writers, but even then, we always wrote a good deal of the stuff. We also developed all the layouts and the characters and the animation. We did the whole schmeer.

"Dave went around during the course of the day, and he'd look over your shoulder to see what you were up to, and would contribute a gag here or there. But the actual direction, I mean the whole damn thing, was done by the animators, and they only get credit as animators," Culhane said.

During the 1930s, the Fleischer Studio developed a system in which several key animators headed up units of artists. These head animators were the actual directors of a film. They supervised the design of characters, worked with the writers and did key animation. Dave supervised the head animators.

Animator Myron Waldman remembered how he became irritated at Dave's habit of coming around and checking a day's animation progress by flipping the completed drawings. One day, Waldman handed Dave a sheaf of blank paper, which

Joe Fleischer in 1912. Courtesy of JJ Sedelmaier.

Dave flipped through with great consternation. He was not amused by Waldman's answer that Dave was holding tomorrow's work!

Where Dave seemed most interested was in the direction of the voice and music tracks and the insertion of gags into the cartoons. He also insisted on a singular trait in the early Fleischer sound cartoons: characters who normally would be stationary in a scene would slightly bounce to a musical beat.

Dave told Adamson with apparent pride that he had "directed" screen composer Victor Young when Young was recording the score for "Gulliver's Travels," the studio's first feature-length production. Dave insisted that Young use his arrangement for a scene and felt vindicated when Young included it in the final score.

Max's son Richard wrote to this writer that part of the conflict between Max and Dave was due to Max's refusal to allow Dave to write the score for the brothers' second feature, "Mr. Bug Goes to Town."

Mae Questel, the voice of Betty Boop and Olive Oyl, characterized Dave as "crude," to this writer and believed he was jealous of his older brother. By the late 1930s, the brothers reportedly were barely on speaking terms.

Animator Gordon Sheehan recalled to film historian Leonard J. Kohl, "I'd see them [Max and Dave Fleischer] at the studio in Miami going down the corridor. One would be going this way and the other – the corridors were only about eight feet wide or so – and I'd see that instead of looking at each other, they would look at the walls. It was hateful. That girl who was out with Dave – sitting in the back was Mae Schwartz. She was a red-headed gal. Very nice-looking gal. One of the first gals I met when I started working at the studio was Mae Schwartz and Dave, of course, had got acquainted with her. I think he used to like to get her out of the girls in the 'Opaquing Department' and inking."

Dave divorced his wife Ida in 1939. He subsequently married his secretary Mae Schwartz in 1945. According to Edith Vernick, some churches in the Miami area called for a boycott of Fleischer cartoons because of the messy divorce.

The announcements that Dave was to leave the studio started in January 1942 and apparently, he never spoke to his older brother again, although he maintained an affectionate relationship with Max's children.

Richard Fleischer described the two men as "bitter enemies who didn't speak to one another for 30 years" in a letter to this writer.

In a newspaper article in "The Miami Herald" in 1978, Joe Fleischer said, "During the making of this feature ['Gulliver's Travels'] things began to go badly for the Fleischers. Max and Dave agreed to disagree between themselves to the point that they did not speak to one another for various reasons."

This rift divided the Fleischer family, and continued to do so for years. It's easy to cast Dave as the villain in the story, although it is also undoubtedly simplistic and unfair.

In its April 15 1942 edition, The Motion Picture Herald announced that Dave was chosen to head the animation unit at Columbia Pictures where he produced the studio's successful "Fox and Crow" cartoons and started a series based on Al Capp's popular "Lil Abner" comic strip.

There was never any additional information supplied about the reasons for Dave's departure in the trade press.

The "Lil Abner" shorts didn't click with audiences. The shorts didn't capture the sly satire and sex appeal of Capp's popular strip and instead had a re-occurring theme in which Mammy Yokum rescues Lil' Abner from a perilous situation. There were striking similarities with the formula of having Popeye rescuing Olive.

Dave's stay with the company was only about two years. Columbia opted to close their animation unit in favor of releasing shorts produced by UPA.

Dave's post-Columbia career is detailed in the second volume.

***

The other Fleischer brothers were employed at the studio at various times. Joe was an electrician; Charlie was a machinist and Lou (1891-1985) was a musician whose skills were essential with the coming of sound. Other than Dave, Lou became the brother with the greatest responsibility at the studio.

Lou studied both piano and violin as a child and found work as a young man playing the piano in theaters accompanying silent movies and in nightclubs. He went to school for civil engineering – a field he did enter– but was working in a jewelry shop when Dave called him to ask if he would join them at the studio "because it needed someone who knew music and mathematics," Lou told animator Ray Pointer.

Lou's first job was to prepare exposure sheets – the charts used by animator to time their drawing to a soundtrack – for a cartoon featuring a recording by popular banjo player Eddie Peabody. Lou's efforts were successful and he left the jewelry store.

He stayed with the studio supervising the exposure sheets and working with the cartoon's composers such as Sammy Timberg.

Lou told Pointer that "it was customary to allow visitors to go through the cartoon studios to see how things are done, but it got too voluminous and disturbing to the artists so it was only limited to celebrities. We had royalty from England and one day [French singer and actor] Maurice Chevalier.

"He had been shown the entire ninth floor of 1600 Broadway and then shown the sixth floor. Last thing [he was shown] was the [production of a] Screen Song (Bouncing Ball) with my brother Joe turning the drum on which the lettering was and I with a black sleeve, black glove and black shirt [to place the ball over the right words].

"After seeing this he remarked, 'Marvelous! Marvelous! Marvelous! Five brothers each in a different capacity and each an expert in his field.' I shall always remember this!"

In the August 1935 edition of the studio's newsletter Joe was profiled. "Joe Fleischer was born on the East side of New York at an address on Third Street, which would indicate the lower East Side. A roster of the famous people who came from that section would fill many pages and who know that Joe may yet become famous? Look at the tradition behind him.

"Joe has four brothers: Max, Dave, Charlie and Louis and the sister Ethel. If the sextette were to line up in consecutive order, which they probably won't do, Joe would be in third in line for the crown. He also holds the honor of being the first of the family to be born in America. He takes this honor seriously and does his best to live up to it.

"His childhood ambition was to be a soldier, but it never materialized. When it came time for him to go to work, [he] got a job with the Brooklyn Rapid Transit subway as a track inspector. Dodging subway cars in the dark, dank tunnels is not the most interesting of indoor sports. There is no future of running around in a subway chasing tracks. Then too, there is always the chance of finding oneself on a southbound track, walking south with the prospect of a train creeping up on your heels. It has been done and is a frightening experience.

"After this ordeal, he enlisted as a law clerk evidently with the intention of studying law, Wrestling with the musty tomes, Kent's or Blackstone's Commentaries. With all the business of contracts, torts, civil actions, briefs, motions to quash, subpoenas duces tecum and all the other paraphernalia of legal clap trap did not appeal very much to Joe. His forte is scientific subjects. His hobbies show his real trend of thought: photography, science and electricity. He finds food in his aesthetic cravings in antiques. He spends many of his leisure hours browsing around the out of the way places, hoping for a real find. Joe likes to read, but confines most of it to scientific subjects. His favorite newspaper is the New York American.

"Joe attended school at P.S. 69 on 54th Street New York, and graduated from P.S. 84 in Brooklyn and Boys High School, also in Brooklyn. Joe always liked school. His good nature and smiles he has carried with him. He always has a good word to a smile for everyone and his good nature is well known around the studio.

"Joe says he is five foot five inches and weighs 150 pounds, before eating. He has blue eyes and brown hair. His habits are very temperate. He doesn't drink, meaning liquor, and five years ago gave up the use of tobacco. Joe has been married 15 years, happily, and he looks it. He has two sons, which have inherited his father's sunny disposition.

"He came to the studio in 1915 which was just two years before the United States entered the World War. When the war finally came around to us, Joe was sent with the Emergency Fleet Corporation.

"He had a nice job playing with torpedoes. You know those long, sleek cigar-shaped mechanical fish, which a nose fill of TNT and no conscience. We wonder if Joe ever heard the saying, "I didn't know it was loaded." East Side luck was with him, however, and he came through all right.

"There may be folks around the studio who will ask what Joe does. The answer is 'plenty.' He is what one might call the chief mechanic. His whole working day is a mess of belts, shafts, cams, eccentrics and oil. It might even be said he works in oil. For the benefit of those who do not know, we have a machine shop and Joe is the factotum.

"Joe has a good appetite; in fact a very rugged appetite and he keeps it in good training by frequent and copious doses of corned beef and cabbage. This food does for Joe what spinach does for Popeye."

***

In the 1979 "Miami Herald" story Joe Fleischer read to the reporter a presentation the then-89-year-old retiree made to school classes. The closing paragraph read: "Finally this to me all seems like a passing dream except to say we remaining Fleischers [Lou and Dave were also still alive at the time] feel grateful for having the opportunity to bring laughter and happiness to people all over the world."

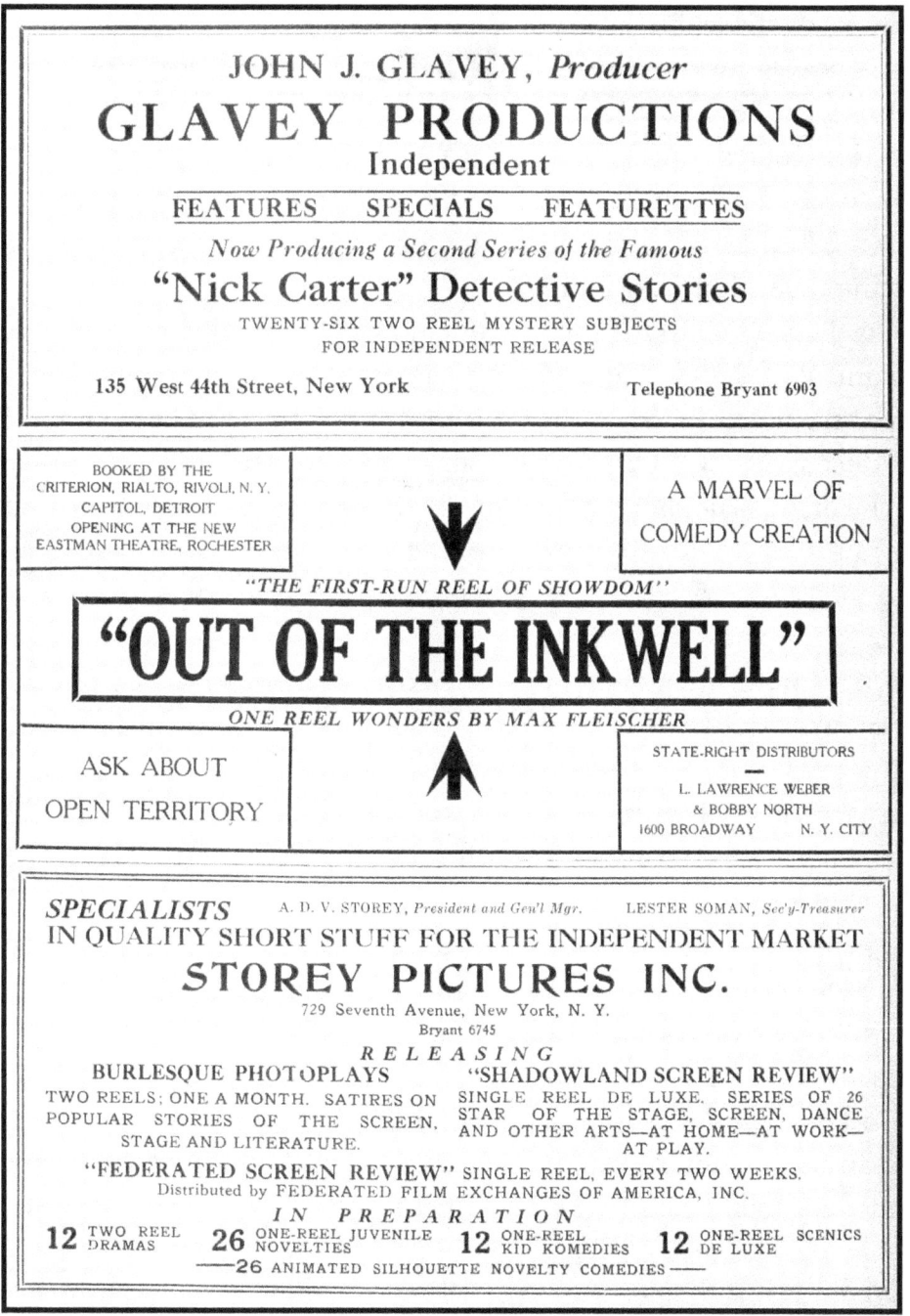

This trade ad from 1922 illustrates the way the Fleischers distributed their cartoons after leaving Bray but before the birth of Red Seal. The state right system allowed people around the country to distribute movies within a set territory for independent producers working outside of the studio system.

Chapter Two

In just a few short years, Max Fleischer went from being a hired hand at the Bray Studios to the head of not just his own studio, but of a releasing company, which expanded and then imploded under its own weight.

It must have been a heady ride for Max and his brother Dave. Breaking off from Bray in 1921, by August 1926 Max's Red Seal Pictures Corp. announced how it was releasing a series of live-action comedies as well as the Out of the Inkwell cartoons, the "Ko-Ko Song Car-tunes," newsreels, the "Animated Hair Cartoons," and many more shorts.

Red Seal had 22 exchanges throughout the country and did not rely on the state rights method of getting their films into theaters.

But, as fast as the rise was to the top, the ride down was equally quick. By November 1926, Max had lost control of Red Seal and was soon an employee in his own company.

The format of the shorts in the 1920s followed the one that had been established by the cartoons Max produced at Bray. Max starred as an artist who is at odds with his creation Ko-Ko, the clown that he draws. The shorts frequently have a sequence in which an animated photo of a hand holding a pen draws Ko-Ko and his setting. Sometimes Ko-Ko would emerge from the inkwell fully formed and very often he would jump into it as a refuge from the chaos he helped to create.

This convention of the artist's hand was seemed to be a reference to a popular act in vaudeville: the lightening artist. These cartoonists would draw cartoons quickly on stage accompanied by comic patter.

Winsor McCay had such a vaudeville act and his landmark "Gertie the Dinosaur" short established the concept of the cartoonist creator dealing with a mischievous pen and ink offspring.

Earl Hurd opened some of his "Bobby Bumps" shorts such as "Bobby Bumps Put a Beanery on the Bum" (1918) with the moving hand drawing his star. In the 1919 short, "Bobby Bumps in Their Master's Voice," Bobby emerges from an inkwell.

This isn't to say that Max's cartoons were derivative. They merely reflected some of the comic sensibilities of their day as well as several of the visual conventions. What made the Out of the Inkwell cartoons so unique was how the conventions were used. Max's use of the moving hand transcended his fellow animators and it became associated with the Out of the Inkwell cartoons.

It's clear looking at trade papers from the 1920s, three most dominant cartoons series were Paul Terry's "Aesop Fables," "Felix the Cat," produced by Pat Sullivan, but developed by Otto Messmer, and "Out of the Inkwell." They were very different in their approaches to comedy and how to use animation.

I compare the Fleischer cartoons to the works of Buster Keaton, whose understanding of the technology of motion pictures produced films that, while may not have been the most popular comedies of their day, have found new contemporary audiences.

At the time, critics saw the Felix cartoons as the most popular animated cartoons of the era and interestingly Felix was often compared to Charles Chaplin – in fact Chaplin "appears" in "Felix in Hollywood" in 1923. The silent Felix cartoons have often been hailed as one of the first examples of character-driven animated humor. The laughs in a Felix cartoon just didn't come out of standalone gags, but out of how Felix would behave.

I'll submit the Ko-Ko cartoons also shared that distinction. Much of the humor comes out of the relationship between creator and creation. Max and Ko-Ko frequently did things out of the nature of that relationship – most often antagonistic. Ko-Ko was a rebellious offspring, a mischievous son.

There is a vitality to the Out of the Inkwell cartoons that I love that revolves around the fact I'm never sure exactly is going to happen and what kinds of animation are going to be used.

The 1921 short "Modeling" is a great example of this try anything approach. Max draws Ko-Ko and the clown complains of Max not using fresh ink – he has "no pep." In an adjoining studio, a sculptor is working on a clay bust of an older man with a prominent nose. After drawing skates onto Ko-Ko, Max comes over to help the sculptor. In a partially rotoscoped sequence Ko-Ko gets the hang of skating. He draws a caricature of the subject of the sculpture client in the ice. He also molds a bust of the man in snow.

When the client spots what Ko-Ko has done, Max takes a lump of clay and throws it at Ko-Ko, knocking him over. All three men come to the drawing board to laugh at the clown, who wrestles the lump of clay off of him and throws it at the face of the client.

Coming off the drawing board, Ko-Ko skates over to the other studio and climbs up into the clay bust. From within he manipulates the clay, tearing off a chunk of crawling back down to the floor like a caterpillar. This frightens the three men who manage to grab the hunk of clay, but Ko-Ko has escaped and skates back to the drawing board and then to the safety of the inkwell.

In an eight-minute short we see the combination of live action and animation as well as three-dimensional clay animation, along with standard cartoon animation.

The relationship between Max and Ko-Ko is perfectly shown in "Fishing," also from 1921, Max is in a hurry to leave and at first only draws Ko-Ko with one leg. Answering Ko-Ko's question, Max tells him he is going fishing, but Ko-Ko can't come. Ko-Ko naturally decides to go find Max especially after he has a wild nightmare about fishing. He concludes that Max has put some "dope" in his ink and that fuels his revenge. Fishing from a small island, Max and his companion find themselves stranded thanks to Ko-Ko and are forced to swim for shore.

It was not only the inventiveness of what was happening on screen that made these shorts so compelling, but the also fact the humor was coming out of a very human dynamic.

In The Clown's Little Brother," (1921) Ko-Ko (still known here as "the Inkwell Clown") receives a little brother by mail. His efforts to amuse the younger version of him are not successful and the younger clown can do everything he can only better. The humor now extends to sibling rivalry.

The studio maintained this level of inventiveness through the run of the Ko-Ko shorts.

***

In a 1937 essay animator Roland "Doc" Crandall wrote for the studio newsletter, recalling the early days with Max and Dave, joining them after his duty in WWI. The insights he shared about the early days of the studio are invaluable.

"I saw J.R. Bray who said I'd have to see Max Fleischer, the production manager. I saw Max and told him Bray had given me a job and I was put on the first 'Inkwells.' I'll never forget an efficiency expert we had around the place. When the job was completed, we'd have to erase our old pencil drawings to have clean paper for a new picture.

"Time marches on. Max and Dave started their own studio and took me with them. Our first studio was in the basement of a tenement. We didn't even have a sign on the door. Max used to help wash cels. We threw the waste film and buckled cels into the furnace until one day it exploded and we landed in the street black with smoke and gasping for air.

"Instead of bowling for exercise, we'd play stud poker for high stakes from Saturday until Monday. The riff-raff from the corner cigar store would invite themselves and dirty up the place while cleaning us up.

"We moved across the street to higher things; a large room over a lunch counter. The girls living over us had so much company combined with the clang of patrol wagons and cops banging on the stairs that we wouldn't concentrate."

He continued, "I remember the way we used to bat out those old Inkwells. Dave would write a scenario in about ten words and in about that many minutes. Max always did the job of running around for a loan to meet the payroll and he never failed us.

"As a typical animator, it was up to me to animate, render my own backgrounds, letter the title cards and make set-backs for the actual. This was done by borrowing my kids' toy houses and bringing in trees and grass from Connecticut. We used everything in our sets from actual photographs from live mice to sick cats. A stuffed Thanksgiving turkey laid around so long it nearly laid us out while stop-motioning it with one hand and holding our noses with the other.

"I remember the camera trips we made on account of Ko-Ko. We went fishing at City Island in April with fish market codfish tied to the hooks. Max fell overboard into the icy sound and nearly drowned as was called for in Dave's script. We shot skyrockets in the middle of May for a Fourth of July Inkwell and explained it to the cops.

"Max and Dave animated with us and photographed nearly all the pictures by the famous 'rip and lash' method and without exposure sheets. Most of the planning, matching and timing was done under the camera. Dem were the happy days!"

***

New York City was the center of the animation industry in this country during this time. John Bray, Pat Sullivan and Otto Mesmer, Paul Terry, Walter Lantz and Max all were in New York producing theatrical shorts.

Despite the popularity of cartoons and the number of studios producing animation it was still a relatively small industry.

Edith Vernick started with Max in the 1920s. She would become in charge of the in-betweening department in the 1930s at the studio and was given an opportunity to animate on "The Fresh Vegetable Mystery," (1939) but reportedly could not produce the number of drawings daily that was required.

Interviewing her in 1977, she said, "Everything was togetherness. There was no jealousy between Aesop's Fables and Max Fleischer or anything like that. All the guys knew one another. This was a field that was different and there weren't too many women in it. I was like one of the boys."

Although she admitted that perhaps there was rivalry between Max and some other producers it didn't extend to the staffs.

"The employees were very friendly," she said.

A short notice that appeared in several of the motion pictures trade publications in 1931 spoke to that relationship. "Victory in a hard-fought bowling match was won last night by the Fleischer Studios (of Talkartoon and Screen Song fame) team headed by Dave Fleischer over Aesop's Fables, the opposing team headed by George Rufle.

"The pins suffered considerable scattering at the hands of the artist: Natwick, Schettler, Bowsky and Dave Fleischer. Even the defiant pin at extreme left was unable to hold up it hand very long against the zigzagging and hurling spheres flung by the husky Fleischer draftsmen.

"The Aesop's Fables boys put up a heroic defense but were unable to break the lead which the Fleischer Boys rolled up at the start and they held by a small lead through each successive game. The third and last game however, developed into a complete rout. The final score of 1,902 to 1,607 meant that a settlement was in order. After a short conference among the rival cartoonists, it was agreed that the Fleischer bowlers were entitled to real money instead of cartoon cash."

***

Despite the use of technology to achieve a unique look, the Fleischer shorts apparently only used cels when necessary. Like the Felix cartoons, the Ko-Ko cartoons used a form of animation in which the characters were drawn on paper and the paper was cut and combined on a background.

The cel system developed by animators Earl Hurd and John Bray in 1915 allowed the use of more sophisticated backgrounds and was part of the overall production technique that made animation commercially feasible.

The use of cels was patented and required studios to pay a licensing fee to use it. Bray and Hurd each received a royalty on every cel used until 1932 when the patent ran out.

Contemporary accounts in trade publications indicate there were issues with studios actually buying a license for the Bray-Hurd Process and instead using the technology without paying for it.

Looking at sharp prints of the Ko-Ko cartoons it's easy to notice shadow lines at the edges of the cut paper.

Here is how writer Milton Wright described the Fleischer use of cut paper in an article in the April 1927 edition of Scientific American.

"To draw 4,000 separate cartoons and photograph them one at a time was the practice in the early days. Then it dawned on some genius that parts of a figure remain motionless throughout several poses and the art of tracing was adopted; the altered parts were added by original drawing. Tracing however was never wholly satisfactory, for it seemed impossible to trace the lines unerringly and an impression of flickers was conveyed when the film was projected.

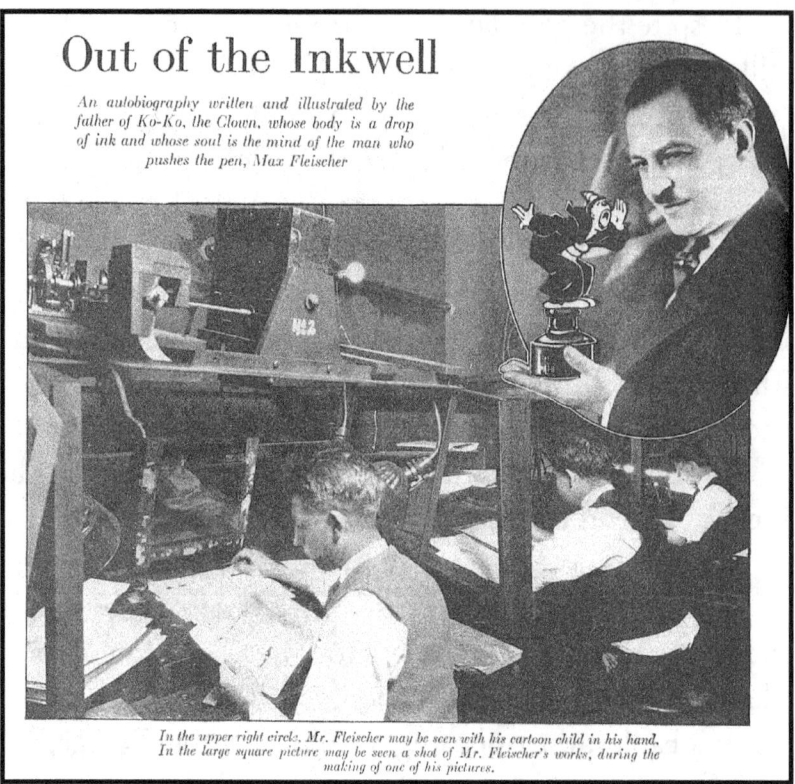

This clip from an article in Film Fun shows a little of how the studio looked in the mid-1920s. (author's collection)

"It was Fleischer's idea – which he patented – to cut out the station parts with a pair of scissors, laying the changed part on top in various positions. Each part could this be used for successive exposures.'

"In the making of an animated cartoon, five sets of persons are called on to co-operate- scenario writers, who build up the story; planners, who assemble and coordinate the scenes for the photographers; editors, who cut and edit the films; animators, and photographers. An animator is a cartoonist. In Fleischer's studios we found eight of them – all men, because women, according to persons in the business, do not seem to make good cartoonists. Each of these animators has practiced until he can draw a dog or a clown – the two standard characters in the Out-of-the-Inkwell series – exactly like all the other animators draw it.

"The animator works over a piece of glass under which is an electric light. On the glass panel he places the drawing of a figure. Over this he places a sheet of blank paper. The light shining from beneath shows the picture on the under piece of paper through the top piece of paper. On this top piece of paper, the animator draws the part of the figure, which is to be in a slightly different position. Then he draws the next slightly different position of the same part, and so on until the whole series making up the complete action is finished. All these little parts of pictures are cut out and numbered consecutively.

"It is essential that all the various portions' fit or 'register' exactly. The method of bringing this about is simplicity itself. All the sheets of paper are the same size and at precisely the same spots 'on each two holes are punched. When any sheet is laid on the table the holes are fitted over two little brass posts. This method of registering is carried throughout all the processes to which the drawings are subjected.

"Now comes the work of the photographer. The drawing is laid on a table. Suspended directly above it is the camera; it has a device on it that makes it possible for the operator to work the mechanism by pressing down her foot.

"Before taking each picture, the photographer presses a pane of glass over the paper. This is to keep the drawing flat. Having taken the first picture, she lifts up the pane of glass, lays down the second picture of the series, puts down the glass panel, and makes the next photograph. This second picture, you will remember, is made up of two, drawings: the main body, which is the same as the first picture, and a cutout drawing laid over the first in a slightly different position. The place where the cut edge meets the original picture dos not show because it is pressed flat by, the glass. The following picture is taken in the same way until the whole scene is completed.

"For showing hand-drawn cartoons in the same scene with photographs, Fleischer has devised the Rotograph. In a horizontal table is set a piece of translucent glass. A projector throws a motion picture through and on to the glass from below. Above is a camera pointed downward. The film being projected is stopped at each frame while the animated cartoon posture is superimposed on the picture and photographed.

"Later Fleischer perfected the Novograph, a slow-motion camera which suspends action at any desired stage. The latest of his innovations is a 'song motion-picture film' which is causing audiences throughout the country to join in singing while a little cartoon runs and skips from one word to another of popular melodies flashed on the screen."

While a description of how the studio's animation technique in 1927 is appreciated, one can only wonder if the reporter knew anything about cel animation. The notation at the end of the article about the popular – and at that stage – long-running Song Car-tune series is especially mystifying.
The other interesting bit about this piece is the implication the photographer at the studios is a woman as well as the fact the rotoscope is never mentioned.

The movie "journalism" of the age was prone to a bit of hyperbole even in the serious Scientific American.

The other aspect about Fleischer studio technique that fascinates me is how Max and his staff apparently soon realized they didn't need the Rotoscope to produce acceptable animation

Another clip from Film Fun shows a model sheet of Ko-Ko drawn in the Dick Huemer style. (author's collection).

and that it was a tool perhaps better used for special effects production.

While the earlier cartoons often include a rotoscoped animation sequence that soon fell by the side. The Rotoscope proved to be essential, though, in combining live action with animation.

***

A key figure at the Fleischer operation in the mid-1920s was animator Richard "Dick" Huemer, who went on to have a long career at the Disney Studio.

In a 1980 essay that appeared in Cartoonist Profiles, Grim Natwick wrote, "What kind of man was Dick Huemer? He spent almost his entire lifetime in animation studios, working first with Raoul Barre on the Mutt and Jeff pictures. This was in 1916. Dick was eighteen years old. He became a key artist at the Fleischer Studio when they produced their famous Out of the Inkwell pictures. In 1930 he moved to Hollywood with the Charley Mintz group and in 1933 he joined the Disney staff. This adds up to about 60 years spent with animated cartoons. The last 40 years he worked at the Walt Disney Studio."

Natwick continued, "He was one of the artists who helped build the early framework of animation. He was a wise and witty man, a droll man who, in a quiet way, pulled rugs from under pompous and false heroes, transformed giants into pygmies and inauspiciously extracted the teeth from snarling paper lions. He was with animation through all its growing pains. Whatever animation became, he helped to shape it, drawing by drawing, idea by idea."

Film historian Joe Adamson did a series of interviews with Huemer in the late 1960s with a finished piece published in Michael Barrier's important animation magazine, "Funnyworld." Huemer told him he began at the studio in 1923 after a stint working on the "Mutt and Jeff" cartoons being produced by Raoul Barre.

At that time about 10 people were employed at the Fleischer studio with Roland "Doc" Crandall as the only animator, Huemer said.

He told Adamson, "As I recall, I would work with Dave Fleischer. Max, of course, acted in all the pictures and had overall say in production. His brother Dave was more or less the director of the cartoon operation. We'd get together and talk about what to animate. The studio, you see, was so small that you could walk from desk to desk. Not like the Disney studio became, full of rooms, and where nobody ever sees anybody or talks to anybody. Then, I could yell across the room, 'Hey, Dave. I want to talk to you. Suppose we do this.' And then we'd sit down and talk it over and laugh our heads off at our great gags, and then it would be my job to animate what we had thrashed out. But, of course, we always had a basic theme. Generally, quite clever. Did you ever see the one about the fly? That's the surviving Inkwell that you see around a lot. A fly is bothering Max; gags, complications, et cetera, et cetera. Take it from there. All in all, it was very relaxed working with the Fleischers."

Another part of the interview detailed the kind of atmosphere at the studio. Huemer recalled of a series of gags between him and Dave, "started when I drew big teeth on Koko… Dave started kidding me about it, baring his teeth at me every time I looked at him. Or he would draw an enormous tooth on my drawing paper when my back was turned. Then finally one night on my way home, I put my hand into my pocket and fished out a handful of teeth. Human ones. He'd gotten them from a dentist friend of his. I forgot what my next move was – probably slipping one or two into his dessert at lunch, or some other disgusting thing. And then came the morning when I raised my drawing board to switch on the light and my hand touched something slimy. There, draped over the light bulb, was the lower half of a cow's jaw, replete with great big yellow teeth and shreds of unhealthy-looking flesh. Naturally I couldn't let him quit while he was ahead. So I sneaked down to the street when he wasn't looking and placed the cadaver on the motor of his Ford. I was only sorry I wasn't there when he started to smell the roast beef on his way home. That kind of ended the whole rib."

Heumer's design sense added much to the way the Fleischer cartoon characters looked at the time and while he was at the studio the practice of "in-betweening" was started. Huemer was assigned artist Art Davis who would create the drawings that got an action from the beginning to the end – those drawings being done by Huemer. It became the standard practice in the industry.

***

How did the film industry, audiences and critics view animation in the 1920s? An interesting perspective is provided by "The Best Moving Pictures of 1922-23" edited by Robert E. Sherwood, a prominent critic of the time whose reviews appeared in "Life" and the New York Herald.

Sherwood introduced his chapter on the year's short subjects by writing, "It is unfortunate that this book must necessarily be devoted to consideration of feature pictures (of five or more reels in length), with insufficient consideration of short subjects: comedies, scenics, animated cartoons, news reels and travel pictures. I do not hold with the notion that a one or two-reel film is not better than 'filler,' and may dismissed as such. Many of the best pictures that have been compressed into brief form.

"I don't want to ignore that short subjects and yet I am painfully aware of the fact that it is utterly impossible for one writer to comment authoritatively on this tremendously wide field. There are so many hundreds of short subjects and their release schedules so uncertain, that I have been unable to cover them with any great degree of accuracy.

"However there have been certain producers whose one- and two-reel products have stood out from the rest …"

Sherwood then details how Buster Keaton was the leader of the shorts performers and writes later in the essay, "Foremost among the animated cartoons have been Paul Terry's 'Aesop's Fables' and Pat Sullivan's 'Felix the Cat.' The romantic adventures of Mutt and Jeff have been discontinued, but Max Fleischer's 'Out of the Inkwell' goes on."

It's impossible to assess cartoons from 1920 until the mid-1950s properly without understanding several important points. Exhibitors competed with one another. In this era in which chain theaters are alike, it's difficult to imagine that theater owners were considered showmen who cared deeply about what they presented in their theaters and how they presented it.

As they had done in vaudeville, owners of movie theaters assembled elements of features and shorts that they believed would attract and satisfy their audience. They did so by building programs. Many of these programs were assembled for both adults and children.

Cartoons were among those building blocks. Just like comic strips were a selling point for newspapers during that time, the right cartoon series could contribute to a theater's success. That's why the trade papers of the day actually paid attention to short subjects and to animated cartoons.

Film Daily, for instance, frequently noted how the larger New York theaters were programmed by announcing that a particular house had certain live acts or performances – many larger theaters had more than just an organist or pianist during the silent era, but a full band. These notices carried which specific feature was shown with which shorts. The goal was to give other theaters owners in smaller markets an idea of what was happening in the larger communities. Max's cartoons were part of that mix in some of the best-known venues in the city.

Contributing mightily to the success of an animated cartoon series was how it was being distributed. Even if a producer made the best series from an artistic viewpoint, it did him little good if he couldn't get his product into theaters.

There were two basic ways to distribute a motion picture. Several of the major studios owned theater chains that featured their own product. Many independent producers needed a middleman to get bookings. One of the most common approaches for them was to sell their films through the state rights system. Essentially, a producer would franchise his product to a booker who had a territory. That booker would seek theaters to show the films he represented.

Max used this system and, in a Film Daily trade ad on Aug. 6, 1922, announced he was "seeking territories through state rights distribution" for his "Out of the Inkwell" cartoons, "a marvel of comedy creations."

In 1921, Warner Brothers had distributed the Fleischer product. It wasn't long that Max attracted the attention of Margaret Winkler, an important player in the history of American animation. In an industry dominated by men, Winkler was a pioneer – the first woman to produce and distribute animated cartoons.

Besides distributing the Out of the Inkwell shorts, Winkler also handled Pat Sullivan's "Felix" shorts and Walt Disney's "Alice in Cartoonland" films. Marrying producer Charles Mintz, Winkler eventually turned more of the business over to him, according to Donald Crafton in his landmark book "Before Mickey."

In the Nov. 3 1922 edition of Film Daily, it was reported that Winkler had "secured the second series of Max Fleischer's 13 single reel 'Out of the Inkwell' comedies for distribution in the United States and Canada." A few days after that the paper announced that Winkler had a distributor lined up for both the Ko-Ko and the Felix cartoons for the greater New York area.

When watching the shorts and their evolution, it's interesting to note how the cartoon became less and less dependent on the Rotoscope. Part of this, I believe, was the development of animation talent. There was a decreasing need to use the rotoscope to achieve acceptable motion onscreen because there were a growing number of people who could animate. The Rotoscope

MADE OF PEN & INK: FLEISCHER STUDIOS

"ENTERTAINMENT and a BOX-OFFICE ATTRACTION", declares Dr. Hugo Riesenfeld, Managing Director of New York's Rivoli and Rialto Theatres.

Edwin Miles Fadman

Presents

"EINSTEIN'S THEORY OF RELATIVITY"

(TWO-REEL AND FOUR-REEL VERSIONS)

Edited by Prof. Garret P. Serviss

Popular Version by Max Fleischer

READY FOR RELEASE ON

STATE RIGHTS PLAN

FOR TERRITORIAL RIGHTS

COMMUNICATE WITH

Premier Productions

17 West 42nd Street   NEW YORK, N. Y.

Telephone Vanderbilt 9548

Contracts closed for Sid Grauman's Theatres, Los Angeles; McVicker's Theatre, Chicago; Mark Strand Theatre, Brooklyn. Ran one week pre-release showing at New York's Rivoli, followed by three weeks at the Rialto. Booked solid over the Marcus Loew Metropolitan Circuit and Paramount Theatres from Coast to Coast.

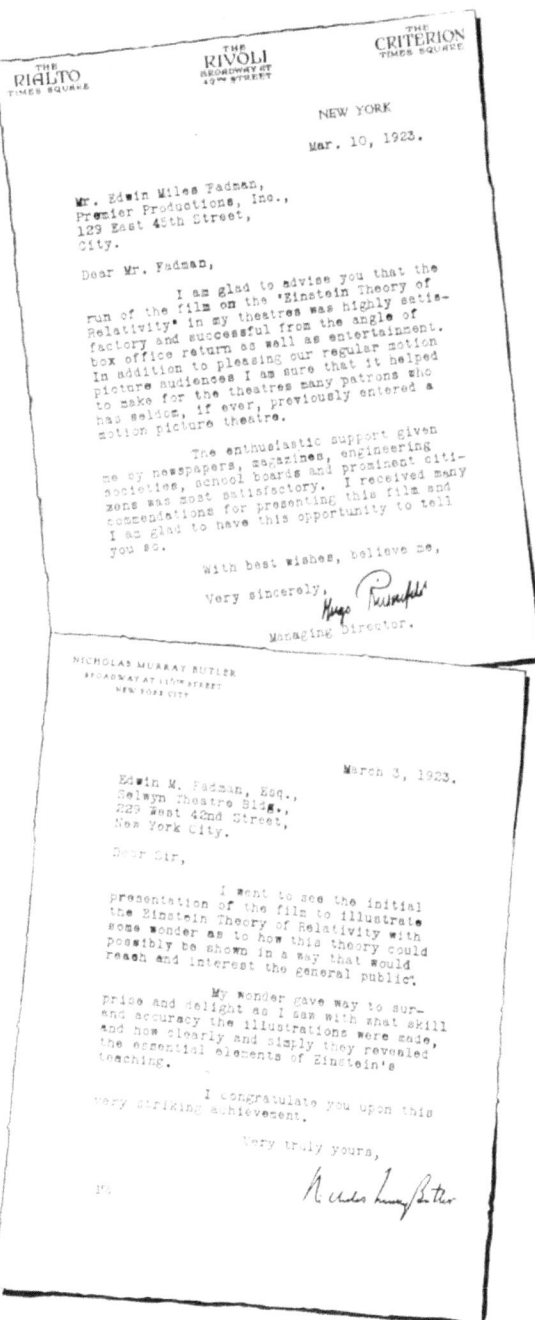

Nicholas Murray Butler, President of Columbia University, was both "SURPRISED and DELIGHTED" with the skill and accuracy with which the Einstein Theory was presented.

Max's documentary about the theory of relativity received bookings in main stream theaters.

allowed people to easily transfer the movement of the live action into cartoon animation. With a growing skilled workforce, the Rotoscope actually added an element to the cost of the production that might not be necessary.

The Out of the Inkwell shorts were being seen and reviewed well. Film Daily's reviewer noted in its March 18, 1923 edition, "This one of Max Fleischer's 'Inkwell' comedies shows the little imp from the inkwell annoying the artist who is trying to sleep. To punish the imp, he draws a high cliff and puts the little clown on its pinnacle so that he cannot get down. The clown goes to sleep and dreams – wild cartoon dreams of a giant and a cave and other things and the artist goes to sleep and dreams that the imp is chasing him all over the city in his pajamas. There are numerous laughs and the reel should have no difficulty in amusing your folks."

The Film Daily critics said of "False Alarm" in Sept. 9 1923 edition, "This latest Fleischer cartoon is well up to the standard set by his previous issues. 'False Alarm' is a clever cartoon number that should fit well on any program. Fleischer's clown performs numerous tricks such as rolling a cigarette and playing fireman. The latter half of the cartoon has some good laughs especially in the bit where the clown goes to put out a fire in a jail, breaks the window, allows the inmates to escape and then discovers the smoke only came from a convict's pipe. The clown meets with his usual fate, that of being put back into the inkbottle to prevent further mischief."

Max's interests during this early success were growing, though, beyond the animated short. From 1923 on, Max produced his own cartoons, but also worked on several documentaries, built a distribution company, started a series of live action two-reel comedies and acquired other shorts to distribute.

Max's first effort out of the realm of short subject animation involved one of the hottest topics of the day and led him to the people who helped him build a distribution company.

The documentaries and how they changed Fleischer's career

It may initially be difficult today to understand just how large a media star Albert Einstein was in the 1920s, but the nature of his fame certainly explained why an independent film producer would gamble on releasing a documentary that explained Einstein's Theory of Relativity.

Considering that Dr. Stephen Hawking made appearances on episodes of "Star Trek: The Next Generation" and "The Big Bang Theory," a film on Einstein's best-known work shouldn't seem too much a stretch to a contemporary audience.

Producer Edwin Miles Fadiman bought the rights to a German documentary on the subject, which he turned over to Max and Professor Garrett P. Serviss for re-editing and the addition of title cards. Serviss was a journalist specializing in science who had written many popular books on astronomical topics. Like Max, he also had a connection to Popular Science. Serviss had been lauded as a writer who could translate science to appeal to "the man on the street."

The two men completed two versions: a two-reel short and a four-reel feature titled "Einstein's Theory of Relativity."

On Dec. 8, 1922 Film Daily reported Max would complete his editing work that week for the feature. Max's interest in the film grew as he was named an "officer and director" in Premiere Productions, which produced the film.

Some people have claimed that this was Max's first animated feature film as it was released early in February 1923. The film is almost all live-action footage designed to illustrate the points of the theory, although Max did produce some limited animation.

The film – apparently the 40-minute version – actually received a three-week run at Rivoli Theater in New York City, according to Moving Picture World. Fadiman then released the film through his Premiere Productions and boasted in a trade ad that he had signed contracts for runs at Sid Grauman's theaters in Los Angeles, McVicker's Theater in Chicago and "booked solid over the Marcus Loew Circuit."

The review by C.S. Sewell in Moving Picture World noted, "because of the large amount of newspaper publicity accorded this revolutionary theory considerable interest was aroused in the average person's mind as to what it was all about.

"The film translated into non-scientific terms and with easily understood illustrations of the different points is a commendable effort to satisfy this curiosity."

Essentially, the movie was an exploitation film, which took advantage of the stir in the press about the theory.

Sewell wrote the four-reel version is "a little more complicated and carries the explanation a little further, which is intended for school and colleges."

As movie trade reviewers would do, Sewell also discussed the box office potential for the films. "So out of the ordinary is this film that is furnishes no definite basis of comparison with any other from a showman's standpoint and it would appear to be a question for each individual exhibitor to decide as to whether it will appeal to his patrons."

"Rush," the reviewer from Variety, certainly had another view of the film. The critic wrote, "The picture occupying just 40 minutes and doesn't hold for that stretch of time. What inspired them to book it into the Broadway film house is a mystery. A title quotes Einstein as saying that only 12 scientists in the world are capable of understanding the theory. That ought to be enough to keep it from boring a mixed lay assemblage of Valentino and Swanson fans and the army of women who do their popular science reading in May Manton and the Butterick publications.

"The film isn't even illuminating in a popular way. It doesn't explain anything that wasn't already clear. It seems a waste of footage to create elaborate and intricate diagrams to demonstrate that if you step off the earth's surface there is no such thing as east and west; that there is no meaning to the conception of large and small unless you establish some fixed standard of comparison and that fast and slow don't mean a thing except in relation to something else. It's just a labored exposition of the obvious. The picture toils through a morass of these elemental matters and then gets down to the obtuse substance of Einstein's theories.

"The conception of bent space and bent light rays is illustrated by elaborate diagrams, but they give no enlightenment. They use up an immense footage to demonstrate that if a man walks toward the stern of a moving boat at the boat's exact speed forward, he is standing still in relation to the shore, but moving backward in relation to the boat itself. A title would have covered that. But when they come to deal with that bending of light, they merely declare the principle and let it go at that.

"The diagrams are extremely ingenious to elucidate obvious things but when they get Einstein into the rarefied atmosphere of pure scientific reasoning they are baffling and the spectator is befogged. The thing is meaningless and gets down to the mere juggling of words. They establish the meaning of the yardstick of 'time space' and then describe the mysterious 'fourth dimension.' If the three known dimensions are up and down, right and left, and near and far, the fourth is 'sooner or later.'

"The whole thing is about as clear and useful as this description of it, and it will probably bore the film fan stiff."

I have seen several prints of the film at several different times but they have always been the two-reel version of the film. It's possible the four-reel version has not survived.

I tend to agree with "Rush," more than Sewell in a contemporary assessment of the film. It's not an engaging film to watch and I've never seen it with a musical accompaniment, which certainly adds a certain burden to it. What does fascinate me about the film is its earnest effort to explain this theory for the masses. There is a certain democratization at work, but of course, with the real motive being to make money about a subject that is in the news.

A trade ad in The Exhibitor's Herald (March 31, 1923) reproduced a letter from the president of Columbia University, Nicholas Murray Butler, who said he as "surprised and delighted" with the film.

Max wrote, "During the production of 'Einstein's Theory of Relativity' I was quite close to Prof. Serviss, an elderly man, somewhat hard of hearing but amazingly brilliant and with a mind that worked with the speed of light. But we couldn't always agree on what should or shouldn't go into the picture. That was in the silent motion picture days. I recall that in the script I wanted to use the title 'When you see the stars twinkle.' Prof. Serviss became vicious in his anger against the use of the word 'twinkle' because he said stars do not do not 'twinkle' – it is merely an illusion. I felt that the picture needed the title in that place and I argued that 'poets make pictures.' They paint with words, but give you a mental picture nevertheless, and since the world has poets and people like poetry, in my opinion it is correct to say that the stars twinkle as I think they do. The professor was absolutely ice cold, until finally he rose from his seat and as kind a man as he was hit the desk with his fist and said, 'I will not go further, nor will I permit the use of my name in connection with a gross misrepresentation of scientific fact.'"

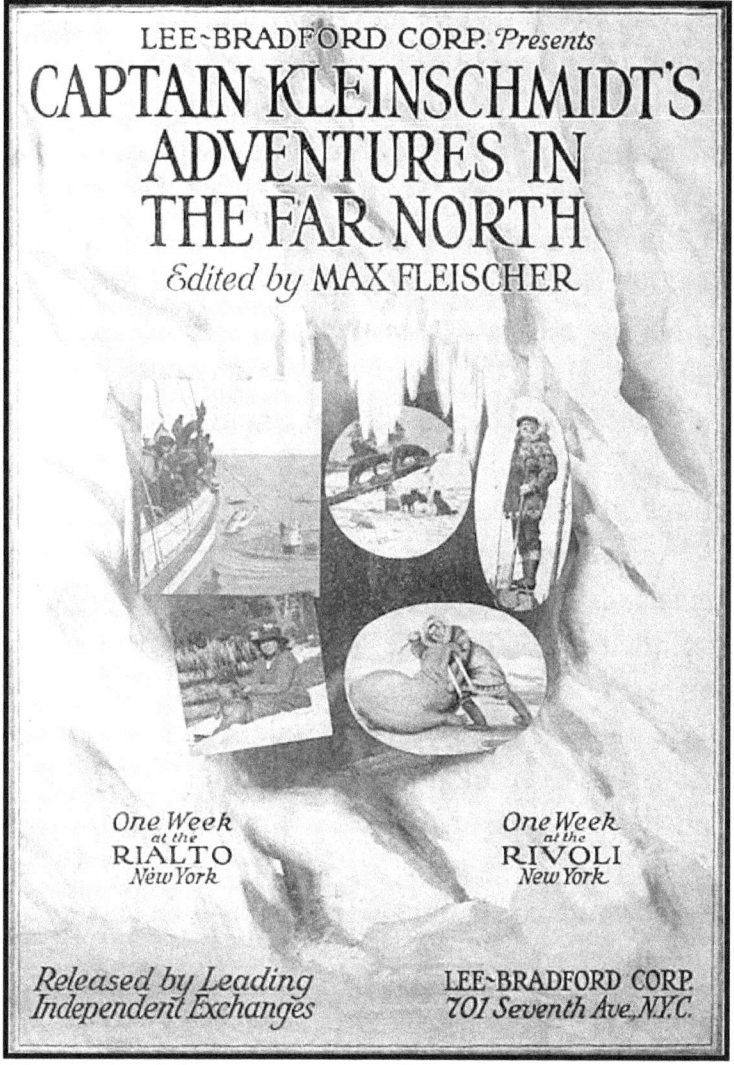

This trade ad from June 1923 is for a documentary featuring an Arctic explorer that Max edited.

Max continued, "I still felt there was nothing wrong with my determination to use that title. He left me, after saying, 'It's too bad that after 60 years of scientific writing for the public here comes Max Fleischer trying to tell me what is right and wrong to say.' I left him alone for a few days and gave him the chance to cool down and than approached him again. 'Professor perhaps this is the thing that you don't realize. I have read your articles for 15 years and they always fascinated me, but when I got to the bottom of the column if something I had read was not clear I went back and read that paragraph over again. Now professor, that's an advantage you have in writing which we do not have in motion pictures, because once we say something on the screen which is not clear the audience can not pull the film back to review it. We must tell our audience these facts in a language which they understand the first time. I agree with you that it is incorrect say 'stars twinkle' but the audience will understand that and won't find it necessary to review the picture.'

"He was sold and I got the title in but every time the reel came to that title, he would put his head in his hands and refuse to look at the screen. It amused me. Professor Serviss was a true scientist."

Max added that he had heard Einstein had seen the film and remarked it "being an excellent attempt to illustrate an abstract subject."

He added, "While we were working on the picture (Serviss and I) his knowledge fascinated me as much as the work of making the picture. I realized that right near me was a mind which I could never attain. He demonstrated, for instance, that the earth traveled at such a terrific rate that in a race with a bullet, the bullet could seem to be going backwards."

"Ten years after the picture was made it was shown again at the Museum of Natural History, which has a theatre seating 1,500. There were 2,500 in there and about 2,000 outside that couldn't get in," Max concluded.

Later in 1923, another documentary on which Max worked was released, "Adventures in the Far North." Max apparently edited the film which was initially released as a five-reeler – about 50 minutes – but later trimmed to a four-reel version.

According to a Sept. 13, 1923 review in Variety, the film was "a consistent digest of the travels of Captain [F.E.] and Mrs. Kleinschmidt through the inner passage to Alaska, which extended over a distance of 5,000 miles from Seattle and return … The trip was made on a former submarine chaser which Capt. Kleinschmidt now calls the 'Silver Screen,' with him supervising the work of several camera men who made the picture. The trip began in May 1922 and lasted seven months … Scenes in Glacier Bay show the breaking up of a 40-foot sea wall and the huge waves caused by the collapse, the capture of a school of whales and the disposition of their carcasses at the whaling station … A thrilling scene is where Capt. Kleinschmidt, his wife and a cameraman are adrift on an ice floe and [are] forced to seek refuge on the top of a giant iceberg."

The New York Times reported the production was at the famed Rivoli Theater and noted, "This production is well worth seeing." It continued, "The second feature at the Rivoli is 'Adventures in the Far North,' a series of pictures taken during a hunting and whaling expedition that lasted seven months. They are singularly interesting. There are some fine scenes showing the harpooning of whales, also pictures of walruses. But perhaps the best picture is that showing a polar bear and her cub. An attempt is made from the ship to catch the cub. When the rope is around it the mother fights and lashes the side of the vessel. Eventually because of the remarkable performance of the mother bear the little one is freed and one sees them both swimming off, the cub keeping very close to the big bear. Captain F. E. Kleinschmidt, who took his wife on this expedition, has had the picture titled as if it were Mrs. Kleinschmidt's diary, which is quite effective. It is a most interesting production and runs for about an hour."

Kleinschmidt was a veteran documentary filmmaker who had risen to some prominence in 1914 when his film "Arctic Hunt" was shown to members of Congress, according to Moving Picture World, "who were then legislating or trying to legislate upon Alaskan affairs. The captain's information in motion pictures was greatly valued by the legislators, who freely declared that nothing less than a trip to a long residence in the territory could have supplied them with the facts recorded by the captain's pictures."

Max's daughter Ruth recounted to me how the sequence involving Kleinschmidt capturing a polar bear cub was a section of the film that Max had deliberately included.

Film Daily's review of May 14, 1923 noted that sequence. "By far the most interesting of all, though, are the pictures of a huge white polar bear swimming with her young offspring hanging on. Remarkable are the shots showing the efforts to rope in the young bear and the frantic attempts of the mother to battle off the captors and her eventual content when the little bear is allowed to go free."

The Film Daily review concluded, "The picture is worthy of exhibition anywhere and should be heartily received."

Considering Max's pride in his work in the Signal Corps in World War I producing instructional films, one might draw the conclusion that these films spoke to his love of science. Perhaps, as well, they added a greater legitimacy to his career than the animated adventures of Ko-Ko.

Max's career as an editor of non-fiction footage took an interesting turn in October 1925 when Moving Picture World announced that he had signed a contract with Urban-Kineto Corp. to be "editor in chief" of two new films series for the company, "Reelviews" and "Searchlights."

"Reelviews" appears to have been a newsreel series and the story reported that "Fleischer will have a staff of cameramen, reaching around the world, ready at a moment's notice to go out and take the needed scenes" – undoubtedly a bit of press release hyperbole.

Charles Urban's company produced non-fiction short subjects, one of which, "Nature's Handiwork" secured a favorable mention in a New York Times movie column in February 1921.

According to an essay written by Luke McKernan, Urban was a film pioneer who had built a large library of stock footage. He was also a proponent of color film technology and had a vision for a film-based encyclopedia that would be sold to schools.

Although he did have two theatrical series of short subjects, Urban's plans did not succeed and in August 1925, a former investor C.M. Bortman bought the assets of the company, which included two million feet of footage.

In the summer of 1925, Max's feature film "Evolution" was released theatrically. Although a trade ad described it as "an Urban-Kineto production edited by Max Fleischer," it was released by Red Seal, the new company headed at the time by Fadiman to distribute the Fleischer product.

The film is comprised of stock footage with some animation by Willis O'Brien from his 1918 film "The Ghost of Slumber Mountain." Max receives director credit with "scientific supervision by Edward J. Foyles of the American Museum of Natural History."

In the film's introduction, man's domination of the planet is shown through various examples and is followed by this title: "Master of all he surveys and standing in awe of his own daring, Man turns to solve the greatest mystery of all time – the mystery of HIMSELF."

The film uses the stock footage to show the development of the earth, the links between various animals and fossil remains of dinosaurs and early man. Its final title card walked the line that divided the nation on the issue; "Some call it Evolution, others the work of God."

The trade ad from Red Seal was breathless: "Everybody is talking 'Evolution;' Everybody wants to see 'Evolution' ... A front-page story in five absorbing reels."

Whether or not the film was a sincere reflection of Max's considerable interest in science is not known. What is definite is that the trade review in Moving Picture World was published on July 25, 1925 is the name recognition of the subject. The review was published just four days after John Scopes, a teacher in Tennessee had lost a court case due to his presenting the theory of evolution in his class, an action against state law.

The nation was obsessed with what became to be known as "The Monkey Trial" and "Evolution," like "Einstein's Theory of Relativity," was in the purest definition an exploitation film.

It proved to be a well-received exploitation film. Moving Picture World reported, "The New York critics hailed the film enthusiastically. Harriette Underhill, in the Herald-Tribune, declared, "Don't miss it whatever you do. We sat through it twice."

Red Seal, which started distributing Max's cartoons, was formed in 1923 as this story announced. Max was the treasurer of the corporation

"The Sun reviewer declares that '"Evolution' is 'an absorbing picture tracing the ascent of man. Your beliefs, pro or con, do not prevent your enjoyment of an exhibition presenting in pictorial forms the beliefs and deductions of the best-known scientists of the world. A wave of applause swept over the audience.'"

"'Absorbing, timely and well-done,' says Rose Pelswick in the Journal. Quinn Martin in The World called it, "Unusually interesting and instructive as well' is the verdict of the Post…

'The Times put is official stamp of approval on it with 'the audience applauded 'Evolution,' which proved interesting as a means of popularizing an abstract question.' 'Applauded for almost a minute,' recorded the Telegraph."

***

It should be noted that Max had not lost interest in the use of film for educational purposes. In 1927, he produced "Now You're Talking," an industrial film for AT&T. Film Daily noted [the film] seeks to teach people how to use and care for the standard phone of the 1920s, the candle stick. Max is credited with the scenario that shows how people abuse this model of the telephone.

"A live action real estate agent falls asleep and dreams of a telephone being taken to the emergency room. The phone's diary reveals all of the inappropriate things people do to him, such as quickly flicking the hanger in which the ear piece hangs, slamming the phone on the desk and twisting the cord. The live action character learns the error of his way," the article noted.

Seen today in the era of cell phone, the film is definitely a curiosity with its depiction of the proper use of a candlestick phone. Handsomely produced, though, the nine-minute short has some funny moments as the traumatized phone recounts his "boss" had treated him.

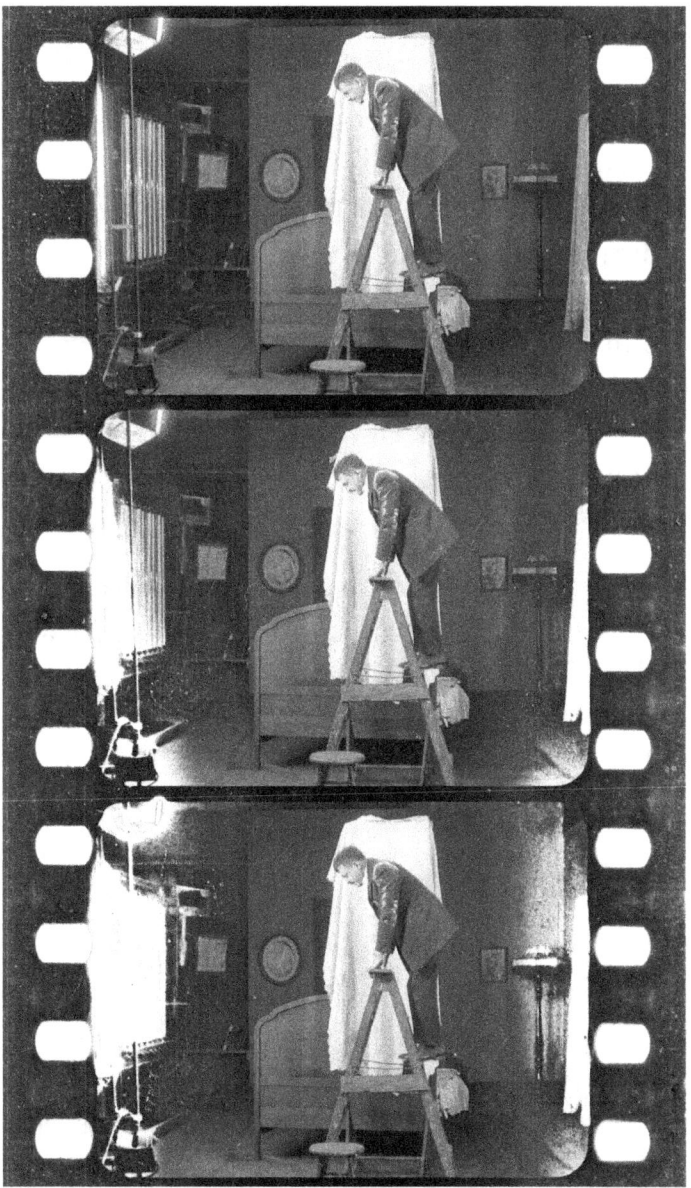

Max clearly was comfortable in appearing in his cartoons. Here is a clip of film from an Out of the Inkwell production with Max looking a a little worse for wear as usual. Courtesy of J.J. Sedelmaier

Red Seal

During his work on these feature films, Max was producing the Out of the Inkwell cartoons and his involvement with Fadiman led to the creation of Red Seal, a company that would allow Max to distribute his own product. Film Daily reported on Oct. 26, 1923, "Red Seal Pictures Corp. has been formed with Edwin Miles Fadiman, president and general manager; Harold Rodner, vice-president and Max Fleischer, treasurer. 'Unusual and distinctive pictures' are promised by the organization which will release via the state right market."

Later that year, Film Daily noted, "Fleischer Closes Foreign Deals – 'Out of the Inkwell' cartoons have been sold by Max Fleischer for China, South Africa, Australia, Poland and England."

The quality of the animated shorts didn't seem to suffer during this time of business reorganization and expansion. The trade reviews were still positive for the Inkwell shorts.

This publicity shot from the mid-1920s shows Max and many Ko-Kos, along with Fitz the dog.

***

An interesting side note reflects the growing status Max was enjoying in the industry. The November 1923 edition of Screenland – a "fan magazine" for lack of a better description – had a fascinating article by Robert E. Sherwood.

Sherwood was a writer whose career was wide and celebrated. A playwright, screenwriter and film critic, Sherwood was awarded four Pulitzer Prizes. His film criticism was in the old Life magazine, among others.

The premise of this article, though, was the importance of "the cutter," the position we call "editor" today.

"However, there is an obscure, unromantic individual who plays a tremendously important part," Sherwood wrote in his introduction. "He is called the 'Cutter,' and although the public never gives him a second or even a first thought he often has the power to unmake the work of a director, actor and continuity combined."

Sherwood described the work of a cutter and then outlined the exercise he was about to undertake. After seeing an advanced showing of Universal's huge production of "The Hunchback of Notre Dame" staring the great Lon Chaney, studio bosses asked Sherwood if he would try to improve the film through his edits.

Sherwood wrote, "My colleagues in the cutting room were Hugo Riesenfeld, director of the Rivoli and Rialto Theatres in New York and Max Fleischer who creates the ingenious 'Out of the inkwell' animated shorts."

He continued, "Our first task was to decide, 'What is wrong with this picture?' each of us picked out the flaw that seemed to be the most glaring and then lumped the complaints together. When we had filed these reports, it looked very much as though there would be nothing left in 'The Hunchback of Notre Dame' except the Hunch."

Sherwood reported the picture had to be "pepped up." He tells how the trio cut out scenes "that had no direct bearing to the story," as well as "too many mob scenes."

He wrote, "When this arduous task had been completed, we set out to work on the sub-titles – and here was the most delicate problem of all. The original titles had been couched in the stilted phraseology of Victor Hugo's novel, so that the various characters were going around saying lines like, "Fie! I know thy reputation. Thou wouldst say as much to any maiden,' and 'Think ye to take our Esmeralda for a plaything? Have done with her or I'll slit your throat.'"

He continued, "These flowery utterances had to be simplified, because many words and phrases that were considered good slang in 1482 are practically unknown to movie fans of the present day. Moreover, the titles were quite inconsistent. In some of them the 'Thee' and 'Thou' from was used, while others were content with the everyday 'You.' And in one title, a lady of King Louis' court was forced to utter the word 'cute.'

"The result was that out of 199 titles, only five remained unchanged. The rest were either re-worded and boiled down to were completely altered to fit the continuity as it had been revised in the cutting process.

"Thus is a strange situation brought about. Dr. Riesenfeld, Max Fleischer and myself revised 'The Hunchback of Notre Dame' to suit our own ideas – although we actually had nothing to so with its preparation and we shall receive no credit or blame for its success or failure."

The clipping ends here, so there is no resolution whether or not Carl Laemmle and company accepted the cuts. There are three people credited for editing the film, but Sherwood, Riesenfeld and Fleischer are not among them.

***

In the Dec. 2, 1923 edition of Film Daily, "Shadows" was given the following review: "Once again the imp from the inkwell becomes involved, this time with the shadows of his own figure. The result is a completely different set of difficulties, chiefly the result of Fleischer's making silhouettes of animals with his figures. These animals annoy the imp and trouble him to such an extent that finally after being chased and crushed he becomes so bewildered that he is glad to jump back into the inkwell. Very laughable, very amusing."

Max was receiving publicity for his studio's efforts outside of trade reviews. Elizabeth Lonergan wrote a piece in the April 1924 Pictures and Picturergoer about the cartoons.

"Have you fallen under the spell of that smallest comedian, that clever and decidedly original 'Out of the Inkwell Clown?' If you haven't there is something wrong with you and you should see a doctor at once," Londergan wrote.

She continued, "I went to the Out of the Inkwell offices to find out for myself all about it. I found out a lot and had a mighty nice time but between ourselves I was almost as mystified when I came out as when I went in. The whole process looked absurdly simple when I was there but once outside I marveled anew at the cleverness of Max Fleischer and his genius in creating a new and delight screen character.

"Mr. Fleischer is almost as interesting as the clown, though not so mysterious a personage and his staff of workers is like a big family.

"Nowhere have I seen the cooperation and the friendly atmosphere that I found in his little office studio. Perhaps the fact that it is small, may account for some of the home-likeness of the surroundings but whatever it is most delightful.

"Max Fleischer told me all about himself, of his coming to a new country from Austria when he was only a lad, of his struggles for an education, his art lessons taken at night after working hours and finally of the position which he secured in a small newspaper where he made cartoons that soon attracted notice. 'But my dream was to make drawings from the screen,' he said. 'At that time there were a number being made but none of them were perfected and the changes from one sketch to another were plainly noticeable to audiences. I made up my mind to perfect a camera that would have the same ease in changing pictures that the regular motion picture ones did and I worked in my spare time perfecting such an invention. The camera must operate more freely to eliminate the difference movement which was perceptible and often annoying to audiences who had hard work keeping their minds on the subject before them. My theory was to make the process so smooth the mechanical side would be forgotten. I gave up my position and as I had no money to waste put all I could spare into the experiment and did away with the problem of office rent by working in my bedroom. After a year and half I was ready to show the results and the getting of a release was the easiest part of it all. Just as we were ready to go ahead the War came and I was sent to Fort Sills to war work. This consisted in making a series of films which were used in the instruction of soldiers.'"

This odd description of the origins of the Rotoscope – never have I seen it described before as simply a camera – also contradicts an often-repeated aspect of Max's story – about the commercial realization a cartoon couldn't take a year to complete, a point made by the distributor to Max.

"A Trip to Mars" (April 13, 1924, Film Daily) received this reaction: "Max Fleischer continues to inject originality and novelty into his cartoon numbers. His latest, 'A Trip to Mars,' on the Rivoli program last week, is a clever and amusing number that shows the cartoonist at his best and with his pen clown performing a series of comedy tricks that will amuse and entertain any audience. The clown is sent, via a skyrocket, to Mars where Fleischer installs all sorts of grotesque, imaginary beings. The artist appears in his film as usual and makes a flying trip to Mars himself through means of trick photography. This is an A-1 cartoon number, a good novelty and quite amusing."

The reviewer is right. "A Trip to Mars" is a fun cartoon tackling a science fiction subject not frequently seen in the movies of the 1920s.

One could say the typical Ko-Ko short was a contest of wills between the creator and the creation. If the shorts were formulaic in that sense, they were not formulaic in how they fulfilled that format. The Fleischer staff was willing to take chances by using different styles of animation and special effects. Other animation studios took notice

Walter Lantz's "Dinky Doodles" series at Bray was as close as an imitation of the Ko-Ko cartoons as one could find, even with Lantz himself as the human star.

Disney's "Alice in Cartoonland" shorts reversed the Ko-Ko format. Instead of a carton character entering a human world, a human is in a cartoon world. Although in one early short, "Alice's Spooky Adventure" (1923), there is a reason given for this interaction – the little girl dreams it – in subsequent cartoons audiences just had to accept it. The other significant difference is the Ko-Ko cartoons were technically superior to the Alice shorts.

The reviews in Film Daily show the wide subject matter of the Ko-Ko cartoons. The basic formula of Max drawing the clown and their often-contentious relationship was broad enough for many variations.

"July 13, 1924 'The Runaway:' Max Fleischer certainly did a lot of work on this Out-of-the-Inkwell cartoon. In addition to the little cartoon clown, there is an actor portraying the devil and, of course, the artist himself. The clown goes through various adventures, finally dropping into the abode of the devil. He is chased by hundreds of little imps and finally after many adventures reaches his inkbottle in safety where he cuddles contentedly in the bottom of the bottle safe. A particularly good example of the method used to make these cartoon drawings move is given. A large stack of drawings of the clown in different poses is shown and when it is shuffled by the artist's hand, the cartoon seems to actually move. This will give many folks who don't know how it's done a good idea of the work entailed in this sort of reel."

"Oct. 12 1924: Max Fleischer has provided some new stunts for his inkwell clown in 'Vaudeville.' As usual the artist at appears with his clown and it's a toss up to see who can give the best performance. The clown offers his bag of tricks and the artist competes by doing some 'quick change' stunt that are made possible by the various camera tricks. Fleischer will be looking for a job on his own account some day, should his clown lose his popularity. He gives his little pet character a close race for comedy honors in "Vaudeville.'"

"March 15, 1925: Ko-Ko, Max Fleischer's cartoon clown who lives in the inkwell feels the urge to be a barber after he sees his boss shaving. So he uses the razor, the clipper and the shears to the detriment of everything and everybody who comes into his cartoon barber shop. The results are funny and quite unexpected. Then he finds a bottle of hair tonic and grows whiskers on everything including a horse, a dog, a cat and the artist himself, until he is finally imprisoned back into his inkbottle. Always amusing."

"May 10, 1925: Max Fleischer's well-known inkwell clown Ko-Ko, is as frivolous and amusing as ever in his latest comedy. 'Ko-Ko Trains 'Em' shows the clown demonstrating the proper way to train animals for a circus. In particular he trains a young pup. Not a cartoon pup, either, but a real live flesh-and-blood dog. The film has been developed in such a way that the cartoon drawing and the real dog seem actually to work together. It has been done before, of course, but it is novel and amusing, just the same. An excellent short reel for any type house."

"June 7, 1925 'Ko-Ko sees Spooks:' Ko-Ko, Max Fleischer's Inkwell Clown, has his share of thrills this time. The artist draws him from the numerals thirteen and the calendar shows the date as Friday, the 13th. Then the colored porter who cleans the office draws a haunted house for the clown's background and throws his hat into it. In vain Ko-Ko tries to rescue his hat without going into the house, but in the end he has to enter it. Numerous incidents then occur with ghosts chasing the clown and his dog, but he is finally rescued. Always entertaining."

During this time, though Max was broadening his business operations. Film Daily reported on May 1, 1924 that Red Seal distribution had contracted with Max for him to produce 26 one-reel newsreels called "Film Facts." Later in August, Max announced a slow-motion process, the Novograph. The next month, this device would be used for a series of shorts called "Marvels of Motion," that Red Seal would distribute.

There are several examples of the "Marvels in Motion" series on YouTube, specifically on the channel established by the Fleischer Studios. The manipulation of ordinary movement from normal speed to slow motion to reverse undoubtedly seemed exotic to audiences in the 1920s. Max's stock in the film world was on the rise. Film Daily noted in its Sept. 21, 1924 issue that Max and Fadiman had entertained "Lord and Lady Mountbatten, cousins of the Prince of Wales, and members of his party," at the Red Seal Out-of-the-Inkwell Studios.

Max produced a cartoon especially for Armistice Week entitled "The League of Nations." A reviewer in the Exhibitors Trade Review Nov. 29, 1924 edition wrote, "This is one of the best Max Fleischer's clever inkwell cartoons, which is praise of a high order as the artist never yet turned out a dull sketch. The idea of the artist playing a joke on the pigmy [sic] clown by holding down a drawing of Mars and other heavenly bodies in front of a telescope and the clowns from every nation in the world answering the call to arms each one popping out of an ink bottle is amusing and entertaining in the extreme. The clown thinks that he sees the Martians preparing to invade the earth and sends forth a distress call to all the clowns wherever they may be. They take an aeroplane in their haste to arrive on the scene in time for the battle and when they discover it is only a joke, they all wind up once more in the inkwell."

By the next year, it was more and more clear the goal of Red Seal was to be like Educational Pictures, a company that specialized in a wide range of short films.

A trade ad for Red Seal in the Film Daily of June 21, 1925, read, "That program – It has got to be built every week. It must be different every week. It must have variety yet it must harmonize with the feature. That is the job of which shows the genius if the showman. He can't get out before the audience and make excuses. He must deliver. Audiences want the goods.

"Edwin Miles Fadiman, president of Red Seal Pictures, hears that from the leading exhibitors in all parts of the country. It is a big problem for them to find real novelties for 52 programs a year.

"The answer, of course was to book Red Seal product such as the 13 new 'Ko-Ko Song Cartunes,' the 13 'Inkwell' cartoons, and the 13 'Marvels of Motion' shorts all produced by Max Fleischer. In all Red Seal offered 93 short subjects to theater owners."

The competition at this time was intense. On the same page, there were favorable reviews for Red Seal's Film Facts one-reeler on the Coast Guard and an "Animated Hair" cartoon, as well as an interesting look at the competing series through its trade ads. Winkler Pictures promoted "Alice Comedies by Walt Disney. Humorous, Novel, New, What a combination!!! … Full of Fun."

Winkler also promoted the Krazy Kat cartoons by Bill Nolan without a mention of creator George Herriman or King Features. Short Films Syndicate promised a "new, better, funnier series" of Mutt & Jeff cartoons.

The Inkwell shorts continued to garner good reviews. The Film Daily's June 21, 1925 edition noted, "'Ko-Ko celebrates the Fourth' is an especially appropriate reel for the Fourth of July or the days just preceding it. Ko-Ko, the Inkwell clown experiments with a box of firecrackers and lands on a cannibal isle. The natives think the fireworks are good to eat and stuff themselves with the unknown food only to blow up and go off after they gorge themselves. Ko-Ko gets himself blown back home safely, however. There are quite a number of hand-colored bits in this, all the fireworks being done in color. A number of shots of actual fireworks are extremely pretty."

This is the first reference I've seen to a Ko-Ko cartoon including a color sequence. They would have been achieved by having painters put color onto the individual frames of the completed prints, a laborious and expensive process. I think it would be safe to assume that these special prints would have been prepared for theaters in larger cities.

Film Daily noted on Sept. 2 1925, "Beth Brown has been appointed editor-in-chief of the Out-of-the-Inkwell Studios and Red Seal Productions, and will assist Max Fleischer in writing scenarios." This is the first reference to an "editor-in-chief" position at the studio. To my knowledge, she did not receive a screen credit.

What makes her name so interesting is that Beth Brown is the name of the author of the novel "Applause" that was turned into the highly acclaimed motion picture of the same name in 1929.

Max assumed the presidency of Red Seal in 1926.

Despite the increasing workload, Max still appeared in the cartoons as noted in the review of "Ko-Ko Steps Out" in the Film Daily Nov. 8, 1925. "A comedy without the ever-present 'Charleston' dance is becoming somewhat of a rarity, and not to be out-done. Ko-Ko 'steps out' in this issue and learns the southern shuffle. His dancing teacher, drawn by Max Fleischer is too old and lame, so Ko-Ko asks for the pen and draws a red- hot dancing baby-doll. This fades into an actual photograph of the girl in action. Ko-Ko, the artist, the cartoon dog. A real puppy and a cat all do the Charleston in fine style. This is a peppy little number with plenty of those cute little touches."

***

"Ko-Ko Steps Out" features Max's daughter Ruth in her film debut. Ruth was interested in a career in show business and the story of her life and her husband's Fleischer animator Seymour Kneitel – is told in series of blogs written by their daughter Ginny Mahoney at http://seymourkneitel.blogspot.com.

Mahoney wrote, "It was natural that Ruth, a fun-loving gal, would want to be part of this exciting theatrical life. Trained as a dancer, by her late teens she was dancing on stage in vaudeville chorus lines. In 1925 Max even created a film, 'Ko-Ko Steps Out,' that was built around Ruth and her dancing. In the film, Max is on screen while Ruth appears first on the screen with Max and then appears to jump from the screen to the stage where they interact. It was a combination of film and vaudeville! … By 1926, when Max's Red Seal venture was floundering, Ruth joined the Ned Rayburn traveling dance troupe as a chorus girl. Ned Rayburn was famous at the time for producing dancing stars … When appearing on stage she sometimes used the name Ruth Dix … likely a play on the name of her younger brother Dick, who she adored. The Rayburn troupe danced in theaters all over the U.S. Ruth would have been about 20 years-old at the time, and her parents, Max and Essie, were not at all happy to have her leading what they considered a wild and questionable life.

"When Ruth returned home from a Wayburn road tour her mother made it clear that she was NOT to go on the road anymore! But Ruth had no interest in sitting idly home, so she proposed that she'd consider staying only if she could work at Max's studio. Max reluctantly agreed – reluctant because he knew the studio had a staff of basically crazy, wild people, and he worried Ruth might contribute too much to that craziness.

"Much to Max's surprise and delight, Ruth became a valuable asset. She worked her way up first to head of the Opaquing (or painting) Department and later she became head of the Inking Department. She also wrote stories for a number of cartoons. Aside from her success in the office, she was still a girl that loved to party, so she was equally popular with the fun-loving staff.

"The studio is where my parents met, my dad was an animator at the time. They were an unlikely pair since Ruth loved to dance and Seymour couldn't dance at all. But he was such a nice guy. Ruth at first thought he had a sweetheart since she'd hear him on the phone saying, 'Hello dear'… I'll be home soon dear.' Turned out he was talking to his mother! My dad was in his late teens when his father died, at which point he became the main support of his mother and sister."

***

Other Fleischer shorts were also receiving attention. The reviewer for the Film Daily Oct. 4, 1925, liked "Marvels of Motion Issue 'D.'"

"In this number of the Fleischer Novograph process series are shown various riders in a steeplechase, and what happens to horse and jockey as they go over the hurdles. First in regular motion you see one take a tumble, then in slow motion is shown in detail exactly what happened. After you have seen this you begin to appreciate just what risks a steeplechase rider takes. Finally, the process is reversed, and the rider and horse get up from their spill and go backwards to the starting point. Another subject is that of a broad jumper. In slow motion the flying figure is held actually motionless in mid-air at one point, so that you can see the tenseness of his muscles and the physical exertion that he is putting into his effort. What occurs when lumps of sugar are dropped into a glass of milk is shown. The novelty of these slow-motion specialties does not seem to wear off, for the various subjects are always new and entertaining."

Not every cartoon received a rave review. In the Film Daily Dec. 27, 1925 edition, "Ta-Ra-Ra-Boom Der E" was described as "a typical Fleischer song cartoon. The verses of the song are projected, while the animated ball jumps from one word to another to time the singing in the audience. The comic cartoons are interspersed. There is little to describe about this reel. Its value consists in the reaction on your audience. If they can be induced to join in the singing, it is a success. If not, it becomes just a filler. You know what you can do with this type."

It was announced in early January 1926 that Max had succeeded Fadiman as the president of Red Seal and later that month he was "touring the east coast visiting exhibitors while Dave Fleischer, of Out-of-the-Inkwell studios is editing a series of novelties which may be released late this spring."

With this move, it could be argued that Max had achieved something that no other animated cartoonist had done and no other until Walt Disney formed Buena Vista in 1953. Max was the head of a studio and a distributor, a company with exchanges in major cities just like MGM, Universal and Paramount. Like those three studios, Red Seal not only produced its own films, but also picked up shorts produced by others for distribution.

There was, of course, a crucial difference. MGM and Paramount, for instance, owned theater chains. Those companies did business with independent theater owners as well, but a solid part of their receipts came within the corporate organization.

Red Seal, like any independent business, had to sell their product and collect the rentals. It could not participate in the business model that helped the majors.

The announcement story in Moving Picture World on Jan. 30, 1926 that Max now headed Red Seal also noted some of his publicity efforts. "Ko-Ko's boss has talked to millions of listeners and has regaled them with chats regarding his clown, these chats being almost as funny as the cartoons. Recently, at WIP Station, Philadelphia, Mr. Fleischer promised his listeners that if they would send their names to him in his office in number 729 Seventh Avenue, New

York City, he would send them a Ko-Ko card. Max graciously promised to print in the names of those who wrote to him. The following day he received 1,082 requests. He was dizzy when the day's work was done. Next morning, on reaching his office he was confronted with 8,391 additional names and was obliged to hire a couple of experts to properly letter the cards to be mailed out. The third day 15,427 urgent requests for Ko-Ko cards arrived! And now, when, Max talks over the radio, he soft-pedals all reference to 'personally lettered Ko-Ko cards!"

In the pages of the film industry trade publications, there was suddenly a burst of advertising for Red Seal releases. On the review pages there was also an increase in Red Seal product. For example, in the Film Daily of Feb. 14, 1926 there are three Red Seal releases – a Ko-Ko cartoon, an Animated Hair cartoon by Marcus and a dramatic short, "The Soul of the Cypress."

Max was clearly expanding his company quickly.

Although reportedly soft-spoken and to an extent shy according to some people, Max was apparently more than willing to publicize his films. In the March 27, 1926 edition of Moving Picture World, Max's trip to Chicago was reported. "When Max Fleischer, president of Reel Seal Picture and head of the Inkwell Studios, was in Chicago a little more than a week ago he spoke over station KYW, shortly after Red Seal's newest exchange opened, discussing the human side of making cartoon featurettes. As a result Max will be doing considerable lecturing.

"Ko-Ko the clown, one of Fleischer's creations was playing in a number of the largest Chicago theatres at the time. Two of the featurettes were Song Car-Tunes, and three others were Inkwells.

"Aided by the fact that Ko-Ko was so prevalent in the town and the interest aroused by Max's talk, the radio-movie fans wrote a trifle in excess of thirty-three hundred letters, begging Max for a cartoon picture of his inimitable clown – and more radio talks are to be made by this film executive before the spring is over.

"'There are intimate and 'back stage' secrets,' Fleischer stated, in explaining the reason for radio talks on the movies, "which will aid the industry as a whole. The great mass of film going folks are genuinely interested in many of the phases of picture making which does not reveal itself when projected, because there is nothing in present day picture making for us to be ashamed of."

The last statement is probably a reference to the lingering fallout in the 1920s from a series of highly publicized scandals, including the Fatty Arbuckle rape and manslaughter trial (in which Arbuckle was acquitted) and leading man Wallace Reid's death due to a drug overdose.

This might have been Max's first appearance on radio, but it wasn't his last.

The same issue of the trade paper reported how Red Seal films had been playing in some of the largest and most prestigious Broadway movie theaters, another selling point for theater owners in small markets.

On April 3, 1926, Film Daily reported, "Max Fleischer stated when he assumed the presidency of Red Seal Pictures, that within a brief period he would have distributing centers in all the principal key cities.

"This statement is being rapidly proved the latest Red Seal Exchange being New Haven and Boston, both of which will be opened on April 15; the New Haven exchange operated in connection with Lester Tobias and the Boston one with Tobias and H.S. Snyder."

MADE OF PEN & INK: FLEISCHER STUDIOS

***

There was one more thing Max had to do to expand his company into new sales territory: produce live action two-reel comedies. Time and time again for both entertainers and producers the two-reel comedies had proven to be the entry level for feature film production. There is no written indication that Max was aspiring for features, but he was clearly heading in that direction.

The new "Carrie of Chorus" series gave Max an opportunity to allow his daughter's interest in show business under his watchful eye. Ruth was to be a member of the cast.

Moving Picture World reported on May 8 1926 Red Seal was planning a series of "Carrie of the Chorus" shorts, based on Irwin Richard Franklyn's syndicated newspaper stories entitled "Memoirs of a Stage Doorman."

Franklyn was to write and produce the series while Max would edit and title each of the films.

"Franklyn has closed for what will materially be as one of the most powerful exploitation angles ever put behind a short subject series. The Hearst chain of newspapers will run in serial form the entire fictionization of the 'Carrie of the Chorus' stores in all of the newspaper guaranteeing credit lines for theaters playing these attractions. This will afford exhibitors booking this series an enviable advertising accessory that will help in no mean way to put over the entire program."

The Film Daily noted on May 12, 1926 "Max Fleischer has engaged Bradley Barker as co-director for his series of two-reel comedies, 'Carrie of the Chorus,' which go into production in a few days at Pathé Studio, Harlem. The initial picture is 'Busting Into Broadway.'"

The June 15, 1926 Moving

This 1926 ad shows the films Red Seal offered theater owners.

Picture World noted that Max was "personally directing" the films. "A taxi cab company supplied two dozen taxis for a 'chase scene.' Manhattan Avenue north of 100th Street was the locale. The Police Department gave its sanction. Assistant Director Dave Fleischer arranged with the motorcycle police to detour conflicting traffic during this 'shooting.'"

The story listed the cast as including Hazelle Harmon, Rolland Flander, Ruth Florence, Ray Bolger, Esther Muir and Venda Case.

The Aug. 15, 1926 edition of Film Daily noted, "Red Seal will start production on the tenth of its 'Carrie of the Chorus' pictures within two weeks, with Dave Fleischer and Bradley Barker co-directing. Six, seven, eight and nine of the series are now being prepared for release."

Moving Picture World reported on Sept. 4, 1926, the first Carrie of the Chorus short "is ready for release on schedule."

The reporter – or publicist – added, "The series, of which there were 13 in all, two reels each in length, marks the entry of Max Fleischer into the two-reel comedy field. Mr. Fleischer has had plans for these comedies under contemplation for some time, ever since the cry arose for more and better short comedy materials, but owning to the press of production activities of his other Red Seal releases, which number among other the Ko-Ko subjects in his song cart-tunes and the Out of the Inkwell comedies, actual production on these had to be delayed until this time."

The Sept. 4, 1926 edition of Motion Picture World noted the first of the new two-reelers, "Morning Judge," was now ready for release. Peggy Shaw played the role of Carrie, the young dancer hopeful. Shaw had appeared on Broadway and acted in about two dozens films and her career ended in 1928.

The director's chair was now shared by Dave and Bradley Barker. There is no mention of Max directing or the involvement of Irwin Richard Franklyn.

In the publication's review, C.S. Sewell wrote, "With 'Morning Judge,' the first of this series Red Seal invades the two-reel comedy field. The action concerns a theatrical troupe stranded in a small town. One of the girls vamps the local judge who gets them out of jail. They are caught by a traffic cop and the judge disguised as a ballet dancer and eventually feels the wrath of his irate wife when the truth comes out. Peggy Shaw is the girl, Joseph Burke the judge and Flora Finch, the noted player of the old Vitagraph days is the wife. There are a number of laughs in this comedy which combines stage

Ko-Ko was still the star of Red Seal, despite the many other attractions. (author's collection)

and rural stuff with a comedy chase and it should amuse the average patron."

The second installment in the series was released the next month and Sewell wrote the following: "The second of the 'Carrie of the Chorus' series show the troupe headed by Peggy Shaw, stranded in a small town with only their ballet costumes. She vamps a local banker who pays their fare and goes with them. Women uplifters arrange to have them arrested at the next station and the girls change costumes with other women and break up the reform convention, then they escape jail by flirting with the constables but the banker comes to grief when his wife, one of the uplifters, played by Flora Finch catches him. This is up to the standard of the previous issue."

There appears that no other 'Carrie' shorts were released, although there are a number of trade publications stories that reported as many as 10 of the shorts were filmed.

Silent film accompanist and historian Ben Model uncovered a 9.5 mm home version of the first short, which he presented on his fourth volume of "Accidentally Preserved" DVD series. The 9.5 mm gauge predated the rise of 16mm and was used for movies aimed at people wanting to build a film collection at home. Model's series is invaluable for those wishing to see silent films that are unavailable anywhere else. The cut-down short ends as the chorus girls are heading off to see the judge.

It's difficult to assess the film with only seeing half of it, but I think it's fair to say that slapstick, rather than characterization, is the backbone of the film. There is a lot of characters milling around doing things without the care or subtle touches that one would see in other contemporary comedies of the period. Dave receives sole directing credit on the print.

On the Fleischer Studios website is an entry from the series, titled "Another Bottle Doctor," which may be the only existing complete print from the series.

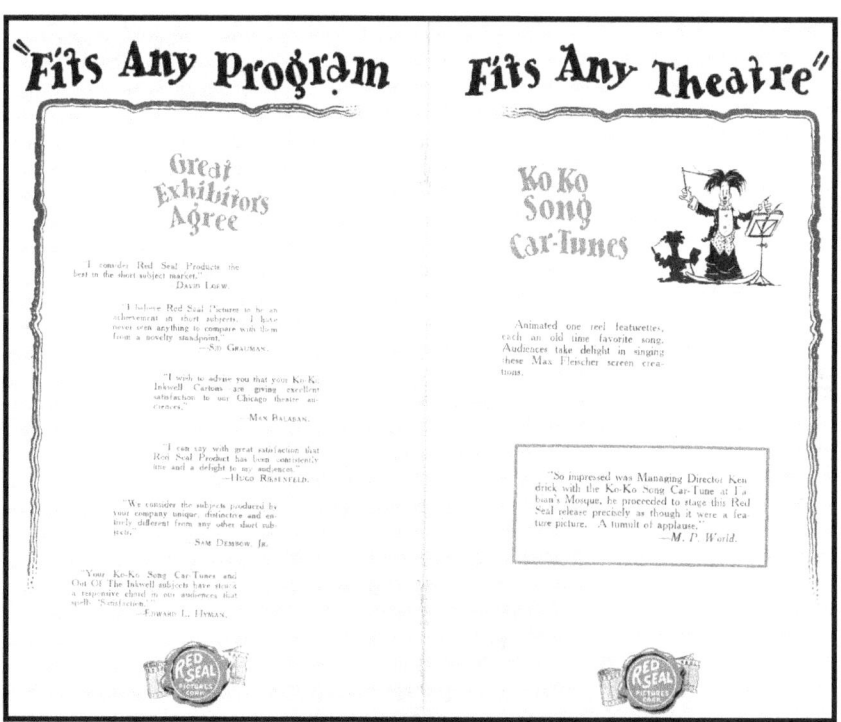

This brochure is a status report of Red Seal from 1926. Courtesy of JJ Sedelmaier.

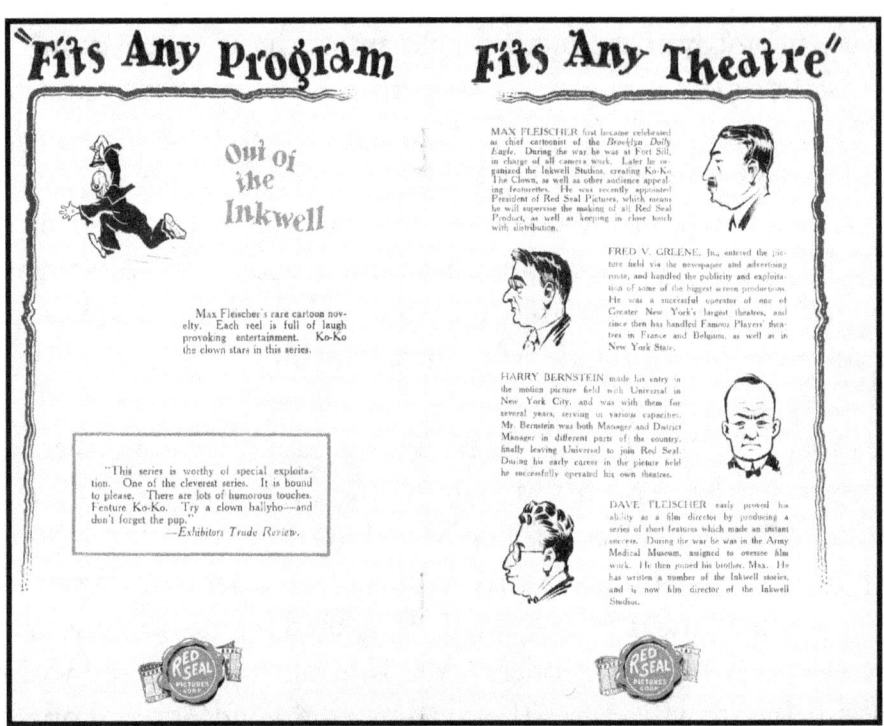

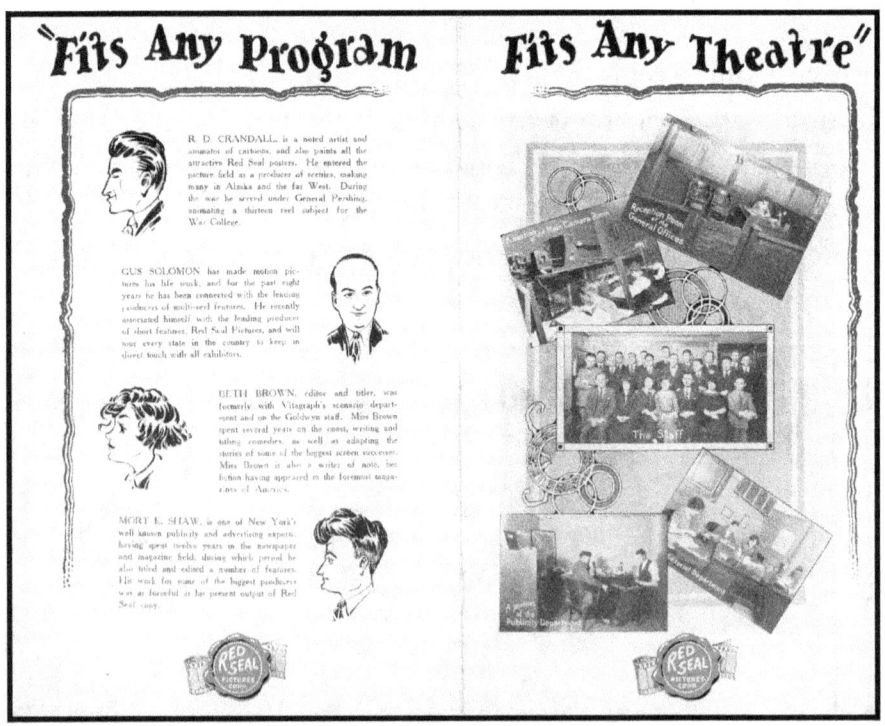
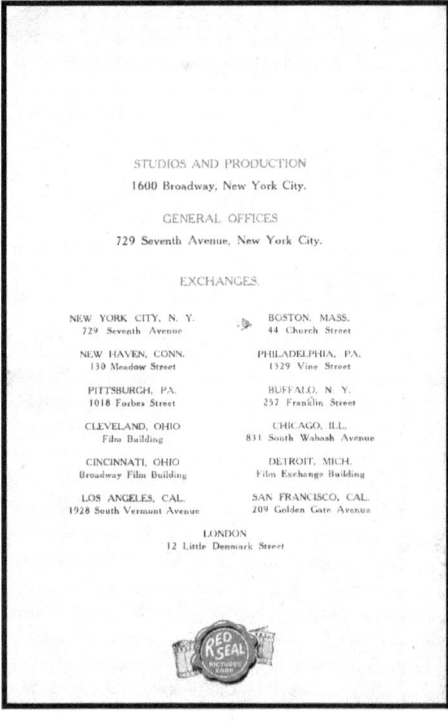

The title card describes the film as a "Back Stage Comedy," and the website characterizes "Carrie of the Chorus" as part of this series. Nowhere in trade ads or review have I seen such a designation.

The film has Peggy Shaw, the star of the series, as a dancing girl with a medicine show. The height of the show is a boxing match in which the troupe's strong man takes on all comers, in this case a doctor who runs a shady sanitorium. He fears he will lose business if the cure-all sold at the show actually works.

All of the action is set outside – undoubtedly a way to keep production costs down – and the short's production seems a bit crude and the story is obviously padded.

***

In the May 30, 1926 Film Daily, Max's name was the by-line for a promotional essay. He wrote, "Give the public good lively short features and you keep picture audiences happy and coming back regularly for screen entertainment.

"I don't mean that the short feature is the only film entertainment which makes them laugh or pleases. But the odds in favor of genuine mirthful entertainment being secured in one or two-reelers are always in favor of the featurette.

"Short features being brief, are of course, spiced well with laughs or interesting topics colorfully presented as seen in such popularly scientific reels like The Reelview, Searchlight and similar subjects.

"When a 'long' feature lacks laughter elements or sustained dramatic interest, it is disappointing to the audience, the very length of short features precludes any such possibility. Exhibitors realize this fact every day in the year. They are getting more and more insistent upon building up their program with short entertainment.

"This is one of the prime factors, which prompted me to go into the production of two-reel comedies. In no way does this interfere with our production of Ko-Ko Song Cartunes, which are given presentation space in the biggest theaters in the country.

"Our Out of the Inkwell Cartoons also maintain the same production schedule. As a matter of fact, we have increased our studio space recently and added to our staff of animators and technicians to insure pictures of smooth and perfect action.

"Even my success in the Marvel of Motion series is being perfected for newer stunts for the coming season.

"Realizing the exhibitors' demands for more shorts, Red Seal will distribute far more product than ever before during the season of 1926-1927. More, and varied novelty reels, as well as newer highly specialized entertainment reels are already in production for the coming season.

"To insure the caliber of our reels I am personally supervising and directing the 'Carrie of the Chorus' series of 13 two-reel comedies. My brother Dave and Bradley Barker, both of whom have made pictures of box office power, are assistant directors. Hazel Harmon, Rolland Flander, Ruth Florence, Ray Bolger, Esther Muir, Vonda Case are the featured players.

"Another new series of colorfully dramatic one reelers are being made by Emery Bronte with his famed dogs, Lassie and Jean. This series will also include a number of stage actors. "Keep 'Em Guessing,' a magic series of one reelers is also in process of completion. These novelties are being produced in association with the Magicians Club of America. Morrie Ryskind devising the titles."

Ryskind is the writer who teamed with George S. Kaufman on the screenplays for three of the Marx Brothers movies, including "A Night at the Opera," as well writing the screenplays for "My Man Godfrey," "His Girl Friday," and "Stage Door."

In the Aug. 14. 1926 of Moving Picture World additional titles were announced for the 1926-1927 schedule including 26 Animated Hair cartoons, 13 "Gems of the Screen" shorts and a series called The Film Reporter, "being intimate moments with screen and sports celebrities."

The July 12 1926 edition of Film Daily reported Mrs. Wallace Reid Productions would establish a short subject unit and produce a series of 12 two-reelers for Red Seal. "A contract has been signed by Max Fleischer and Cliff Broughton, business manager for the Western organization, who is returning to the coast from New York."

Max's celebrity continued to grow. One could argue that during the silent era the only other person associated with the creation of animated cartoons who was better known was Pat Sullivan of Felix the Cat. The Motion Picture News ran a photo in June 5, 1926 edition showing the crowd that turned up at a Brooklyn theater to see Max.

The Out of the Inkwell cartoons were still receiving good notices. On July 25, 1926 the Film Daily critics noted of "Toot Toot," that "Max Fleischer produces in this one another clever combination cartoon in which part of the action takes place on a real train and ties up with the cartoon train which Ko-Ko, the clown, operates. The artist in person is seen on the train creating the cartoon characters, and every-once-in-a-while a shot of the train and its passengers creates the illusion that it is the cartoon train which Ko-Ko and his dog are operating. The tricks and gags that are worked into the wild ride of the train make this a diverting cartoon number."

Red Seal had proven itself very effective in getting attention from the trade papers but this all stopped in the early fall of 1926.

End of Red Seal

When Red Seal and Max returned to the pages of the trade publications, the news was not good. Out of the Inkwell Films Inc. was headed to receivership.

On Oct. 5, 1926, Film Daily quoted Harry Bernstein, an unidentified executive of Red Seal, that "this development does not affect the solvency of the Red Seal of which Max Fleischer, president of the Inkwell is also head. 'We shall go right on with all of our pre-arranged plans for the Red Seal production and distribution,' said Bernstein."

In the next day's edition, it was reported that Spiro Film Corporation, a laboratory used by Fleischer had brought the legal action. Red Seal and Fleischer had liabilities of $109,737 and assets of $310,613. "Appointment of a receiver for Out of the Inkwell Films, Inc., will assure continuance of the corporation, with Max Fleischer, president, in charge, the latter stated yesterday. The company submitted a bill in equity to the Federal Court,

This trade ad from 1928 shows part of the new line-up of short subjects distributed by Paramount.

stating the firm was solvent, and asking appointment of a receiver. Action of a laboratory forced the company 'to seek the protection of the courts in order to work out its problems,' Fleischer said. E. Bright Wilson has been named receiver under $15,000 bond."

On Oct. 16, 1926, Merritt Crawford writing in the Moving Picture World, commented on the company's problems. He noted, "Out of the receiverships of the Max Fleischer organization, announced in the press last week have grown some ugly rumors which in no way reflect upon the originator of the Out of the Inkwell cartoons and his associates but which it is hinted will prove a sensation in the industry should they eventually find their way into public notice.

"Max Fleischer needs no introduction to Moving Picture World readers either as an artist whose clever film cartoons have earned him a unique position in the motion picture industry or as a business man engaged for six years past in a profitable and growing enterprise, whose name and reputation is second to none.

"Consequently, it is with real astonishment and sympathetic concerns that many heard the news – that for some reason not entirely apparent – a receivership had been applied for in the United States District Court for all the Max Fleischer organizations.

"According to court records, serious differences had arisen between Consolidated Film Industries Inc., or one of its subsidiaries and the companies headed by Max Fleischer, and the application to the court, instituted by the latter, was, in nature, an appeal for the court's protection in the form of an equity receivership.

"No further details are available from the court records at present, but there is a distinct feeling in many quarters that some phases of the situation should speedily be given publicity.

"Until this can be done properly and with due regard to all the legal aspects of the case, we would prefer not to take sides, but as a matter of principle it would seem that of it is possible to eliminate companies like Red Seal and Out of the Inkwell with reputations so high for quality and integrity of personnel as they all the facts should be known.

"Meanwhile, it is hoped that the trade will suspend judgement despite current rumors, until such time as Mr. Fleischer decides to speak further for the receivership or until the present problems of the corporation are fully ironed out.

"We have known Max Fleischer as an able newspaperman and artist, as square-shooter and as a good game fighter and from all we hear, as we go around film row, this goes double."

The company was taken over by Oct. 27 by Alfred Weiss of the American Multi-Color Corp. "Yesterday's session in federal court was concerned chiefly over a dispute over the fee of the receiver and receiver's counsel. Weiss offered to advance the $50,000 provided creditors agrees in an extension, permitting the firm to pay off its obligations in monthly installments over the period of a year. A compromise suggestion by the court, in the demand and offer with respect in settlement for $6,000. Creditors whose claims are under $100, are to be paid in cash it is stated," the Film Daily reported.

Moving Picture World reported, "The new organization already shows its excellent judgment in electing Max Fleischer vice president of both corporations [Red Seal and Out of the Inkwell Corp.] putting him in charge of production. The name Max Fleischer and his Inkwell clown with his clever antics are known all over the world. Fleischer is an artist with originality and ingenuity that has never been equaled."

One doubts the glowing words made up for the fact that Max was now an employee of his own company. If one wanted to speculate, one might draw the conclusion that this was a defining moment for Max about how he should operate as a producer. He had tried to set himself as not only an independent producer, but also one with his own means of distributing his product and acquiring the short subjects made by smaller companies. That effort had failed.

Max's subsequent deal with Paramount took away a level of independence, but gave him relatively more security when it came to distribution and marketing. Many years later Walt Disney would form his own distribution company. Max's vision was the same, but his expansion has been deemed by some as too fast.

The Film Daily reported on Nov. 15, 1926, "Launching of an immediate plan of expansion by Red Seal Pictures Corp. is planned by Alfred Weiss, new president of the company and Out of the Inkwell Films. Reorganization of the two firms was completed with Weiss in control, following dismissal of the receivership action against the companies. Weiss paid $218,000 of the liabilities and furnished the working capital on which the companies could operate.

"Red Seal now operates 21 exchanges throughout the nation and new ones are to be added as rapidly as possible, says a company statement. Max Fleischer is vice president of both corporations placing him in charge of production.

NO short subject in sound during the current season leaped to more universal popularity than Paramount Screen Songs. Scores of theatres of all classes voluntarily wrote wires and letters of enthusiastic praise for these novelties. The words of the songs appear in unique and humorous style on the screen, with the celebrated "bouncing ball" to keep time. With instrumental and vocal accompaniment. The entire audience joins in singing—and signifies its approval at the end by thunderous applause. Prove this for yourself!

Twelve releases, one reel each, of Paramount Screen Songs in 1929-30. Including such popular favorites as "Good Bye, My Lady Love," "Chinatown," "Oh, You Beautiful Doll," "Smiles" and others.

PARAMOUNT Talkartoons are something entirely new and entirely different from anything ever seen and heard before. For the first time cartoons will be actual talking pictures, not merely cartoons synchronized after their creation. By a special process, the cartoon figures will actually talk. The novelty value alone of the Talkartoons will make them successful. But, in addition, they will tell complete stories and will be brilliantly entertaining.

Six Paramount Talkartoons, one reel each, will be released in the coming season. Both the Screen Songs and Talkartoons are presented by Max Fleischer. Directed by Dave Fleischer.

The new deal with Paramount distribution came after the take-over of Red Seal, as seen in this trade ad.

"Reorganization of the company makes the return of Weiss to the field. He has been a factor in the industry since the days of General and was one of the originators of the Triangle Film Corp,"

Dave Fleischer renewed his contract with Weiss in December.

"Ko-Ko's Queen" from 1926, shows the lengths Max and his staff were willing to go for a one-reel cartoon. Dressed in a tux, Max informs Ko-Ko that he was going to a beauty pageant to watch "my girl" win. Max draws a beauty for Ko-Ko and Fitz and, of course, neither woman nor dog are good-looking. K-Ko attempts to alter his date's looks to enter her into a beauty contest but fails. He draws his own version of a beauty who jumps from the drawing board to a nearby table, transforming into a miniature human.

That sequence was filmed on a set with over-sized props and with some impressive animation of cartoon Ko-Ko with the live action actress. It's all very impressive, although the sexual politics depicted in the film are a little difficult to watch.

Under the new regime, the cartoons were now known as starring "The Inkwell Imps." The shorts were still well received. The Film Daily critic noted about "Ko-Ko Gets Egg-Cited" on Feb. 20. 1927, "Perhaps Ko-Ko doesn't 'know his onions' as well as he might. In his latest escapade he trails a chicken to gather in eggs for Max Fleischer, his boss, but he frolics too long in a hennery and before he knows it Ko-Ko is the father of a fine brood of little Ko-Kos. Good laughs if not always strictly refined."

This cartoon was still described as a Red Seal release.

Red Seal as a distributor was given an apparent death blow when Paramount made the decision to distribute 26 Inkwell Imp cartoons by late April 1927 when Max was introduced to the Paramount sales force. A trade ad appearing on May 11, 1927 stated, "The Inkwell Imps are known wherever short features are show. Presented by Alfred Weiss. Produced by Max Fleischer."

There appears to be some overlap, though as noted in the July 22, 1928 edition of Motion Picture News. The trade magazine listed film currently in release and although there was a long list of Inkwell productions in the Paramount section, under state's rights was "Ko-Ko Makes 'Em Laugh" listed as Red Seal.

Despite his business problems, Max was still a celebrity. In July 1928, he began a weekly appearance on WLTH radio in Brooklyn speaking about motion pictures.

Even under the Weiss reign, the production of the cartoons carried on with a high level of quality. One of the best of the later Ko-Kos is "Paradise" (1929). Max announces he's going to do some indoor duck hunting, which is his term for firing a gun at an indoor Coney Island style range. Naturally Ko-Ko and Fitz wind up shot and they go to heaven. Dog heaven for Fitz is loaded with available bones to chew and female dogs with whom to flirt.

People heaven isn't too bad for Ko-Ko, either, although he has trouble getting his wings to work. When they both leave their respected heavens, they wind up back on the firing range.

In "Ko-Ko the Convict," Max gets angry at how Ko-Ko and Fitz have treated his new puppy so he sends them to prison. A plethora of prison gags abound with the capper being one in which Ko-Ko mistakes the electric chair for a barber's chair.

In "Ko-Ko Explores," (1927) Max is seen at his typewriter working on the scenario for a new film. He tells Ko-Ko and Fitz he's writing a cartoon about head hunting cannibals and right on cue one appears from behind a nearby globe. He snatches Max's head off his body returns to the cartoon universe where he rolls up the photo images like a poster. Ko-Ko and Fitz now attempt to get the "boss's" head back. Meanwhile, Max's headless body is staggering around the studio.

When they finally find Max's head, he is now the king of the cannibals and is hanging between trees being fed by tribesmen. Luckily for Ko-Ko and Fitz, the cartoon turns out to be one of Max's many tricks. Yes, the portrayal of the cannibals is an objectionable stereotype.

In "Ko-Ko's Kane," (1927) Max is hard at work on a multi-use walking stick. Ko-Ko and Fitz jump into his drawn plans and wreak havoc. The cane's many buttons perform a number of surprising functions for them and what follows is a typical free form association of gags and images. When Max has perfected his "real world" invention, he doesn't know Ko-Ko and Fitz are inside of it and in a clever live action climax they wreak their revenge.

The Fleischer shorts did indulge in ethnic humor and there are some gay jokes, but largely sex wasn't part of the studio's stock humor. Perhaps that's why "Ko-Ko's Catch" (1928) is unusual. Max is busy flirting his new secretary (!) and assigns an automatic drawing devise to set up the scene for Ko-Ko and Fitz, that involves a mechanized, coin operated barber. The pair discovers other coin-operated devices, a dancing flapper and then a clockwork police officer who chases them.

Once the cop has crashed into a wall, they turn their attention back to Max who is putting the moves on his secretary. Ko-Ko and Fitz place a loaded rat trap on the secretary's shoulder, which catches Max's hand and back into the inkwell they go.

"Ko-Ko's Haunted House" (1928) features a device that forecasts the use of three-dimensional sets years later at the studio. An artist working next to Max used the inkwell to make a haunted house which goes from a drawing on a page to a large model. Ko-Ko then explores the interior of the house and runs into ghosts. The artist tortures Ko-Ko and Fitz by banging as drum out outside of the model and shaking it. Ko-Ko complains to Max about the artist and Max responds by drawing multiple Ko-Kos to "haunt" the studio.

The last Koko cartoon was "Chemical Koko" in July 1929. Ironically, it doesn't follow the long-established Max and Ko-Ko format and instead has the clown interacting with a scientist who can change an African-American into a white man, a gag that is disturbing decades later. Ko-Ko is set up in a lab and is given a chemical that can alter those who ingest it. He soon has a line of customers, including a momma giraffe who has a baby hippo, something at which Ko-Ko wags his finger. When the scientist gets a dose of his own medicine he shrinks down to Ko-Ko's size who spanks him and drops him into the inkwell.

The cartoon is really not up to the standards of those released in the final year and certainly doesn't give the character the send-off he so richly deserved.

***

Ko-Ko's series was replaced by a new one "Talkartoons," that initially starred Bimbo and eventually gave birth to Betty Boop.

In the first several years of the Boop series, Koko – the hyphen had been dropped – was a co-star, along with Bimbo. It's notable the studio never settled for a voice for Koko, as it seemed to change from short to short.

Perhaps one of his best outings was in the Betty Boop cartoon "Boop Oop a Doop." Set in a circus – Koko's being a clown fits nicely – he is the hero of the film rescuing Betty from the lecherous ringmaster of the show.

He is also used as Cab Calloway's cartoon stand-in in "Snow White" in which he sings "St. James Infirmary Blues."

1934's "Ha! Ha! Ha!" was the character's swan song. Apparently inspired by the silent cartoon, "The Cure," the sound short is set up as an Out of the Inkwell cartoon. "Uncle Max" draws Betty, but leaves the studio, as it's closing time. Koko emerges from an inkwell and spots a candy bar on the drawing table. His eating of it causes a toothache and Betty then plays dentist, dragging Koko into the drawing of a dentist's office. She administers "laughing gas" to kill his pain and naturally the gas enters the "real" world. Just as the in the classic Out of the Inkwells, photos of objects, such as typewriter, are then animated as laughing.

With the gas escaping to the streets of New York, there is a live action scene, undoubtedly studio personnel crossing a street breaking up in uncontrollable laughter. Betty and Ko-Ko go back into the inkwell.

I have no idea if this was designed as Koko's farewell. In Betty Boop's world, which was increasingly becoming situational in comedy, a clown – and for that matter an anthropomorphic dog serving as a boyfriend – really didn't have a role.

After 1934, he then only made a cameo appearance in the 1949 Screen Song short "Toys will be Toys," co-directed by Myron Waldman for Famous Studios. Koko appears as a doll flipping his way through a parade of toys. He is also seen in the background of the parade scene.

It was a sweetly nostalgia moment. Waldman told me that Koko was a favorite of his as a child and it was a thrill for him to animate the character when he worked on the Betty Boop shorts in which Koko was a co-star.

His 1960 television revival will be discussed in the second volume.

Perhaps the Ko-Ko short best known to audiences in the last 30 years has been "Ko-Ko's Earth Control (1928), which has been seen in various video collections. Ko-Ko and Fitz are drawn walking the globe. They come into a building in which there are various controls and instruments that control the planet's weather. Fitz is naturally attracted to a lever with a sign that read, "Danger. Beware. Do not touch Earth Control. If this handle is pulled the world will come to an end." Ko-Ko's efforts to prevent Fitz from pulling the handle fail and all hell breaks loose. The sun melts the moon. Inanimate objects become alive. Ko-Ko encounters a demon. The short features some psychedelic effects as well. It's an amazing cartoon.

Ko-Ko was among the cartoon stars who can be spotted in "Who Framed Roger Rabbit."

One could speculate that at the dawn of sound Max and his staff either wanted something new to offer their audiences, despite the clown's name recognition and popularity or didn't know if the silent format of the clown interacting with people in the real world still would work with sound. It's interesting to me that they didn't try at least one sound short starring Koko as a pilot.

The coming of the Bouncing Ball and sound

In 1924, Max started releasing the "Song Car-tunes," which served as the prototype for the later "Screen Songs" series.

What this series did was to take the convention of glass slides that would be projected in theaters with the lyrics of popular songs on them. The theater's pianist or organist would play the song with the projectionist changing the slides with the lyrics.

According to Rick Altman, a film historian and professor of cinema and comparative literature at the University of Iowa, the slides were part of the nickelodeon era as early as 1896.

The Fleischer Studio took the concept of the communal song singing one step farther. They produced animated cartoons that presented the lyrics within an animated framework and they used popular songs that were undoubtedly well known to audiences.

This series brought to popular culture the "bouncing ball," which nearly a century after its introduction is still recognizable and is still a healthy part of popular culture today. The ball was designed to provide the rhythm for the song as people sung the lyrics.

The Song Car-tune was announced in a story in the Exhibitors' Tread Review on Aug. 16, 1924. The story was a preview of the new season of Red Seal offerings and reported, "There will also be something brand new in the way of a fun novelty, which will be released as 13 Song Cartoon reels composed of well-known old time and modern songs done in funny cartoon form and adapted for audience singing where desired, perfectly timed, scored and synchronized and released every four weeks."

The story continued, "The first of these reels went on for a pre-release run at the Rialto, New York, and was composed of the three old time Charles K. Harris songs, 'Mother, Mother, Mother Pin a Rose on Me,' 'Goodbye My Lady Love' and 'Come Take a Trip in My Airship.' The trade papers commented freely on the unusual success of this novelty. The New York Tribune said, 'These things are simply impossible to describe. You must see them for yourself.'"

That first "Song Car-tune," also reviewed a rave from the Film Daily reviewer on Feb. 24, 1924. "Here's a new idea in song reels, presented by Charles K. Harris, the music publisher who is responsible for the songs and Max Fleischer whose animated cartoons skip nimbly from word to word of the song and lend much charm and some laughs. There is no picturization of the action described in the song – simply the words which run along the screen in large single-line type that moves slowly from right to left in time to the music and on which the tiny cartoon figures dance. The songs included are 'Mother, Mother, Mother, Pin a Rose on Me,' 'Come Take a Trip in My Airship' and 'Goodbye. My Lady Love.'"

In "Tramp, Tramp, Tramp, a silent Song Car-tune," (1926) Ko-Ko holds up a card that essentially explains the concept. "The Ko-Ko Glee Klub marched all the way to this theatre to cheer you up with the tune that made grandpa 'step out' in the good old days. 'Tramp, Tramp, Tramp' (The Boys are Marching). Watch the bouncing ball, join in and sing, everybody!"

These cartoons were one-reelers and one could argue had less actually animation than in a regular Ko-Ko cartoon. The bouncing ball would appear for one set of lyrics and then animated figure or figures would walk, run or jump on each word for another stanza.

"Sweet Adeline" (1926) opens the same introduction as "Tramp, Tramp, Tramp." There is animated footage of a band going into a theater with Ko-Ko holding a sign urging people to sing. In part the sign reads, "We will guide your voices in song. So raise your chests as I raise my baton." The sign promised, "The loudest voice wins."

Many of these shorts shared a reverse design with solid black backgrounds and the animation and song lyrics in white.

Not a landmark

The Song Car-tunes marked a significant historical point in film as the first sound cartoon – made with the Phonofilm process by Dr. Lee De Forest – was in this series "Oh Mabel" in 1924.

The question is how true is this statement and subsequent others about the Fleischers and sound films.

The book "Empire of the Air: The Men Who Made Radio" by Tom Lewis is essential reading about De Forest and his career. He is characterized as having stumbled on the invention of the vacuum tube and subsequently spent most of his time involved in self-promotion and a string of failed business ventures.

His sound-on-film system relied heavily for its success on the inventions of Theodore Case and Earl I. Sponable of the Case Research Lab in Auburn, N.Y.

The problem with the Phonofilm releases is that few theaters were willing to invest in installing sound systems for the films. The Phonofilms had no major studio or distributor behind them.

According to a story published in the March 15, 1924 edition of the Exhibitor's Trade Review, Dr. Hugo Riesenfeld, a key figure in the creation of Red Seal and the managing director of three prominent New York City theaters: the Rialto, the Rivoli and the Criterion, endorsed the Phonofilm. He gave a continuous three-week run to several Phonofilm live-action subjects. The publication called the run "the highest compliment that has been paid to Dr. Lee de Forest's Phonofilm."

According to the www.silentera.com, a reference source about silent films, Paramount filmed at least part of its 1923 film "The Covered Wagon" in Phonofilm in 1923 to provide a prerecorded musical score. However, that print was apparently only shown in its New York City engagement at The Rivoli.

Another 1923 Paramount release, "Bella Donna" also had a Phonofilm musical soundtrack. Both of these Phonofilm efforts predate the Fleischer's use of the technology.

De Forest never produced a feature himself and the longest format movie that he produced was a two-reeler. His shorts were one-reel musical or comedy acts, although he did distribute a Phonofilm recording of President Calvin Coolidge.

Some writers have asserted online that Red Seal was created to distribute the Phonofilm cartoons and that De Forest was a partner in the company. This is difficult to believe as the announcement in 1923 that Red Seal was being formed did not mention De Forest, who was infamous for his self-promotion.

A 1926 promotional booklet for a Red Seal event does not mention the Phonofilm shorts or de Forest. In fact, the slogan used through the six-page booklet was "Fits Any Program. Fits Any Show." Certainly that did not describe the Phonofilm shorts.

None of the trade ads for Red Seal that I've seen mention the Song Car-tunes in their sound versions. A full-page trade ad in 1926 listed all of the film series Red Seal was either making or distributing and there was no mention of the sound versions of Song Car-tunes.

A trade ad for "Has Anyone Here Seen Kelly?" again doesn't mention any sound version but did note there are hand-colored prints available at Red Seal exchanges.

Film historian David Gerstein shared the results of his work that casts doubt on part of the accepted Fleischer story about sound.

Ruth Kneitel described the accomplishment this way in a chronology of her father's career she gave me: "made first talking animated cartoon experiment with Dr. Lee de Forest at Rialto Theater, New York, 1924." Other historians note the location for the screening was not the Rialto Theater in New York City, but instead the sister theater The Rivoli.

Her brother Richard referenced the use of sound preceding Disney's "Steamboat Willie" in his memoir about his father by discussing the relationship between Max and Dr. Lee De Forest, whose vacuum tube was the needed component for the electronic age of the 20th Century. He said the cartoon "My Kentucky Home," which contained one line of synchronized dialogue, was released in 1924.

He added the sound cartoons were not a financial success as there were few theaters wished to convert to De Forest's Phonofilm technology. Richard noted the other cartoons made using the sound process could be shown silently.

In Max's 1939 autobiographical essay he does not mention any of the experiments with sound. Although people I've interviewed who worked at the studio all assert Max was a humble person, it would be logical for him to stake that historical claim.

To add to the confusion, some on the Internet have claimed the dog character is Bimbo, which is incorrect as that character and name would not be used for years.

While "Oh Mabel" had a recorded musical score, the "My Old Kentucky Home" entry of the series (1926) had one line of synchronized dialogue – another first – "Follow the ball and join in everybody," a cartoon dog told the audience. With the exception of that line of dialogue, the cartoon seems to be designed to have been shown as a silent, which would have made financial sense.

Interestingly enough, neither Ko-Ko nor his dog Fitz appear in the print "My Old Kentucky Home" that is supposedly part of the Song Car-tune series. I've wondered why the studio did not want Ko-Ko to be the character to speak the first line of dialogue in an animated cartoon? Ko-Ko was an integral component of many of the Song Car-tunes in the role of an emcee introducing the short. He is missing from "My Old Kentucky Home."

The reason is shockingly simple: Gerstein has shown the cartoon we have come to accept as the 1926 version produced by the Fleischers was not produced by them and not in 1926.

Gerstein noted, "Despite decades of past confusion, it appears the seven 'Biophone Screen Tune' bouncing ball cartoons, released by Alfred Weiss and Red Seal in late 1929, are mostly not reissues of earlier Ko-Ko Song Car-tunes, but are mostly original non-Fleischer material. A few parts of bouncing ball segments are some reused from Fleischer, but not always. The Biophone Screen Tunes have Inkwell Studio end titles but only because Weiss continued to use the Inkwell Studio trade name after he and Red Seal split from Fleischer."

He continued, "The original Fleischer Ko-Ko Song Car-Tunes originally all featured opening cartoon sequences of Ko-Ko (and sometimes Fitz) leading their band to a theatre or preparing for a show. The Weiss Biophone Screen Tunes, by contrast, all feature opening cartoon sequences starring the black-furred dog character we know from the common 'My Old Kentucky Home.' His name (taken from period reviews in multiple trade journals) is Pinkie the Pup and he seems to be unique to these shorts."

He concluded, "So, the big takeaway is this: the famous dog segments in the Screen Tune "My Old Kentucky Home' and these other Biophone shorts are post-Fleischer creations from 1929, so Pinkie the Pup's famous 'Follow the ball' dialogue was not a Fleischer 1926 innovation – unfortunately!"

Gerstein said there are other "Screen Tunes" that seem as early Fleischer sound experiments but are not. They include "Down in Jungle Town," "Jingle Bells," "London Bridge is Falling Down," "Pack Up Your Troubles in Your Old Kit Bag," "Summer Harmonies," and "Tramp, Tramp, Tramp,"

He added, "Many of the same songs were reused from the Ko-Ko Song Car-Tunes to the Biophone Screen Tunes, but this didn't always mean animation was reused."

So now, the question is what about "Oh Mabel?" Gerstein did find a newspaper ad from the New York Herald-Tribune which mentions the cartoon but no designation about sound. The official Fleischer filmography maintained on the family's website noted "Oh Mabel" was a Song Car-tune and was released in 1924, but it has no designation as being a Phonofilm collaboration. It is characterized as a lost film.

A 1924 story in the Exhibitor Herald trade paper discusses at length De Forest's Phonofilm and its growing acceptance – I'm fairly certain this is a press release from De Forest – but it does not mention any of any animated cartoons.

A 1925 article in March 15 edition of the Film Daily by the general manager of Phonofilm mentions how the company produced shorts of presidential candidates and how a recent short of Eddie Cantor performing showed how Phonofilm lent itself to musical and comedy performances, but again no mention of Max Fleischer or animation.

Joe Fleischer's business card shows the studio's address at 1600 Broadway, steps away from Times Square. The building, a center for the New York City-based film industry, has been demolished.

The Film Daily reported on April 1, 1927 that De Forest Phonofilm was planning to make installations of equipment with a range of price between $2,500 to $4,000 per theater with six installations planned. This alone would prevent all but the largest of theaters to be able to afford showing De Forest's films.

The battle for a predominant sound system was now on. Vitaphone used sound recorded on large phonograph records that were coordinated with the projection of the film. Movietone used the sound-on-film technology was similar to Phonofilm – but superior – developed by Case and Sponable. Case had broken off his partnership with De Forest. De Forest was embroiled in lawsuits about Movietone.

De Forest's company – never a major player – sank.

Paul Terry used the RCA sound system in 1928 to produce his first sound cartoon, "Dinner Time." Terry's star, Farmer Alfalfa makes an appearance and there are some wild lines shouted but no synchronized dialogue. It was released several months before Disney's "Steamboat Willie," and featured music and sound effects.

It's a rough, plot-less Terry production and the sound effects really don't add appeal.

The Disney cartoon that propelled the animation industry into sound, "Steamboat Willie," in 1928 was recorded with a knock-off version of the Phonofilm system owned by producer Pat Powers.

Somewhat ironically, years after his supposed brush with Phonofilm, Max co-directed "Finding his Voice" with F. Lyle Goldman for Western Electric Company in 1929. The film depicts how the Western Electric sound system for movies worked. The story credit ("by W.E. Erpi") is actually an in-joke and stands for "Western Electric Electrical Research Products Inc."

In the short, "Talkie" solicits the help of "Dr. Western" in helping his mute friend get a voice. Step by step the sound-on-film process is illustrated from the recording the set to the speakers behind the screen at a theater.

With the success of Disney's "Steamboat Willie" in October 1928, it was only a matter of time that Max tackle sound production.

It was under the Weiss regime that Max made the switch to sound with the release of the newly re-christened "Song Cartunes" to the new series known as "Screen Songs." The first short, "The Sidewalks of New York" was seen in February 1929.

The release was actually the earlier cartoon with a new soundtrack. One exhibitor wrote about the short, "A little cartoon to the tune of 'Sidewalks of New York,' and it was liked." It was followed by "Yankee Doodle Boy" in March and "Old Black Joe" in April.

The new series, which had initially the same format as the silent cartoons, were received well. The Film Daily wrote in its May 19, 1929 edition, "Screen Songs – Novelty Cartoon Type of production. Animated song Max Fleischer gets a big break on the sound angle, for it gives him a chance to show something in the way of a real novelty with his clever cartoon stuff. He has a college cheerleader putting his gang through some of the old tunes. Then the words are flashed on the screen, with a variety of comedy manipulations of the letters and animated figures such as autos, dancing balls and college boys sliding over the letters in harmony with the tune. A fine male quartet is used on the one number, and the popular melodies had a Broadway audience humming out loud—which is quite a record in itself. Will click in any type of house. Time, 9 mins."

Other reviews followed: "June 9, 1929 Daisy Bells. Paramount Screen Song. Very Clever. In the days of B. S. – before sound – Max Fleischer's song cartoons always provided diversion. Now that the ear hears while the eye sees, the entertainment qualities of this series is considerably enhanced. The cartoon work is clever and the sound effects fine. Sure-fire for any type of audience. Time, about 6 mins."

Film Daily noted on June 23, 1929 that "Max Fleischer drew some fine praise for his production of sound cartoons. Max has been ringing the bell for a long time, so little wonder [Paramount exec] Manny Cohen is enthusiastic."

A new era

Variety reported in its Nov. 30, 1929 edition that Dave has received a settlement against Weiss for $27,000 in a court proceeding. Max "had a similar action pending."

Both men were bringing suit against Weiss because he had "ousted them from the studio without paying them the remainder of their five-year contract."

With the drastic changes of Red Seal and the on-going distribution deal with Paramount, The Film Daily reported on Oct. 21, 1929 that "Fleischer Studios, at present located in Long Island City, will move to New York at 1600 Broadway, after Nov. 1, according to Max Fleischer, president. Fleischer Studios Inc. have no connection whatsoever with Out-of-the Inkwell Films, Inc."

The independence from Weiss was celebrated, according to the Film Daily, at Christmas

1929. "Max Fleischer, giving in to the holiday spirit, will play host to about 40 employees of his Fleischer Studios, Inc., at a Christmas spread to be staged Dec. 23 at Roth's Restaurant," it reported.

What Richard Fleischer noted in his book is somewhat different. Richard maintains that Max and Dave had quit the Weiss organization and were broke. The space in Long Island City was donated by a friend of Max's since Max did not have the money to rent space.

But clearly Max rebounded with a distribution deal with Paramount, which according to Richard, owned the cartoons Max produced. Max retained the ownership of the characters created by the studio.

With sound and the end of the Ko-Ko cartoons brought an end to the design style established by Huemer. Existing model sheets Huemer drew of Ko-Ko show his clean draftsmanship. Now the designs of the characters were in what is now called the classic "rubber house" style. The characters were built on circles.

It is a radical approach to change a look so drastically and one wonders with Heumer's departure, if this was an issue that was addressed by Max and Dave. Among the responsibilities of a "director" in other studios included the designs of characters, but then again, most animation directors were artists.

As noted, many people thought Dave was a great gagman, that Dave loved working on the music for the shorts and that Dave directed voice actors. Dave's signature is on the model sheets for films such as "Gulliver's Travels" and "Mr. Bug Goes to Town" signifying his approval.

I've never heard anyone speak about Dave as a cartoonist or a designer. It's difficult to imagine today that an animation studio wouldn't have a central approach to the design of its characters, but it would appear for at least the time in the late 1920 and early '30s that was the case at the Fleischer Studio.

One cannot underestimate the effect of Walt Disney's success of "Steamboat Willie" and the sound revolution. The popularity made Disney the only true "star" among animators and eclipsed the only two men who had achieved public recognition for their work: Pat Sullivan of the Felix cartoons and Max Fleischer.

In September 1928 edition of Popular Science the advent of sound was described as "making over the movies." Writer Alden P. Armagnac quoted a number of people in the industry. "'In five years, there will be no silent pictures,' says Jesse L. Lasky, vice president of the Paramount-Famous-Lasky Corporation. 'Motion pictures are as much entitled to embrace sound as is the stage,' D. W. Griffith, independent movie producer declares. 'We will have to learn when to add the whistles, and sirens and fire-wagon gongs and when to leave them out,' cautions Al Christie, maker of Christie Comedies.'"

Sound was so revolutionary that some people didn't know what to call it. The term "talkie" was commonly used, but in its Feb. 2, 1929 edition, the trade paper Exhibitors Herald-World printed a list of suggested named including "Vision-Tone," "Showvox," "CNHear," "Cinetone," "Photovox," and "Vocafilm."

In 1929, theaters owners were making the transition to sound and different studios competed with several systems. Initially studios were making two versions of some releases: one sound and one silent. Looking at the trades, by the end of 1930, the only silent films made were considered low budget and fare for only the bottom of a program.

To get a sense of Disney's new status and impact on the field, Gilbert Seldes, author of "The Seven Lively Arts" and the noted critic of American popular culture, wrote in an essay about animation in "The New Republic" in June 1932 that is quite revealing.

He wrote that Disney's "Silly Symphonies" were "the perfection of the movie; they are the movie developing in its own field, borrowing not at all from inappropriate sources and transforming draftsmanship and musical composition to its own ends. They have reached the point toward which the photographed and dramatic moving pictures should be tending, in which as in the silent pictures everything possible is expressed in movement and the sound is used for support and clarification and for contrast."

Seldes was somewhat critical of the role Mickey Mouse was playing in animation and said, "The success of Mickey Mouse is so great that it overshadows not only the competitors of Walt Disney in the field of animated comics, but Disney's own more interesting work, the 'Silly Symphonies.'"

Seldes saw animation as a pure kind of cinema, a radical opinion at the time.

It is interesting to note the only other animator mentioned in his essay by name was Max Fleischer.

"Disney's nearest rival with whose work I am acquainted is Max Fleischer and the best of his cartoons is one called 'Sky Scraping,' in which a variety of animals carry the skeleton of a building beyond the crescent of the moon and desert it at the five o'clock whistle. The plots of drawn comics are seldom more complicated than this and that is another point in which the regular movie might take a lesson from them."

The sound era was a completely different time for the motion picture industry and that certainly included animation. Although Max saw initial success with his new sound Screen Songs, the success of his studio and everyone else's – Seldes' opinion aside – rested in the quest to find animated stars.

***

In 1981, animator Al Eugster spoke to me about working at the studio during this transitional time. Eugster had started in the business in 1925 at the Pat Sullivan Studio working for Otto Mesmer on the Felix the Cat shorts. He was an inker.

"At Felix the Cat we had our drawings on paper, rather than cels. We photographed the inked paper drawings …I started in just filling in Felix," he recalled. He added with a laugh, "Technically I was blackener rather than an opaquer."

He said in the spring of 1929 he and fellow artist Rudy Zamora walked over the Queensboro Bridge to apply for as job at the Fleischer Studio in Long Island City. The two told Nelly Sanborn, Dave's secretary, that they had inked and animated, although neither had actually animated at that point.

They were hired for $35 a week with the promise of a raise to $40 in two weeks if they were satisfactory. They had been making $25 a week at Sullivan's operation.

"That was a pretty good raise for us at the time," Eugster said.

In the fall of 1929, the studio moved back into Manhattan to 1600 Broadway, a building that was well known as a center of the New York film industry. Eugster was still inking, but was promoted in January 1930 when many of Max's more experienced animators went to other studios.

Eugster noted that Zamora, George Canata and James "Shamus" Culhane were instantly promoted. "We were thrown right into it and began animating with a contract. It worked out somehow. I enjoyed it. I really did. My first opportunity as an animator. I have fond memories of it."

He said that at the time he was hired the studio had a staff less than 30 people.

"There wasn't any direct contact with Max in 1929. Our contact was with Dave. The head animator would work with a group of three animators. He would do the layout and would be the go-between between Dave and the animators. Dave would make a daily walk-through."

He continued, "I never saw a script at that time. We just ad-libbed as we went along. Dave would make his daily rounds and suggest gags we could put into the picture. While we were working on a scene, we would add a bit of business in that scene."

Later on, Eugster said, "We did have a story conference and the animators would join in. Max was present at those conferences. Dave, we would just pick a subject … and get some ideas we could tie onto the theme of the picture. The head animator would break it into scenes … that was probably the closest thing to a script. I guess in a way that was a script. I don't recall any formal scripts."

Animator and director James "Shamus" Culhane told me in an interview that in 1929, "I was working at Krazy Kat as an inker and they moved out of the city and went to Hollywood. They didn't take everybody and they didn't invite me to go. So, I went over to Max's.

"In those days it was very easy to get a job if you were any good. The whole animation industry, the year before that, had given a banquet for Winsor McCay. It wasn't a big industry. I don't think there 60 in the whole business.

"So, I went to Fleischer's as an inker, but it was quite a different operation. Max had 120 people working and where Krazy Kat has only four animators Max had six or seven. So, I was given the chance of doing some in-betweening,

"When I was there a while doing both inking and in-betweening, which I hated, I found it restricting, all of sudden he got sound. It was a big explosion; all kinds of problems. One of the things that happened is Lou [Fleischer], who was a ragtime player, he didn't know enough animation to edit a piece of music. I did. It just happened I had been playing the violin since I was nine, two hours a day for all that time and at that moment I didn't really know if I wanted to be a professional violinist or an artist. I hadn't made up my mind, but this made up my mind right away because I knew how to edit a piece of music, I figured I'd really be important.

"I soon became an animator. I could have been an animator before but I couldn't get the opportunity. Very soon after that there was an exodus – Dick Huemer, Sid Marcus, a whole bunch of them left and went to various outfits. Dick went to Walt's; Sid Marcus went to Columbia.

"But anyhow, there was a big exodus and they had an emergency meeting one morning. We walked in and the whole wall where all the animators were, at that moment there were three animators there. So [Willard] Bowsky and [Al] Eugster and me were made animators. We were all put in as animators all in one few swoop. It scared the hell out of us.

"The first picture we worked on was a thing call 'Swing You Sinners' (1930). It was a tough nut, too. There was this crazy old character with long ghostly hands and a high hat and long hair that trailed down the back that was a bitch to draw. However, we managed to do it," Culhane recalled.

It was this early sound period that one could see the Fleischer Studios struggling to find its way. The emphasis was on showcasing sound, rather than a central character such as Ko-Ko. While many of the Ko-Ko shorts were not heavily plotted, most had a definite beginning, middle and end. The early sound cartoon's largest failure was in the stories.

This assessment, though, was not reflected in the reviews of the cartoons at the time.

The first Talkartoon, "Noah's Lark" was released on Oct. 25, 1929. Set on an ark, but certainly not the Biblical ark, this cartoon opens with a series of musical vignettes. The animal crew – Noah is the only human – spots a Coney Island like amusement park. The ship drops anchor and the crew departs for shore leave. There are gags centered on the amusement rides and a parade. Eventually the crew and others rush back to the ship, which sinks with the weight. Noah is last seen chasing a mermaid.

This trade ad shows an early version of Bimbo.

The cartoon is rather formless and there is little of the studio's design style established by the silent cartoons. At a time though in which any production with sound attracted attention, the short was still unique to audiences.

"Chinatown, my Chinatown" (1929) has the clean Dick Huemer design sense of the classic Ko-Ko shorts and is essentially one ethnic gag after another concerning a Chinese laundry. It one of the best-looking early sound cartoons, but it is blatantly racist. "No singee, no washee," the narrator warns in his introduction to the song.

Another example of either a Mickey Mouse swipe, homage or inside gag was seen in "I'm Forever Blowing Bubbles," also released in 1929. The mouse is washing various animals ranging from a cat to an elephant to a pig. The freshly scrubbed animals run into a circus tent where they form a band and the leader introduces the song in what appears to be a painfully constructed and carefully constructed moment of dialogue. Each syllable of the few words of dialogue is haltingly spoken and animated.

A Felix-like cat is the central figure in "Oh You Beautiful Doll" (1929). The cat runs a music shop and when a female cat comes in there is an attraction. She casts a come-hither look and the male cat looks at the audience and says, "Monkey business, meow!"

Like so many of the Screen Songs in 1929 and 1930, "I'm Forever Blowing Bubbles" was performed in a near dirge-like pace in the first sing along sequence and then sped up a bit for the comic second rendition.

Variety hailed "I'm Afraid to Go Home in the Dark" Screen Song (Jan. 25, 1930) as having "Immensely amusing effects and music added to the inimitable Fleischer cartoon touch send this soaring over the top. 'I'm Afraid to Go Home in the Dark' is the theme song of this funny episode of a cartoon character drunk and afraid to go home. The audience is invited to join in the chorus and did – when this was caught at the Rialto, New York. Surefire stuff. Time, 9 mins."

In the short, Ko-Ko's co-star, Fitz the dog, stars as the titular character. There is a funny bit in which he fights with his own shadow. I think this may be the last appearance of the character.

"Hot Dog," released March 29, 1930, marked the first appearance of the studio's first recurring character during the sound period, Bimbo. Although roughly a dog in appearance, the first incarnation of the character had a slender build, a white face and sometimes carried a cane. He wore a derby hat.

In his initial outing, Bimbo is literally driving his car along a city street looking for women. He eventually picks one up – actually kidnapping her – and is confronted by a police officer who brings him to court. There the judge asked him, "Well?" Bimbo responds with playing a "St. James Infirmary Blues" on a banjo he produces. There are some gags along the way of the song at its conclusion he rides the banjo out of the courtroom.

This short shows everything that was great about the early Fleischer sound cartoons and everything that was wrong with them. There was no story, but yet they had some inventive gags and a sense that anything could happen. There is a keen use of music, though.

There was no character development. Bimbo here was simply a lecherous dog/man who gets away with his abduction. He isn't even cutely drawn.

It's amazing to note this was the same studio that had defined a cartoon series from almost its beginning in a way audiences could understand and relate. It's as if the addition of sound and the elimination of Ko-Ko from the roster threw the studio for a collective loop.

Another jarring note in these early sound cartoons was the use of vocal talent. Not only did Bimbo have little personality, the character's voice wasn't consistent from appearance to appearance.

Little is known about the vocal artists, although a group of music researchers contributing to a website (www.denvernightingale.com) dedicated to singer Billy Murray listed Murray's contributions to the Fleischer shorts between 1929 and 1931. Murray provided incidental voices for characters as well as singing songs in some of the Screen Songs such as "In the Good Old Summer Time," a song he recorded in 1905.

Murray had been a popular recording star at the turn of the 20th Century but by the late 1920s his style of singing was no longer in vogue. How he was selected to appear in the Fleischer shorts is not known, although Max had used him in "Finding His Voice" in 1929.

***

It's interesting to note that during 1930, the Fleischer Studios went legit about using cels. The International Photographer reported the lawsuits against Max, along with Aesop Fables, Inc., Winkler Pictures Inc., Winsor McCay and Paul Terry has been dropped by Bray Hurd Process Co. because all of the entities had agreed to pay the licenses to use cels. The story noted the company was now pursuing lawsuits against any studio that had not yet bought a license.

***

The Screen Songs were a very mixed bag at this time. "The Prisoner's Song" (1930) melds the song very well with the framing sequence set in a prison and has a spoken introduction that implies we're all prisoners in one way or another. In this short, the ball is replaced by a tear, which matches the mournful quality of the song.

One would suppose "Take a Ride in my Airship" (1930) would involve gags centering about an airplane or dirigible. Instead, most of the cartoon setting up the sing along portion involves a cat eagerly waiting for the delivery of her new piano.

"In the Good Old Summer Time" (1930) is a plotless one-reeler involving a group of animals parading to a park.

Variety reported on May 28, 1930 there was increased demand for cartoon shorts "that every company in the industry next season excepting Warner Bros., Fox and United Artists will include cartoon comedies on programs."

The story continued, "Paramount-Publix has song cartoons and other series with animated characters. That company was so astounded with the demand early last season for cartoons it took on a new series from Max Fleischer and halfway through the film year trebled the output."

Motion Picture News reviewed "Firebugs" on April 19, 1930. "Some of the absurdities of this cartoon subject are good for plenty of laughs. It's one of the series produced by Max Fleischer. There is some funny business when the fire department is called to answer an alarm, and its efforts to induce the piano-playing fiend to escape the burning building. Running time, six minutes."

Animated by Ted Sears and Grim Natwick, the short features Bimbo as a firefighter whose staff includes his horse Sparky and apparently dozens of mice. At the fire of a multi-story apartment building, he tries to rescue a classical pianist intent on playing. Bimbo's efforts to get him out of the building aren't successful and when his horse eats the keyboard to the piano, the musician plays on. Only at the conclusion of the melody is the pianist happy, even after he has fallen out of the building with his piano, Bimbo and the horse.

The popular song, "Yes, We have No Bananas" was given the Screen Song treatment in May 1930. Motion Picture News reported, "These song cartoons continue to maintain an extremely high average. The words and music of the well-known popular number lend themselves to clever animation. Joseph [sic] Fleischer has done it again. It's all a lot of nonsense, but so ridiculous, it's funny. This will make any audience go in for chuckling on a wholesale scale. Running time, 8 mins."

Some of these early sound cartoons foreshadowed the kind of humor and themes that would characterize the studio just a few years later. Variety noted (June 14 1930), "Wise Flies. There are quite a few laughs in this Max Fleischer cartoon. It has some novel gags, and for those who enjoy these exaggerated affairs, it has lots of laughs. The kids will pronounce it a wow. The spider and the fly fable here is given the funny treatment that only these cartoons can provide. Running time, 7 minutes."

A villainous spider, complete with Victorian top hat attempts to seduce a female fly but is rebuffed. He returns home to his wife who asks, "No flies?" He hangs his head in shame and replied, "No flies." A female fly does fall into his web, while the spider plays like a mandolin and sings the song "Some of These Days." The fly escapes, but continues the song on her banjo. When things are looking bad for her, the spider's wife looks out the window and is elated, as are their four spider babies. That elation turns to jealousy as Mrs. Spider realizes her husband is more interested in having a fly girl friend than a fly meal.

This is one early Talkartoon that holds together. It has a marginal plot, but it flips our expectations about the villain. The humor is dark and sexual at times and it features an excellent sound track.

Animator Willard Bowsky is generally credited for injecting spooky backgrounds and themes in the early Fleischer shorts. Ghosts, graveyards and consequences of a person's actions are all on display in "Sing You Sinners." Motion Picture News (Oct. 11, 1930) wrote, "The clever cartoon pen of Max Fleischer again demonstrates itself in this Talkartoon. An offstage chorus sings the lyrics to the rhythm of the action and the result is usually diverting. The cartoon hero is this time taken into a graveyard with the absurd results that you might well imagine. Worth a play. Running time, 9 minutes. O.K. for heavy feature."

"The Stein Song" (1930) was the first Screen Song to feature live action footage of a celebrity singer – a staple for the series in a few years. With a cartoon intro set at a Yale-Rutgers football game, crooner Rudy Vallee sings the song that is a rallying song for the University of Maine.

"A Hot Time in the Old Town Tonight" (1930) features more Mickey Mouse doppelgangers – a recurring image in early Fleischer shorts – drunk jokes and racial images as well as an amorous spider, a very potent combination to modern viewers, although not a very good cartoon.

"Put on Your Grey Bonnet," (1930) continued the practice of presenting songs from 20 to 30 years previous. Perhaps there was a sense of nostalgia for that era or perhaps the rights to those songs were less expensive. In this short the cartoon set-up is a band attempting to perform. The treatment isn't very remarkable, but at least there is a logical tie-in the song. The post sing along sequence actually is about hitching up a horse to a carriage!

"Mariutch," reviewed on Nov. 30, 1930 by Motion Picture News, is another example of the raciness for which the studio became known and also for it's hit or miss approach as reflected in the contemporary review. "'Mariutch' has had a number of better predecessors. The song, however, is known up and down the land and is 'way ahead of the cartoon work that accompanies it. In high spots, there is one: when the curtain behind which the violently active hootchy-kootchy dancer doing her stuff goes up and demonstrates the gyrations belong to three acrobats. Running time, 7 minutes."

For Max the dark days of losing his studio and working under Weiss appeared to have turned a corner, despite the country being in the depths of the Great Depression. Film Daily reported on Dec. 24, 1930 that Max was "distributing $10,000 in Christmas bonuses to 100 employees of his cartoon organization. Half of that is being handed out now and the other half will be in salary increases over the year."

Film Daily announced on Oct. 23, 1931 that Max would start two more series of cartoons because of the on-going finance success of the studio's productions.

***

A diversion for the studio at this time was a brief flirtation with sponsored cartoons. In 1930, Variety reported that Paramount-Publix had earned $212,000 in a nine-month advertising program in its theaters. One of the ad spots was for Lysol disinfectant.

"Lysol picture is a Fleischer cartoon ["A Jolt for General Germ"] that's to be showed into selected spots of Massachusetts, New Jersey, and New York… contract calls for a series of about six regular advertising shorts to be shot into about 30 or 40 towns of the Publix circuit operation."

The shorts had a budget of "about $5,000."

When it played at the Paramount Theater in Brooklyn, NY, Variety reviewed it (Nov. 12, 1930). "This first of the Paramount's commercial advertising shorts is no bad starter. Cartoonist Max Fleischer made the action sufficiently entertaining to file most of the rough edges off the advertising.

"Lysol, disinfectant, is the product mentioned and used prominently in the typical cartoon short yarn. There were snickers in the audience at the Brooklyn Paramount when the bottle and trademark were close-upped but no other expressed reaction at any time outside of the frequent laughs secured by the drawings.

"An army of germs is attacking the country. The defender's bullets bounce right off the impregnable enemy – the shells come limping home with tears in their eyes and it looks bad until a messenger rides back to a drug store for Lysol. A few drops of that kills off Gen. Germ's army including the general who had attempted to kidnap the heroine. Fleischer's frightful looking germs and the sound effects added become part of the entertainment.

"With the commercials, if confined to cartoons, it depends on the artist. His work and thoughts can make a commercial sufficiently amusing to cover blunt mention of the product, but he can also make the product and the theater seem ridiculous.

"If properly entertained it probably makes slight difference to audiences what the motive might be or what product is plugged. The radio is proof of that."

Fleischer returned to the sponsored cartoon in 1931 with "In My Merry Oldsmobile" for the Olds Motor Works. For a commercial, the cartoon has plenty of sex gags. There is a strip tease, an ass joke and pronounced cleavage, among others. There seemed to be some extra effort taken with the short with some archival footage of an Olds from 20 years earlier providing the background for the first song sequence.

***

It was one Talkartoon in 1930 that would change the course of the studio forever. It established a star for them and an identity for the sound era. That was "Dizzy Dishes," which gave birth to Betty Boop.

The Motion Picture Herald reported in 1931 that Max (see photo at bottom) was in attendance of a Paramount sales convention conducted in Atlantic City. The Fleischer cartoons were an important feature of the Paramount line-up.

Chapter Three

The legend is that in the crowded studio at 1600 Broadway in mid-town Manhattan, Grim Natwick was given the assignment of animating part of the Fleischer Studio's newest Talkartoon "Dizzy Dishes." Part of Natwick's assignment was creating and animating a nightclub singer. For inspiration, he was handed a photo of then-popular Helen Kane, a bouncy brunette who was acclaimed for her high -pitched child-like, but none-the-less sexy, singing voice.

That was the humble beginning of Betty Boop, quite possibly the most popular female cartoon character in the world. Despite the fact the Betty Boop cartoons stopped being a staple on local television stations decades ago and two contemporary versions of the character failed to ignite a revival, Betty's popularity in licensing has guaranteed the immortality that few cartoon characters have been able to maintain.

Type in the phrase "Betty Boop merchandise" into a search engine and you might be amazed at what you get. Amazon alone has hundreds of items. One could make the argument the character is generating more money today for its owners than it did when the cartoons were in their heyday.

And one might safely say that many of the teen and young adult women who buy the Boop tee-shirts, purses and other merchandise may never have seen a single Betty Boop cartoon. The cartoons themselves have only had a limited release on DVD. The Boop shorts seen the most are the ones that have fallen into the public domain.

When the Betty Boop cartoons were released on home video in a boxed set in 1996, they were met with critical success and proved to be a good seller. Their qualities still seem to attract an audience 70 years after they were made. The more recent official DVD release was also seen as welcome news to animation fans.

The often times surreal and risqué Boop cartoons are revered today for their imagination and hipness. Their funky urban qualities continue to delight audiences 90 years later. Of all the studios producing animation in the 1930s, the Fleischer Studio made cartoons that best reflected the blend of emotions that characterized that time; a contradictory blend of hope and despair and of domesticity and running wild.

Beginnings

The late Myron "Grim" Natwick was a fairly recent addition to the Fleischer operation. An animation vet by 1930, Natwick had entered animation prior to the First Word War at the studio set up by publisher William Randolph Hearst to publicize his newspaper's comic strip characters. Later, Natwick studied art in Europe for three years and came back to the United States where he worked on Felix and Krazy Kat shorts.

Producing shorts at the Fleischer Studio in 1930 was a far looser process that one could imagine. Animators had more responsibility for plots and gags, and there wasn't direction in the accepted sense. The early sound Fleischer shorts were, more often than not, merely a collection of gags linked together by a very general "plot." The creative process was a carry-over from the silent days, but it was clear a more standardized method of production was needed to meet the demands of sound.

Grim Natwick recalled to me in a 1978 interview, "The animator simply received a scene or a group of scenes or a whole picture. An animator like myself would receive an entire picture, and they'd put a couple of younger animators to work with us. The animator was virtually the director of the picture. If there were any characters necessary, the animator created them and animated them. There was no supervision.

"I remember on this picture ["Dizzy Dishes"] there was a 'Boop Oop A Doop' song and it had been recorded by Helen Kane, and I believe at the time, before the unions got tough, they may have even used her original track.

"In the first picture ... I animated a big part of it. I created the character [who would become Betty Boop]. They had this little dog Bimbo. She had to sing and dance and I forgot about the dog thing. She became looking more and more like a girl. In her early pictures, the first two or three perhaps, she retained those long poodle ears."

Natwick said his animation skills attracted Walt Disney who came to New York, had lunch with him and recruited him.

"Dizzy Dishes" is a remarkably crude affair. There really isn't a plot, but instead a string of gags centered in a nightclub. The Bimbo character is a waiter trying to accommodate the needs of his customers. He was attracted to the singer – clearly a caricature of Kane – who sang one song.

Kane looked like the stereotypical flapper from the 1920s. She wore her hair short in curls and her fashion included the shorter dresses preferred by many young women at the time.

Natwick's time at the Fleischer Studios was brief. He accepted an offer in 1931 to join the Ub Iwerks Studio in California. In 1934, Walt Disney hired him where he eventually did his most significant work on "Snow White and the Seven Dwarfs," and by 1939, he was back with Fleischer working on "Gulliver's Travels."

"Their [the Fleischers] comedy is typical American slapstick comedy the way it impressed them. You look at some of the Betty Boops and they are wild. They're really wild. Disney never got that wild," Natwick said.

Natwick worked on the first six shorts, which featured Betty as part of the cast. He insisted to me that, other than changing her dog-ears to earrings, the design and personality changes to the character were "insignificant." While Natwick was a trailblazer, the ultimate success of the character rested on the animators, writers, voice actresses and composers who would follow him after he left the studio.

Among animation historians and fans, this version of how the character came to be was accepted to be true. In Max's autobiographical writings he never took credit for Betty Boop's creation. In his son's Richard's memoir of his father, "Out of the Inkwell: Max Fleischer and the Animation Revolution," Richard wrote: "The script for 'Dizzy Dishes' called for a female entertainer to play opposite Bimbo. Since Bimbo was a dog, Max devised a character that was half dog and half human female. In its first appearance the character was nameless, but what a character is was – gross, ugly with an enormous bouncy behind. However it did have round, saucer-like eyes and shapely feminine legs.

"The executives at Paramount flipped for the dog-lady and wanted more films made with her. Max was delighted to oblige and made her the lead in every cartoon. But Max immediately began to work with his animators on refining the character. The dog-like features didn't last very long …

"Since my father's death in 1972, Grim Natwick, one of Fleischer Studios' oldest and most talented animators, has often been quoted as claiming to be the creator of Betty Boop. But before his death, my father had sworn under oath in two lawsuits that he, Max Fleischer, was the sole creator of the character. He acknowledged that many animators contributed to her development, not just Natwick, but also Seymour Kneitel, Myron Waldman, Doc Crandall, Ted Sears, Willard Bowsky and Al Eugster. I find it more than passing strange that, to my knowledge at least, Natwick never made such a claim while my father was alive."

Stephen Worth is the director of the animation archives for ASIFA-Hollywood, the southern California chapter of the international association that promotes animation. Worth sent me the following reaction to Richard Fleischer's claims:

"At the ASIFA-Hollywood Animation Archive, I have an exhibit hanging on the wall that proves conclusively that Grim created Betty Boop.

"Included in the exhibit are Grim's character designs for Betty from 'Dizzy Dishes,' 'Barnacle Bill,' 'Accordion Joe' and 'The Bum Bandit,' as well as a studio gag drawing of a beautifully drawn Grim Betty from 'Mysterious Mose' asking a horribly drawn Betty Boop, 'What happened to you little girl?' The badly drawn Betty replies, 'Boo hoo! Eggy made me!' On the back of the sketch is a note from Grim saying, 'Rudolph Eggeman's drawings were messy.' This confirms Grim's stories about how after Betty became successful, they tried to have other animators draw her, but none had the chops to draw a pretty girl like Grim did.

"I believe Grim's account of how Betty Boop was created.

"Grim said that Dave Fleischer told him they had found a girl who could do a perfect impression of Helen Kane. They wanted to do a cartoon with her, so Dave gave Grim a photo of Helen Kane clipped from a magazine and told him to make the girl look like the photo. At ASIFA, we have the inked key cleanup of Grim's design. It isn't crude and grotesque the way the film looks. Grim said that he was rushed, trying to do all the girl animation himself, while Ted Sears focused on Bimbo and the restaurant gags from Grim's thumbnail layouts. Grim animated the girl very loose and fast, expecting the assistants to follow his key cleanup, but they weren't able to. I attended a screening of 'Dizzy Dishes' with Grim at the LA County Museum of Art, and Grim grumbled through the song. After the cartoon, Charles Soloman introduced him from the stage as the creator of Betty Boop, and Grim took a bow. After he sat down, I asked him why he had been grumbling during the film. He said, 'The damn assistants messed up my lip-sync!'

"The most telling drawing in the ASIFA exhibit is a drawing that Grim referred to many times in interviews. Grim said that Dave Fleischer came to his desk one day and said, 'Mickey Mouse has Minnie. Do you think Bimbo needs a girlfriend?' Grim thought about it and said he would come up with an idea for a girl for Bimbo. Dave explained he had the idea to do a Talkartoon based on the song 'Barnacle Bill the Sailor,' and told Grim that he would check back to see what Grim came up with for the 'fair young maiden.'

"Grim had just finished 'Dizzy Dishes,' so he proceeded to adapt his Helen Kane caricature to serve as Bimbo's girlfriend. He drew a sketch of Betty Boop looking out a window as if to say 'Who's that knocking at my door?' Dave returned to his desk and Grim showed him the sketch. Dave said, 'I like the face, but Bimbo is a dog. Shouldn't she have a dog body?' Grim grabbed his pencil and drew Betty Boop's head with a four-legged canine body and pointed at it and the voluptuous one leaning out the window and replied, 'What do you want? A dog's body or a pretty girl's?' Dave laughed and said, 'You're right, Grim.'

"Grim told me these stories on his front porch in Santa Monica. After he passed away, his family asked me to sort through his artwork that had been in storage for decades, and I found the very drawing from 'Barnacle Bill' he was referring to. It shows Betty Boop leaning out the window, and below it, in the margin, is a small sketch of Betty with four legs and a stubby tail. The dog Betty is circled and a line from the circle points to the Betty in the window. When you look at the drawing, you can see Grim gesturing with his pencil as he says, 'What do you want? A dog's body or a pretty girl's?'

"Grim spoke very highly of Dave Fleischer. He said that he considered him a fine director, even if he didn't do his own layout or timing like the directors at other studios did. Grim said that Max was a fine gentleman too, but indicated that Max was more interested in running the 'front office' and working with the camera department on technical developments. His day-in, day-out creative supervision was from Dave. The only aspect of Betty Boop that Max could possibly have had a part with is the casting of the Helen Kane sound-a-like, but I tend to think that was most likely either Dave or Lou Fleischer.

"Grim told me a story about the last bit of Betty Boop animation that he did. When he was working on 'Gulliver's Travels,' Max came into his office one day, (which was unusual). Max told Grim that he appreciated that Grim had created Betty Boop. He told Grim that they had had a good run with her, but they were making the last Betty Boop cartoon, and he wanted Grim to work on it 'for old time's sake.' (My guess is that the last cartoon would have been 'Musical Mountaineers,' because there's quite a few scenes in there that look like they may be by Grim.)

"Grim said that Max told him as a sign of his appreciation, that after the completion of this cartoon, he would make a gift of the character to him. Grim thanked Max for the gesture, and shook his hand. Grim went on thinking that he owned the character, until years later, he read in the trades that Max had licensed his rights to the Fleischer characters for a great deal of money. The article mentioned that Betty Boop was one of the properties Max had licensed.

"Grim was always on good terms with Max, so he picked up the phone and called him.

A woman (Max's daughter?) answered and Grim asked to speak with Max. She asked who was speaking and Grim told her. She went away from the phone and was gone a long time. Finally Richard came to the line and told Grim that his father was sick and couldn't be disturbed. Grim asked when would be a good time to call back because he had a question about the licensing deal he had read about. Richard told him that there was no good time, told him never to call the house again, and hung up on him.

"Being treated like this rankled Grim. He spoke to a lawyer who filed a claim with the Fleischers for a portion of the money from the licensing deal. Grim ended up losing, because he had never filed the paperwork necessary to prove the transfer of ownership."

The authorship of the character has become more and more important with the increased amount of licensing. Natwick wasn't the only person who had a claim. Long-time Fleischer animator Myron Waldman created Betty's dog Pudgy that is prominent in currently licensed products. Waldman never received any money for his contribution.

Here is a rare example of Bimbo merchandising: a Bimbo embroidered patch front the 1930s. (Author's collection).

Who's the boss?

Dave Fleischer took the screen credit as director of nearly all of the Fleischer shorts through the demise of the studio in 1942. For animation fans and scholars who understand the role of a director, Dave's constant screen credit makes him appear an animation genius or that "director" meant something else than at other studios.

The truth is that Dave was not a director in the same way as Chuck Jones or Tex Avery. Directors such as Jones and Avery headed their own animation units, and were responsible for working with writers on a short, overseeing the design of the characters, drawing key poses, directing the voice actors and even animating sequences.

Dave acted as a line producer. He was more of a general supervisor of the shorts rather than the primary creative force. He did direct the voice actors in the recording schedule, and, according to ASCAP records, he also dabbled in composing some of the music for the cartoons.

This could certainly account for the differences in how characters such as Betty Boop looked from cartoon to cartoon in the early sound era. Characters often even looked differently within the same cartoon due to the use of several animation units and how each would draw the characters.

A more traditional animation director would have insisted there would be greater artistic continuity between scenes worked on by different units. These variations seen today give the early Fleischer sound cartoons a sort of loopy charm – a fly by the seat of your pants look.

A story on the studio in the Dec. 28, 1930 edition of "The New York Times" described the story process at the studio during the early sound era.

"The complex, efficient mechanism which transfers Bimbo's madcap adventures to the screen is not a little prosaic. Properly speaking, there is not even a scenario. Somebody, anybody, one of the photographers, perhaps, suggests an abstract subject – a bullfight, a mailman, a steelworker, and a sailorman. Thereupon the idea is approved, the basis of approval being simply the probability of its being fertile in humor and the gagmen consult in Dave Fleischer's office.

"The whole thing is quite informal. Anyone who is not busy at the moment drops in [Dave Fleischer's office] and takes a hand in the proceedings. A rough scenario emerges from the discussion. The cartoonists then receive their assignments, each to draw a sequence in the mad narrative. The artists are informed of the hatching plot and instructed to prepare backgrounds and scenery, which will later be blended with the action drawings of the cartoonists."

Even after the studio began to use a separate story department, Fleischer animator Myron Waldman told me that he remembered getting scripts without an end, "They hadn't thought of a gimmick, yet," he said.

Fleischer animator Gordon Sheehan shared his perspective on Dave's accomplishments to film historian Leonard J. Kohl:

"Dave and Max Fleischer were equal partners in Fleischer Studios as far as I know. At least, they took equal salaries out of the company's profits. Max got producer's credit – Dave got director's credit on all cartoon productions but this was an honorary credit. He didn't draw so he wasn't actively involved on the laying out or animating of the film. However he did check over every script before it went into production, made changes and offered suggestions usually in the line of supplementary gags or humorous situations. And he supervised much of the music writing and recording of the cartoons.

"But the actual work of drawing up a storyboard from a cartoon script, 'roughing it' – making rough layouts of the action – timing the action, and handing it out to animators to draw up, was done by one of the group-head animators. In New York before we made the move to Miami, Florida, in 1938, there were five groups of about six animators each, including assistant animators and the group heads were: Willard Bowsky, Seymour Kneitel, Dave Tendlar, Tom Johnson and Myron Waldman. These five talented cartoon animators were the real directors of the films they handled, and so, were almost totally responsible for the quality of each film, as well as keeping the production costs within a predetermined budget.

"Dave had the authority to make changes in the rough film, but I doubt that he often used it."

"In respect to Dave's contribution to the studio's animation output, although he appeared to take very little part in the drawing end of animation he was credited with having a keen sense of timing and pacing of a cartoon, and the head animators consulted him frequently on this very important subject and on general animation problems that might pop up from time to time. Dave also sat in on most animated cartoon recordings, and played a big part of selecting the music and sound effects that helped make Fleischer films an important contribution to the theatrical animation move industry.

"Of the customary two screen credits awarded for animation on each film, one went to the group head (the real animator), and the other went to the animator in the group who furnished the most film footage on the production."

In a 1987 edition of Animato magazine, Shamus Culhane wrote in a letter to the editor, "Recently, I was given a retrospective evening by the Mill Valley Film Festival. One of my films was a Betty Boop cartoon, 'Bamboo Isle.' I animated a hula-hula by Betty which probably was my best animation at Fleischer. Al Eugster and I wrote, directed and animated the film. Yet when the credits came on, I saw to my anger that the animation credit was given to Seymour Kneitel and William Henning, with direction by Dave Fleischer. I had forgotten that when I had originally saw those credits, I went on strike for three days. It took all of [William] Gilmartin's persuasiveness to stop me from quitting." [Note: William Gilmartin was the animation production manager at Fleischer's at the time.]

"… As for animation credit, for some reason the Fleischer's decided that only two animators would be given credit on a picture. Since three or four animators often worked together, they decided to rotate the screen credit, regardless of the fact that in many cases the animator didn't do a foot of the film.

"… For people to continue to follow blindly this charade of screen credits does an injustice to the artists involved. Better to inform your readers that screen credits are completely unreliable, and omit them entirely."

Animator Dave Tendlar offered this assessment of credit to Kohl:

L.K.: "Every single Fleischer cartoon that I've ever seen says 'Directed by Dave Fleischer,' but he really didn't 'direct' any of those, did he?"

D.T.: *"Well, very greedily, he took that 'title' on every picture! But, the 'Head Animators' were the 'directors,' actually, because they did all the work! Dave took the credit!"*

L.K.: "What did he do?"

D.T.: *"He used to 'O.K.' stories, talk to the story men about ideas – develop ideas for pictures, add gags - things like that. He also directed the sound track – the dialogue – he'd show the dialogue men [voice actors] how to read lines."*

L.K.: "He would coach them – Jack Mercer, Mae Questel – as far as getting the voices to sound the way he wanted them to?"

D.T.: *"He would sit in on the voice recordings and tell them just how he wanted them to read [the] lines."*

L.K.: "Now, I think he wrote some of the music for the songs, right?"

D.T.: *"No! Dave didn't have anything to do with music. No. He may have made some suggestions for the songs. But he didn't finish [writing] the songs. The professional musicians did that."*

***

Although animation was a regular part of the movie experience for audiences for years, the process was fascinating to people. In the Paramount Pictures internal newsletter, "Pep-o-Grams," from Oct. 22, 1931, writer Dick Engel presented the following version of how the Fleischers made the cartoons: "To begin with a story which is adaptable to this type of picture is decided upon. Music is then arranged and gags are developed.

"After the proposed cartoon has reached this stage, it is turned over to the animators or cartoonists, as you prefer, who in turn make drawings of the action as described in the story. Not all of the cartoons are drawn by one person. The animators divide up the story between them after a discussion in which all details are decided upon. Each animator then develops a series of penciled drawings and then in turn are transferred to the 'in between' department which furnishes cartoons. That completes the actions between those sequences, which the animator has made.

"From this procedure the cartoons are then 'traced' and 'inked in' on a clear celluloid sheet. The figures are than painted a sharp white and black for contrast. This process is called 'opaquing.'

"The next step is the make up of backgrounds, which are appropriate for the locale as called for in the picture.

"All drawings are finally assembled and checked for motions, completeness of detail, etc. The next process is the timing or layout of the of exposure sheets for photographing the cartoon. Drawings are now put in sequence to fit the music.

"Each drawing in then photographed in order. Incidentally, it will be interesting at this point to know that it takes on an average of 7,500 individual drawing to make up a complete song cartoon. Unbelievable perhaps for so short a picture, yet the song cartoon's life on the screen is but for several minutes.

"After the film has been developed the entire cartoon is shown in a projection room where a check-up is made for smoothness in the moving of the figures and the general make-up of the film.

"The final addition to the then complete cartoon is the synchronization of music sound effects and voice which tend to give the picture life. Nearly every sound from gargling soup to a skeleton walking on a tin roof is accomplished by technicians experienced in this art.

"To those of us who have seen the Betty Boop character in these cartoons we do know that her voice has a certain charm. Betty Boop is growing more popular every day with movie fans. This character is portrayed by a very real person who synchronizes her voice to that of the young lady in the cartoon.

"The average Fleischer song cartoon takes ten weeks to make. Approximately one week is spent synchronizing the sound and the balance of the time is devoted to the structure of the cartoon itself.

"It is hard, tedious job and Max Fleischer and his co-workers are to be lauded for their wonderful efforts which we all know are enjoyed by the theatre-going public."

It's interesting that Engel made sure he didn't name the voice actress who supplied Betty's voice nor did he mention Dave's role in the production of the shorts.

I believe that Max enjoyed participating in the production of the cartoons as revealed by his continuing role as Koko's straight man in the silent shorts. When the new Fleischer Studios was set up, though, there was an apparent arrangement that Max would handle the business end of the studio while Dave would oversee production. Dave's role apparently included the screen credit as director often to the chagrin of the real directors of the Fleischer cartoons. Max's interest in the production of the shorts, though, can be seen in his inventions, such as the tabletop 3-D process.

Ruth Kneitel, Max's daughter, showed me documents that suggested that Max did get involved with the creative side of the company after the coming of sound. She had an undated script for a cartoon involving mermaids that had numerous notes in red pencil, which she explained were made by her father. The mermaid short was never made, though. By the look of the existing artwork it may have been destined as one of the Color Classic cartoons.

The Birth of a Star

Considering the somewhat haphazard way the Fleischer Studio used to create cartoons at this time, it's little wonder that it took them a while to figure out what exactly to do with Natwick's Helen Kane-ish singer.

Bimbo was the star of the early Talkartoons, but he was a character with little or no definition. His physical appearance changed three times – from an almost stick figure with a bowler hat and floppy ears to a transitional design with a porkpie hat and small ears to the more dog-like creature wearing a sweater.

It's difficult to take Richard Fleischer's version of the early reaction to the Betty character seriously – that someone at Paramount recognized the potential of the character from her debut in "Dizzy Dishes." Looking at the Talkartoons in order one can see the transitional pains from silent to sound production and from having a very established character – Koko – to starting from scratch.

In "Barnacle Bill," (1930), we see the second appearance of the still unnamed Betty character. Here she is the "fair young maiden"

Paramount had an in-house newsletter which in one issue had this header.

and the object of the rough sailor's attention. Although the lyrics are cleaned up from the sexually explicit ones from the drinking song, it is still a sexually charged cartoon and typical of the Fleischers' work prior to the Production Code in 1934 that censored sexual material in films. As in "Dizzy Dishes," the star of the show is Bimbo.

There is a noticeable difference with this short. It's about something. Bimbo is a lecherous sailor on leave trying to find sex. The song provides a framework for the action and the gags. The Betty character provides Bimbo with something he needs: a foil.

"Swing You Sinners" (1930) is a problematic cartoon for contemporary viewers. Bimbo, or a version of Bimbo, is attempting to steal a chicken. He fails and is chased away from the henhouse by a cop. He finds himself in a graveyard where spirits haunt him.

The animation by Ted Sears and Willard Bowsky is quite good and the music is sophisticated for its time. The problem is that Bimbo is portraying a racial stereotype of an African-American. The spirits sing, "Chicken you used to steal!' Bimbo replies, 'I don't steal no more." "Craps you used to shoot!" "I don't shoot no more." "Dames you used to chase! "I don't chase no more."

He escapes to a barn where the ghosts pursue him to an upbeat rendition of "Swing You Sinners." The end of the short is a wonderful psychedelic musical number.

Here is a cartoon in which the strengths of the animators – Bowsky and his love of spooky motifs – is perfectly matched with two great songs. The problem is the ethnic quality of the humor.

"Sky Scraping" (1930) is another example of a series of unrelated gags centered on the building of a skyscraper. Bimbo appears in several scenes but really has little of the action.

This short illustrates the wildly uneven approach to the character and to the studio's style. "While "Swing You Sinners" has the thinnest of plots, it works well. "Sky Scraping" lacks any plot.

Bimbo is solo in "Up to Mars" (1930). While lighting off fireworks, Bimbo is taunted by a mouse who he tries to kill with Roman candles. Instead he is tricked and winds up on large rocket, which takes him to Mars. There he encounters Martians who essentially do things in opposite of Earth, i.e. a thief gives his victim money and valuables. He joins a Martian army unit (!) and there are now a series of marching gags. The short just ends.

"Mysterious Mose" (1930) has Betty in a prominent part. She is alone and scared on a stormy night– so scared her nightshirt jumps off of her twice for a glimpse at her cleavage. She sings the title song and Bimbo appears, as the character who is haunting her. Naturally within Talkartoon logic they fall in love. At the end Bimbo is revealed to be a clockwork robot.

This cartoon shows the Fleischer free association that some might interpret as sloppiness – a fish from underneath Betty's carpet, an odd enough image, is transformed into a saxophone-playing caterpillar for no real narrative reason. It just happens.

"Trees Saps" (1931) Bimbo is a logger who is teamed up with what is apparently a seal dressed in logger's clothes. All the audience knows is that Bimbo must occasionally toss him a fish.

There's a risqué gag when the seal chops down a utility pole occupied by a linesman who yells, "Hey Goddaaaaaaaaaaaaarn you." Bimbo runs out of fish but is saved when a tornado appears and ultimately blows the seal away.

"Teacher's Pest" (1931) features Bimbo as a student going to school. Mayhem in the classroom ensues. Betty appears as a classmate but is no longer a dog, but a cat. Bimbo tells the teacher he has to use the lavatory, but instead goes to a closet to get out a banjo for another musical number, "School Days."

In "The Cow's Husband" (1931) a cocky Bimbo is a toreador on his way to a bullfight. The bull is crying about having to go into the ring and one of his calves tell him, "Don't worry daddy, We'll collect the insurance."

The two meet in the ring and sing to each what they think of each other. A struggle ensues and Bimbo loses the fight with two horns stuck in his backside. The triumphant bull is carried by other bulls into what we think is the arena, but as the door closes, we see it's a wholesale butcher shop.

The song and the gags work pretty well and there is a better structure to the short.

"The Bum Bandit" (1931) features Bimbo as a hold-up man and all-around tough guy. He prepares to rob a train, but Betty warns the engineer. Bimbo stops the train as he is walking through the frightening passengers he is confronted by Betty in a Western outfit. She is the sister of Dangerous Dan Magrew, she sings, as she manhandles Bimbo. It turns out she is Bimbo's wife. "Remember the night you went out for quart of milk and left me with the kids?" she asked him as she displays a photo of their large family.

The design for Bimbo switched back to the original for this short, instead of the second one. "Twenty Legs Under the Sea" (1931) has Bimbo deep-sea fishing. An obliging large fish hooks himself on Bimbo's line and drag him to the bottom. Through an undisclosed plot point, Bimbo winds up as the king with two matching Betty Boop mermaids at his side. Bimbo manages to lure his subjects to what appears to be an amusement park that in turn brings them to a fish canning plant!

"Silly Scandals" (1931) is another example of what was right and wrong with the early Fleischer sound shorts. The plot involves Bimbo sneaking into a theater to see Betty perform. After she sings her number, the gags shift around a stage hypnotist. Nothing remarkable has happened in the short until the very end when Bimbo, under the spell of the hypnotist, has hallucinations that seem to have come straight out of the psychedelic era of the 1960s.

At least the character was given the name "Betty" in this short.

"The Herring Murder Case" (1930) opens with a gorilla shooting a herring, who said as he expired, "They shot me! Holy mackerel! Is this the end of the herring?" This line is a parody of the last words Edward G. Robinson's Little Caesar character said in the conclusion of "Little Caesar."

This is the first sound appearance of Koko, who would play a supporting role in several cartoons. He appears out of an inkwell and walks into the drawing of the background for the cartoon's setting. He tells Bimbo, who is a private detective, about the herring's death.

It was also the first appearance of the final design for Bimbo, a recognizable dog.

Betty did not appear, although the Boop voice is used for the herring's widow. Although her very next Talkartoon was a quantum leap over "Silly Scandals," she was still just part of the punch line.

"Bimbo's Initiation" (1931) has been included in various lists of outstanding cartoons and for good reason. Here the Fleischer "looseness" served the cartoon well. There isn't really a plot; Bimbo, innocently walking the street, stumbles into a trap laid by an anxious secret fraternity who would like him to join. When he refuses, he is put through a variety of tortures and perils designed to make him change his mind. He only changes his mind when the ominous figure who keeps asking him "Wanna be a member? Wanna be a member?" turns out to be Betty.

"Bimbo's Initiation" is one of the studio's best shorts. Genuinely creepy at times with a truly surreal concept – who are these guys and why are they so insistent? – it's quite funny and very well animated. It's only marginally a Betty Boop cartoon, though.

Throughout these early cartoons, Mickey Mouse, or a character that looks very much like Mickey Mouse, kept making little cameo appearances. In "Bimbo's Initiation," he appeared as Bimbo disappears down a manhole for his first encounter with the fraternity. Why the Fleischers were winking at their colleagues at Disney has never been explained. It was one of many such appearances in the Talkartoons.

With "Bimbo's Express," (1931) Bimbo had to share the billing with Betty and the two had a memorable exchange of dialogue. "I can't let you in. I'm in my nightgown," Betty said. Bimbo replied, "I'll wait until you take it off."

In "Minding the Baby" (1931) Bimbo, in the midst of doing laundry, is told by his mother he has to mind his baby brother, who is a brat. From the next building over, Betty sends Bimbo a note "Ma is out. Come over." Bimbo can't, though and Betty sings a song about the two of them "playing house" an innocent song in a not so innocent situation. He does go over, though, balancing on the laundry line between the two buildings which only causes his brother to use a piano roll to try to escape from the building.

"Mask-a-Raid" (1931) is the first appearance of Betty as a human and that she is now the star of the Talkartoons. Bimbo is billed as her co-star. She is the queen of a masquerade ball and the subject of Bimbo's affections.

Betty's footage increased in "Dizzy Red Riding Hood" (1931) as she had the title role, but it was in "Boop-Oop-A-Doop" (1932) in which the Boop character really started to gel. Betty is more than just an attractive accessory. She is definitely the star of the short, while Bimbo and Koko are her co-stars.

Betty plays a circus performer who is the object of unrequited affection from the ringmaster. This is one of the most openly sexual of the Boop shorts. The ringmaster corners Betty in her dressing area and rubs his hand up and down her thigh. He then tells her if she wants to keep her job, she'll... and he whispers something in her ear that horrifies her. She then launches into the song "Don't Take My Boop-Oop-A-Doop Away." Koko manages to save her and winds up the hero.

So what is "Boop-Oop-A-Doop?" The refrain that singer Helen Kane made famous was essentially meaningless, but when used in the right context it could inspire risqué interpretations. Betty prevails over her unwanted suitor with the help of Koko who receives a literally burning kiss as his reward.

"Boop-Oop-A-Doop" marks the first phase of Boop's cartoon persona. She is the sexy but innocent star in a no-holds-barred cartoon universe. Sometimes her co-stars are animals, sometimes humans, sometimes something in-between. A few of her cartoons resemble the classic silent Kokos in which Betty emerges from an inkwell into the "real" world.

The Film Daily reported in its Sept. 6, 1931 edition that Max had declared Betty to be star and that "in the future the cartoons will be built around Betty with the other characters 'also in the cast.'"

"The Robot" (1932) is a true puzzlement. Here is the first version of Bimbo being used after the new character design had been established. Bimbo takes his girl friend, who is an off-model Betty Boop without the distinctive voice, for a ride in his car. They crash outside of a carnival and the female character refuses his proposal of marriage unless he can defeat a boxer prominently billed as an attraction. Bimbo builds a robot out of his crashed car to defeat the boxer but is thrown out of the ring. Coming to his rescue is the girlfriend who now is Betty – clearly the scene was animated by someone else. Naturally Bimbo defeats the boxer in the second round and he and the faux Betty drive off.

An early Betty Boop model sheet which shows the character as most people know her.

It almost looks as if "The Robot" was made earlier and held for release because with the next short, Betty's character gelled even more.

With "Boop-Oop-A-Doop" Betty's character began to be more developed as a working-class person, often times involved in some sort of performing. One could see in these early cartoons, the Fleischer animators struggling to present Betty as something more than just a sex object and more than just a foil for gags in the surreal Fleischer universe. Sometimes Betty could be as innocent as a child and other times she was as knowing as Mae West.

Koko the clown had been a cinematic version of "Peck's Bad Boy," the brat you love or hate rebelling against his father, but Betty was far more difficult to define.

It should be noted that short subject were seen by the film industry as one element that had been affected less by the Depression, than as the rental charges of feature films. The Film Daily noted (Oct. 23, 1932) that Max was planning two more cartoon series. "Cartoon grosses generally are making a better showing under present business conditions, declared Fleischer yesterday. This type of picture is only off between five and six percent as compared with greater drops suffered by other kinds of screen entertainment receipts, he said."

Betty was certainly popular enough by October of 1932 that Max made a personal appearance at the Earle Theater in Philadelphia. There was a display at the theater with several hundred cels, as well as "the original glass table top table used to sketch the first Fleischer cartoon." Mae Questel also appeared at the weekend event along with "Cookie" Bowers "who creates the 'noises.'"

Bowers was a vaudeville performer known for his mimicry according to a 1931 story in the Hollywood Filmograph. He provided some of the voices for the "Dogville" shorts produced in the early 1930s. A mention in a column in the Aug. 1, 1933 edition of The Film Daily noted he was performing in New York City and described him as "who furnished sound effects for many cartoon shorts." He was also described as a "wonderful imitator of animals and musical instruments."

A trade ad in the June 11, 1932 edition of the Motion Picture Herald declared Betty Boop as "the Box Office Baby." The ad continued, "The most popular entertainers on the air are singing and playing Betty Boop, the hit song that sweeping the nation! Kids everywhere are joining Betty Boop & Bimbo Clubs! Betty Boop thrills and Betty Boop strip cartoon are delighting the young and old of the world! She's the country's latest craze this master creation of Max Fleischer, master showman! Now featured in Paramount Screen Songs and Paramount Talkartoons, Betty Boop has become so tremendously popular that after August 1st she will be starred! In Paramount Betty Boop Cartoons! … but more big news later."

It became clear that because Betty was based on Helen Kane, the element of music was increasingly important in shaping her cartoons, especially popular music.

The Fleischers, with their base in New York and ties to Paramount and its Famous Music division, began using well-known singers and big bands in their Betty Boop and Screen Song cartoons. Radio stars such as Arthur Tracy, Singing Sam, Broadway performers such as Lillian Roth and Ethel Merman, and recording artists such as Rudy Vallee, the violinist Rubinoff and the Mills Brothers were among the stars featured in Fleischer shorts.

Betty soon eclipsed Bimbo as the studio's star.

In "Kitty from Kansas City," (1931) Betty is traveling by train along with a cat and parrot. She's grabbed by the mailbag hook of a passing training and while hanging, hears Valle sings. Valle then appears singing the song while wearing an 1890s outfit.

The novelty song had been a hit for Valle and his appearance in the animated short was significant enough to warrant a trade ad for that short alone. In many ways the cartoon was a forerunner to the modern music video.

If nothing else, the Fleischer Betty Boop and "Screen Songs" provide a fascinating musical time capsule of some of the best-known popular artists of the time. No other animation studio during the 1930s seemed as interested in presenting contemporary music as the Fleischer Studio. Dave had a keen interest in music, while Lou was a violinist. Sammy Timberg was the studio's composer during the period and he had a strong Tin Pan Alley background.

Lou and Timberg worked on the musical tracks for the cartoons and were able to use songs that had appeared in Paramount films. Sometimes these songs are used to accompany the action, while at other times Betty performed them.

This interest in music was coupled with the use of live-action footage that was part of the Koko silent cartoons. The result was that in the period of 1930 to 1935, the Fleischers' cartoons, with their use of popular music and live-action, continued to be singular. No other studio at the time was apparently willing to go to the extra expense and trouble of filming performers to be used in an animated short.

In 1931, Rudy Vallee was red hot in popularity and made his first contribution to a Fleischer cartoon.

The next Talkartoon cartoon was another milestone. "Minnie The Moocher" (1932) featured Cab Calloway and his big band playing one of their signature tunes. "Minnie The Moocher," like "Bimbo's Initiation," is almost plot-less. Betty, living with her parents, decides to run away from home, accompanied by Bimbo. At nightfall they stay in a cave, which they discover they're sharing with a variety of ghosts who launch into the title song. The lead ghost, who sings and dances, is a rotoscoped Cab Calloway. His antics scare the two back to their homes.

Calloway's song of the life and death of a drug-user was a popular hit, but one wonders if people at the studio understood what the urban slang meant.

The eerie backgrounds and the macabre jokes in the cave are typical of the sense of humor of Fleischer vet Willard Bowsky who worked on 11 of the Betty Boop shorts. A significant talent at the studio who contributed much to the Popeye series, Bowsky was a controversial figure. He was among the "inner circle" of confidants surrounding the Fleischers, but had a reputation, ironically, for anti-Semitism among many of his co-workers, according to Waldman.

Lou Fleischer, who headed the music department at the studio, told animation historian Ray Pointer about Calloway's reaction to the short.

"When Cab saw this [his cartoon form] he screamed in laughter and stretched himself out on the floor! Some months later I met Cab Calloway and asked, 'Did our cartoon help or hurt your show when it went on the road?' He said, 'Are you kidding? We had your cartoon shown the week before we arrived at every theater, and on its account none of the houses could accommodate the crowds that came. Are you kidding?'"

According to his 1976 autobiography, "Minnie the Moocher and Me," Calloway said the Fleischer "Minnie the Moocher" was his favorite of the cartoons in which he and his band starred.

The Film Daily (Jan. 10, 1932) called the cartoon "swell" and added, "This Max Fleischer musical cartoon is one of the best turned out so far with the cute pen and ink star, Betty Boop, who seems to be getting more sexy and alluring each time and her boy friend Bimbo. The musical portion is supplied by Cab Calloway and his orchestra and what these boys can't do to the 'Minnie the Moocher' number isn't worth mentioning. Cab and his boys are shown only for a brief moment at the opening. Then a cartoon character, a big walrus with serpentine hips, performs the gyrations to the tune of the 'Minnie' song. The effect is little short of a knockout, especially to those familiar with Cab's radio, stage or nightclub. Betty Boop's part on the action concerns her running away from home because of her bad parents. With Bimbo she goes into a cave, where spooky figures give them such a scare that they beat it back home."

Betty is shipwrecked with Bimbo and Koko in "S.O.S" (1932) but are picked up by pirates who chant when they are playing jacks, "Pepper, salt, mustard, cider, we're so tough we'll crush a spider!" Naturally Betty attracts the attention of the irate chief and Bimbo and Koko rescue her before anything bad can happen to her.

"The Dancing Fool," shows just uneven the series could be, especially when compared to shorts such as "Boop Oop a Doop" and "Minnie the Moocher." The plotless cartoon opens with a series of gags with Bimbo and Koko and their efforts to raise and lower a scaffold. They paint Betty's window of her dance school and join in. The rest of the cartoon is simply a series of repetitive gags and movements performed by the members of the class.

In "Chess-Nuts (1932)," the short opens with two middle-aged men playing a game of chess and studying the board intently. The shot shifts to the board itself where the pieces move by themselves before the three-dimensional animation switches to cel animation. The last shot of the short shows an altered photo of the two men now with long grey beards.

Characters who resembled Betty had popped up in cartoons from other studios, and in 1932 Max bought an ad in Film Daily that asserted his rights. "I hereby serve notice that the character Betty Boop is fully protected by copyright registration and I intend to protect my interests to the fullest extent of the law against anyone attempting to use to imitate this character."

The progress of process

Even if the character was used in cartoons of uneven quality, it was clear that Betty and the studio were attracting a lot of attention.

These stories show an evolution in the way the cartoons were made. A piece appearing in the New York Times on Dec. 28, 1930 noted, "The whole thing is quite informal. Anyone who is not busy at the moment drops in and takes a hand in the proceedings, A rough scenario emerges from the discussion. The cartoonist then receive their assignments, each to draw a sequence in the mad narrative. The artist are informed of the hatching pot and instructed to prepare backgrounds and scenery, which will later be blended with the action drawings of the cartoonist.

"The first pencil sketches of the action are done by 'animators.' These young men who spend their working hours in a phantasmagoria where only their pencil and the white drawing board are real, concoct the weird action of Bimbo and his playmates, each successive drawing reveals the characters in a different but consecutive pose. Bimbo, in one drawing, will be affrighted by the approach of a monster; in the next he will be turning slightly to flee; in the next his foot will be off the ground and so on until he is in full flight.

"The 'in-between man' gets the 'animator's' work. His job is to make the drawings between each of the animator's sketches to fill in the action so that when tun off rapid succession the thousands of finished pictures will produce an impression of smooth motion. Meanwhile in another room the background men who are known by their fellows as the 'artists' because of their talent with the brush, are painting background scenery on sheets of exactly the same size as those used by the animators and in-between men."

The writer then described that Max H. Manne in a studio at Eleventh Avenue and 43rd St. in New York City, would add the dialogue and sound effects. "In the studio Max and his three assistants sit a long table each with his cue sheet telling him what, when and how to make a noise. Around them in neat rows are the implements of their trade, ready to be grasped and laid down again with one motion. Each has his own microphone. The picture is flashed on the screen and the boys get to work."

The Film Daily, one of the most prominent trade publications for the motion picture industry featured a regular column "Along the Rialto" written by "Phil M. Daily." In the June 24, 1932 column, Betty was the subject.

"Why does the animated cartoon holds its popularity throughout the years while every other type of picture rises and falls in cycles? This question has been mulling through our bean for a long time. We figured that Max Fleischer, pioneer cartoon creator and developer, could tell us. His answer was, 'If you'll stroll through the cartoon plant with me and absorb what you see, then you'll have the answer.' And here is a glimpse of what we saw.

"An entire floor of a big office building devoted to cartoon creation, 18 Betty Boops and 18 Screen Songs a year. This tight program keeping a staff of 50 to 100 people busy throughout the year. Over 30 special mechanical appliances, most of which invented by Mister Fleischer himself. For his animated process is radically different from any other, being a mechanical engineer as well as a fine creative artist darned unusual combination. He has 20 individual patents of his own on various cartoon systems and devices.

"It takes nine weeks to pack a completed cartoon up in the can from the time the scenario department starts with an idea. This department consists of highly specialized gagmen who work entirely different from gag men on a Hollywood lot who plan a gag to start and break in two to three minutes with regular actors. In cartoons, a gag must develop and break in an average of five seconds. They must plan an average of 30 gags for each cartoon figuring and audience response to about 10 then they have a sure fire animated.

"Only seven minutes of screen time to play with yet every cartoon requires the detailed system of a regular studio production, music dialogue, costumes, story treatment, direction with a very tough problem of visualization; for they cannot tell 'til they see the finished product on the screen just how the production has gone over. The studio director sees the actors before him, the action, the atmosphere gets the person reaction. All this is denied the cartoon creator. He relies on visualization and some special sixth sense that tells him whether he's on the right track or not.

"Take the remarkable case of Betty Boop, cartoon gal who rose from a lowly extra to a dazzling star. The audience reactions showed the unknown extra in insignificant bits had caught on so they started grooming her. Mister Fleischer gave her a doll-like face with those baby eyes but also a mature figure with oo-la-la curves and a boudoir languor in her walk – if you get what we mean. And Betty became an overnight hit, something brand new in cartoon characterization. They talk of Betty around the Fleischer studio as if she was Greta Garbo and she is to them with a million dollars wrapped up in her come-hither eyes and sexy seductiveness. So that's why animated hold their perennial appeal: they're short, scientifically and cunningly created with humor, humanness, sure fire gags, clever artwork, psychological appeal, directness, punch, action. They furnish a diversity of entertainment in the shortest space of time."

Animator Gordon Sheehan, who joined the studio in the early 1930s, told historian Leonard Kohl about how he worked. "Animation was more than a job – it was a creative venture and getting paid for doing this was like getting icing on the cake. As far as freedom with gags was concerned – as soon as we received a new script from the story department, Willard Bowsky, my boss, would make a pencil story board on 11" by 14" white paper. He would spend several days laying out each scene in sequence, very much like a long comic strip, staging and sketching out key action poses and rough timing the movements, also noting camera pans, dissolves, etc.

"When the story board was complete it would be gummed up on a bulletin board and the whole group, assistants as well as animators, would gather around as Willard went through the whole story, acting out special scenes. This finished, everyone in the group was invited and encouraged to make comments and gag suggestions that might make the production funnier and later, if possible, incorporated in the film, By this method we could quite frequently make a mediocre script into a lively, entertaining animated cartoon."

Sheehan also explained to Kohl about the use of sound. "Before the middle of the 1930s, most of the animation was drawn first, then recorded later. To visually guide the recording musicians of the tempo, cartoon characters were animated to bends their knees and wave their arms or perform some other obviously repetitive action in time with the beat. Usually the tempo of the movement would start out slow, pick up speed as the film progressed and end up fast at the climax.

"Around the mid-1930s, the Fleischers expanded their music and sound department and initiated a system whereby music, voice and sound effects were pre-recorded and marked on lead sheets which were very much music sheets and informed the animators exactly what frame of film the cartoon character moved on, how long the action should be and where to place the accents on the action.

"This made for more refined synchronization between cartoon action and the soundtrack but some animators complained that this system allowed less freedom to animate. I believe that all in all, it improved the quality of animated films."

Crazytown

Once there seemed to be some stability about the name and character of Betty Boop, some of the kind of experimentation that was fairly common in the silent Ko-Ko cartoons began to be seen in the Boop series.

Calloway was delighted with the results of his first cartoon and returned to the studio twice to do more. He and his band appeared in "Snow White" (1933) and "The Old Man of the Mountain" (1933). No other musician, other than crooner Rudy Valle, appeared as many times as Calloway and his band.

Max and his star.

The Fleischer version of "Snow White" takes the basic plot of the fairy tale and presents it in seven minutes. The centerpiece of the film is a performance of "St. James Infirmary Blues," another Calloway hit and another song rife with drug references. Once again, the action takes places in a cave in which the wicked witch has transformed Koko into a singing ghost who accompanies the seven dwarves as they transport Betty's body to its resting place.

"The Old Man of the Mountain" has Betty daring to confront a violent recluse who is terrifying a mountain town. As Betty travels up the mountain, she is met with a parade of refugees who all cite "The Old Man of the Mountain" as the source of their unhappiness. One woman pushing a baby carriage flips the carriage open to reveal three bearded babies; a gag that couldn't be used after the Production Code was implemented.

Jazz legend Louis Armstrong appeared with Betty in "I'll be Glad When You're Dead, You Rascal You" (1932). The Armstrong band not only performed for the soundtrack, but Armstrong was transformed into a cannibal in this less-than politically correct cartoon.

Perhaps the most elaborate use of a guest star musician was in "I Heard" (1933). Instead of performing a song or two, Don Redman and his band provided the entire soundtrack to the cartoon.

Guest musicians were often filmed before a non-descript curtain, but Redman's band was shown in front of an elaborate backdrop with mechanically animated Fleischer animal characters.

A great use of the Fleischer Rotoscope process was in "Betty Boop's Bamboo Isle" (1932), in which the Polynesian musical group The Royal Samoans performed. The male dancers were rotoscoped for one scene and a female dancer performed a hula that was the basis for one of Betty's most memorable moments. Animator Shamus Culhane has said he did the hula animation without the help of the Rotoscope, but the motions appear to have the quality of rotoscoping, especially since a female dancer appeared in the introductory live action title sequence with very similar movements.

Betty's dance is a bit notorious because of the amount of cleavage that is shown. The short has Bimbo traveling to a Polynesian island encountering Betty with whom he instantly falls in love. The native tribesmen are fooled by Bimbo's make-up and install him as their leader until a rain storm washed his make-up away. The depiction of the native tribe is less than complimentary.

The humor of the Boop shorts was definitely anything goes and ranged from sentimental and almost cloying at times to adult and cynical. In "Mother Goose Land" (1933), Mother Goose comes alive and takes Betty to meet the characters from her nursery rhymes. As she and Mother Goose are flying off, Betty's house says goodbye and tells her not to worry because it will keep "the home fires burning." With that statement, flames envelop the house, and it burns to the ground.

"I Heard" is one of the more impressive uses of popular music in a Betty Boop cartoon.

In the early 1930s, the Fleischer artists loved surreal "cartoony" images. A great example is the conclusion of "Betty Boop's May Party" (1933) when an elephant accidentally taps a rubber tree, spraying the entire area with sap which gives everything the ability to stretch and bounce like rubber. The resulting animation is a lot of fun.

The American cinema before 1934 was a time when filmmakers constantly pushed the envelope on adult themes. The Fleischers took advantage, as did several other animation producers, to give their cartoons the same kind of openness. The results are cartoons that seem delightfully naughty today. They maintain an innocence that keeps them from appearing to be simply pandering towards cheap laughs.

If the Fleischer animators could think of nothing else in these shorts, they would toss in a gratuitous underwear scene. While Betty's standard costume looked as if she wasn't wearing a bra, Depression audiences knew she did because they saw it often enough.

The sexual humor can be seen today as potentially offensive. In "Betty Boop's Big Boss," (1933) Betty uses her charm to get a job, and then fights off the unwelcome advances from her boss throughout the cartoon. When she is rescued from him, she decides the boss is not so bad.

References to homosexuals are made in several Betty Boop shorts, as well. In "Betty Boop for President" (1932) there is a sequence of gags in which the audience can see what a Boop administration would be like. One of the scenes shows a hardened criminal in an electric chair. When the switch is thrown, he doesn't die, but is transformed into a swishing lisping character.

"Minnie The Moocher" also had, as many other Fleischer shorts of this time, gags aimed at Jewish audiences, whether they are inscriptions in Hebrew (such as the Hebrew word for kosher on a ham) or the use of Yiddish phrases. Ethnic humor can be seen in a number of Fleischer shorts, some of which could be seen as offensive today. The cartoons were made during a time in which ethnic humor derived from offensive stereotypes was ubiquitous on radio, in vaudeville, the movies and in print. Rather than stating a point of view, the jokes were simply part of the cultural climate of the time, right or wrong.

The Jewish jokes not only reflected much of the ethnic background of the staff, but also brought a distinctively city flavor to the cartoons as did the cartoons backgrounds and settings. The Fleischer shorts were the most urban of any of the cartoons of the era.

Animated photographs were featured in "Ha! Ha! Ha!" (1934) when Betty, attempting to play dentist for Koko and his aching tooth, releases laughing gas into the city. Photos of buildings are animated to literally laugh along. The film was essentially a sound remake of the silent short "The Cure."

"Betty Boop's Rise to Fame" (1934) was a bit of cheat as it used the cost-cutting measure of recycled animation from older cartoons, but the short is really a delight. A reporter visits the Fleischer studio to write a story about Betty and Max – in his only sound cartoon appearance – draws the character that obligingly recreates scenes from some of the earlier triumphs. The short features some accomplished blending of live action and animation, staples of the studio's silent shorts.

"Betty in Blunderland" (1934) is another illustration of the studio's relationship to Paramount. Paramount had released in 1933 a live action adaption of "Alice in Wonderland,"

It really didn't take too long for Betty Boop to become a star as this trade ad attests.

which used nearly every actor under contract in elaborate make-ups replicating the look of the original drawings. The film was not successful, but it undoubtedly inspired Max and Dave to do a version with Betty as Alice.

A review of the cartoon from an exhibitor in Piedmont, MO, was reported in the Aug. 25, 1934 edition of the Motion Picture Herald. "It is one of those cartoons that patrons stay to see the second time."

The short, which is more enjoyable than the feature in this writer's opinion, also has another link to Paramount. Betty sings a re-worked version of "Everyone Says I Love You,' which was written for the Marx Brothers movie "Horse Feathers" in 1932.

Although the storylines and the animation itself were far more coherent and consistent by 1934, it's clear the sexual nature of the Boop cartoons, which distinguished the series from others, was still alive and well in "Betty Boop's Trial' (1934). Betty plays an actress who attracts the attention of a motorcycle cop who tries to pull her over. When he is successful, he brings her to court, where what saves her is her sex appeal

A black face gag is included in the short. Unfortunately, there are instances in the Boop series in which there are depictions and gags involving African-Americans that are cringe-worthy today.

***

In 1934, the studio produced its only Betty Boop color short, "Poor Cinderella." Since the superior Technicolor process was contractually unavailable to the studio, the staff used Cinecolor, a two-color process with the base colors of red and green. The result is not very satisfactory as the color process has a limited palette. The animation is quite good, though, and the backgrounds are impressive.

"Poor Cinderella" also used the 3-D process developed by Max, one of two prominent efforts to bring the look of three dimensions to cartoon animation. Ub Iwerks, the former partner of Walt Disney and the driving force behind Mickey Mouse's earliest successes, developed a multi-plane camera that allowed a series of background and foreground drawings to be combined with an animation cel when he had his own studio in the mid-1930s. When Iwerks returned to Disney, he perfected the camera.

Max's approach was literally three-dimensional. He developed a system in which a background model was built on a revolving turntable. The animation cels were photographed in front of the background model, which was turned to match the movement in the animation. Sometimes the models were cut-out paintings mounted on cardboard to give the illusion of depth, but often times the models would be three-dimensional constructions that would result in even more impressive results. The results could be spectacular. In the Betty Boop series, "Betty Boop and the Little King" (1936) has some great 3-D sequences, as does "House Cleaning Blues" (1937).

The 3-D process was also the focal point in helping to sell the Color Classic series as we'll see in the next chapter.

Paramount announced the new process in a story in the Motion Picture Herald on Nov. 3 1934. The story said Max has been working on the process for two years but remained silent about it until he perfected it.

The Paramount press release said, "The illusory effect, however, can be used in feature pictures to even greater advantage than in cartoons, Mr. Fleischer was quoted as saying. He estimated his method will not increase production budgets over 15 percent."

The story continued, "The Fleischer process embraces a huge machine, weighing over a ton, and composed of 500 working parts."

Although this writer does not know what Max meant by using the process in a feature film, the studio certainly used it in shorts.

Max's technique was described in the November 1936 edition of Popular Science.

The uncredited writer reported, "Like immense slices of pie on a twelve-foot plate, curious miniature movie sets made of clay, wood, sponges, plaster, and cardboard now add new realism to animated cartoons by creating an illusion of depth. In the New York studios where Popeye, Betty Boop, and other famous characters of the screen cartoons come to life, such sets are replacing the flat, sketched-in backgrounds familiar in the past.

"The conventional method of producing a cartoon reel has been to sketch the successive stages of the action on thin sheets of clear celluloid, called 'cells,' and then to photograph them against a background drawn on a strip of paper. Between photographs, each forming one frame, or picture, in the finished film, the celluloid sheets were changed and the background strip moved slightly. When run through the projector at sufficient speed,

This photo from a Popular Science story from 1936, shows an annotated breakdown of Max's 3-D process. (Author's collection)

these successive movements give the impression of continuous action.

"In the new-technique, just introduced, the background strips are replaced with a three-ton, twelve-foot rotating table mounted on a framework of steel and holding midget wedge-shaped settings. The celluloid sheets are placed in a window in front of the camera with the buildings, streets, trees, or mountains of the set showing through. The resulting photograph makes the figure sketched on the celluloid sheet appear to be in the midst of the scene formed by the scale-sized objects on the table behind. After each picture, the 'cell is changed and the table rotated, just as the strip background was moved in the older technique described above.

"Operating a series of gears, a small hand crank moves the table. Markers indicate exactly how far it should be rotated between the shots. In some instances, the rotating mechanism is connected with the motor that operates the camera, so that movements of the table are automatic. To ensure precision adjustments of the camera and the 'cell' holder, both are mounted on a heavy lathe bed.

"All of the work of designing, building, and perfecting the apparatus, with its elaborate combination of trusses, cranks, and gears, was carried out in the experimental machine shop which forms a part of the New York studios. This research room is completely fitted up with electric machinery for working in both wood and metal.

"The 'slice-of-pie' shape of the sets gives them the proper perspective. Streets grow narrower as they recede from the camera; buildings diminish in size, and the ground slopes upward. The result is a realistic and natural perspective from the angle of the camera. If the sets were made square or rectangular and moved like a train of cars past the lens, they would give the impression of depth, as the sets do now, but the farthest objects would move as fast as the nearer ones and the effect would be unconvincing. The vanishing point, or place where parallel lines seem to meet on the horizon of the sets, is at the center of rotation of the table, six feet from the sheet of celluloid.

"To increase the sense of depth in the new cartoons, characters are seen walking behind trees and posts. This is accomplished by moving silhouettes, mounted on a special carrier, between the lens of the camera and the figure sketched on the sheet of celluloid. The silhouettes used for this purpose are made from flat plywood or cardboard and carefully proportioned.

"Backdrops behind the sets are mounted on vertical rollers. These rollers can be turned at any desired speed to give varying effects that range from summer clouds drifting lazily across the sky to storms rushing past at top speed.

"If full-color films are being produced, the objects in the set can be painted to give the hues desired. Also, colored lights playing over the miniature building and landscapes can be employed to create spectacular effects such as moonlight and sunset scenes.

"In addition to rotating, the table, which holds the sets, can tilt vertically. The impression of rising over a set in an airplane is achieved by tilting the table downward. In some mountain scenes, the set is tilted up to give the view from the valley and down to give the view from the peak. This permits using the same set throughout, and results in a saving of both time and money.

"Several sets can be prepared on the rotating table at the same time. As soon as the filming of one set is completed, the table can be swung to the next. Max Fleischer, who has patented the new technique, predicts that similar methods may be applied on Hollywood sound stages in the production of feature pictures."

It was a literal approach to the concept of imitating three-dimensions on the movie screen and while no cartoon was ever done entirely with the effect, it could be very effective.

***

It may surprise some people to learn of the growing importance of short subjects to the motion picture industry during this time. In the July 20, 1935 edition of the Motion Picture Herald, a story about short subjects which included both one and two-reel features, live action and animated – the writer noted, "That the short subjects surrounding a feature may make or break a program on the theater's bill is not necessarily true. But that good shorts, well diversified may make a good program decidedly better and considerably enhance audience enjoyment, there can be no questions."

The writer also noted how "the increased use and more importantly the improved quality of color have been vital factors in the improvement of the short subject."

As noted in an earlier chapter, the people in the mid-1930s who owned movie theater were still using the vaudeville premise of building a program with the use of shorts and double bills, whether it's "A" picture supported by a "B" movie or two "B" films.

While the article did not address Betty Boop, it did say, "Popeye the Sailor, of the comic strip, has done more to increase the infantile consumption of the much-maligned spinach than any single factor of the generation, will appear again. His popularity last season was matched only by Disney subjects. A special, in color, featuring the indomitable Popeye in two reels should be something to pre-sell."

The following year the first of three Popeye two-reelers, "Popeye the Sailor meets Sinbad the Sailor" was released in Technicolor and with 3-D sets.

Media crossovers

One of Walt Disney's many accomplishments was his understanding of how merchandising works to exploit and extend the popularity and profitability of a cartoon character. Although comic strips characters had crossovers into other mediums, it wasn't until the success of Disney's Mickey Mouse did people see the advantage of licensing animate cartoon characters for various toys, games and other consumer products.

Betty Boop was a Fleischer property to be sought for licensing, but it was not without some pain. Max apparently did not appreciate the idea of Betty Boop toys that could generate additional profits. Myron Waldman told this writer that when he a conversation about merchandising, Max's reply was "We're not running a toy factory."

That certainly didn't prevent other people from seeing money in the character's popularity.

This page in the Motion Picture Herald illustrates how exhibitors viewed short subject. They are promoted with the features to create a full program of attractions to lure audiences.

In the Feb. 20, 1934 edition of Variety, it was reported that Judge Woolsey would award an estimated $100,000 to Fleischer due to an infringement by a doll maker, Ralph A. Freundlich on the Betty Boop copyright. The dolls were made without a license. The case was pending for a year and Fleischer's lawyer was Louis Nizer, who said at the time he believed the ruling was a first as it dealt with a three-dimensional object based on a drawing.

Max began seeking licensing deals for the character after the judge's decision. Cameo produced a joined wooden doll that carried a copyright notice in a red heart on the back of Betty's dress. Another product was a combination doll and purse that also carried the Fleischer copyright notice.

Bimbo also was the subject of merchandising. There was a joined hand-painted wooden doll, similar in design to the one of Betty, several pin back buttons and a detailed embroidered patch.

Bimbo and Ko-Ko joined Betty in her debut Big Little Book in 1935, "Miss Gulliver's Travels" and the three characters were the stars of a toy projector set manufactured by the Duracolor Toy and Novelty Company in New York City. The "films" were actually rolls of translucent paper on which were printed a series of multi-color drawings.

Perhaps the most intriguing crossovers are two live-action versions of Betty, both produced by Max's distributor Paramount Pictures. In 1931, Sammy Learner (who composed the Popeye theme song) and Sammy Timberg (see the section below on the music of the series) wrote a short starring pop superstar Rudy Valle entitled "Musical Justice." Valle is the judge overseeing the court that hands out punishment for musical transgressions.

"Miss Gulliver's Travels" was one of two Big Little books starring the character. The inside illustrations were not always "on-model." (Authors' collection)

Betty Boop, in the form of Mae Questel, is one of the people on trial, however she wins over the judge and is pronounced by the jury as not guilty.

One of the "Hollywood on Parade" shorts from 1933 features a plot set in a wax museum, The statue of third-rate comic Eddie Borden comes to life (Borden himself) and he attempts to flirt with the wax figure of Clara Bow. Bow's husband (played in the flesh by her real husband, cowboy star Rex Bell) advises him to leave his wife alone, but perhaps he should meet Betty Boop, whose statue is across the hall.

The actress played Boop is unbilled but it's not Helen Kane, Betty's model, although she had been in several Paramount films and it is not Mae Questel. Most historians believe it is

This is part of the roll of translucent paper on which "slides" were printed for a home toy projector set. (Authors' collection)

Bonnie Poe, an actress who performed the voice prior to Questel taking over the role.

The short is notable not only for its surreal plot, but also that Bela Lugosi in his complete Dracula cape and evening wear coming to life from his wax statue to attack Betty. His memorable line as he heads towards her throat is "You have booped your last boop." Naturally, Betty is rescued from the living dead.

"Betty Boop Fables," a 15-minute weekly radio program was produced and broadcast by the Bamberger Broadcasting System from Nov. 15, 1932 to Jan. 27, 1933. The show featured Questel as Betty and William Costello, the first voice of Popeye.

Betty also had her own comic strip from 1934 to 1936, which was distributed by King Features. As comic strip historian Bill Blackbeard noted in his introduction of a collection of the Sunday strips, Helen Kane actually negotiated a comic strip for herself ("Helen Kane, The Boop-Boop-A-Doop Girl") with King Features, while talks to finalize a Betty Boop strip were still going on. The strip only lasted for a few months in 1933 and 1934, Blackbeard noted, and the Betty Boop strip replaced it.

The Kane strip was firmly set in the world of the stage with Kane as a performer and the Boop strip carried the "real" world show business theme as well. By the time strip had made its debut in 1934, the studio had left the surreal world of funny animals behind and the comic strip presented Betty as a struggling motion picture star.

Although well drawn by Bud Counihan, it did not have a long run. Just like the Mickey Mouse strips carried Disney's by-line (although he had little to do with them), this strip was credited to Max.

Interestingly to note, King Features had tried out a Koko strip in 1933 with the clown as a pantomime character but Blackbeard reported newspaper editors showed little interest.

Times change

The installation and enforcement of the Production Code in 1934 had a major impact on the Boop shorts. The Fatty Arbuckle scandal in 1921 had brought about the first wave of self-policing by the motion picture industry. The former Postmaster General Will Hays was hired by producers to enforce a content standard. This was mostly a public relations move as Hays had little power over the producers.

By 1934, though, the Catholic Legion of Decency had become a force for change. The group regularly condemned movies with objectionable content and there were calls from some people that movies had gone too far. In the face of potential censorship from outside, the studios started adhering to the code.

The early talkies contained rather frank depictions of sexual material and violence, although audiences certainly seemed to approve. Mae West, the comic actress who built her career on double entendrés, was credited as having saved Paramount Pictures from financial ruin.

In many parts of the country there were already state and municipal censorship boards, and the film industry wanted to prevent the establishment of a federal board. Hays hired Joseph Breen to enforce a new tough content code for motion pictures that detailed what was acceptable and what wasn't. A film could not be released from one of the mainstream Hollywood distributors without the Production Code seal of approval. Not until 1953 and the unsanctioned release of "The Moon Is Blue" did the strangle grip of the Breen Office begin to loosen.

The Fleischers were not the only studio that had laced their cartoons with adult humor, but were the most well known and popular. For instance, in Paul Terry's "In A Cartoon Studio" (1930), there's not only a female cat character with considerable cleavage, but also a gay reference as well, a marked departure from Terry's standard mouse and cat gags. At the Van Beuren Studios, a series featuring the comic strip character The Little King frequently featured adult material, including the King fathering a group of children with a mermaid.

Another Van Beuren cartoon, featuring Sentinel Louie, a character from the Little King comic strip, has the nastiest non-racial gag ever featured in a theatrical cartoon. In "A Dizzy Day" (1932), the sound of a woman screaming with pain can be heard, and the cartoon's nominal hero follows the cries. He discovers a woman being beaten by an obvious criminal type. The two men look at each other and Louie delivers the knockout blow himself. With the woman now silent, the two men shake hands.

Betty's antics did get her into trouble. There is one often-repeated story in which the Hays Office, responsible for the self-censorship of the film industry, allegedly ordered Max to remove Betty's garter, but letters from outraged fans brought it back. While I've not been able to confirm this incident, one Betty Boop short was definitely banned in Great Britain. "Red Hot Mamma" (1934) has Betty literally freezing Hell over with her disapproving look. British censors found this comic depiction of damnation to be too blasphemous to show in their country.

The Boop cartoons began to change to meet the new standards and the change in the taste of the movie audiences. The cartoons were more polished and the Boop universe was more defined. Gone were the inkwell and references to Uncle Max. Gone were her trademark short

Betty's appearance evolved by the mid-1930s.

skirt, as well as Koko and Bimbo. Betty had a re-occurring boy friend, Freddie, a younger brother, a grandfather, and a dog, Pudgy. In many cartoons, she was portrayed as a working girl with a career far from show business. There was greater emphasis on the gags coming from the character or the story rather than just being inserted into the cartoon.

Popeye the Sailor had made his cartoon debut in what was technically a Betty Boop cartoon, and now in the post-1934 period, several other King Features characters would do the same.

"Betty Boop with Henry, The Funniest Living American" (1935) is less than successful. The Henry character, a long-standing fixture of many newspaper comic pages, was a pantomime character that was strictly gag-driven with little or no personality. The highly stylized design of the character (supposedly a little boy with no hair, an odd nose and no mouth) was not attractive in animation.

The studio fared better with its next effort "Betty Boop and the Little King" (1936). Otto Soglow's comic strip had a little more substance than Henry and, as noted above, the character had already been featured in a series of cartoons produced by the Van Beuren Studio. This short, featuring the Little King sneaking out of the opera to watch Betty's vaudeville act, is a delight.

The last of the comic strip try-outs came with "Betty Boop and Little Jimmy." Jimmy Swinnerton was one of the true pioneering geniuses of the American comic strip, but this cartoon didn't capture the themes or the visual style of the original strips.

For some modern fans, the post-1934 Boop cartoons are frequently too tame. Although the studio was definitely redefining the character, there are many gems, which wisely used

the Grampy and Pudgy characters.

"Betty Boop and Grampy" (1935) introduced the new character that one can assume is actually Betty's grandfather. Grampy is an inventor, and considering Max's interests, a perfectly logical character to come out of his studio. When in a spot, Grampy whips out his thinking cap (a mortarboard with a light bulb) and invents a solution with whatever materials are handy. Other good Grampy shorts include "Be Human," "House Cleaning Blues," "Grampy's Indoor Outing."

Pudgy, Betty Boop's dog, was designed by Myron Waldman to give the series more story potential and made his debut in 1934 with "Betty Boop's Little Pal." The addition of the little dog gave the series more potential for sentiment. Waldman called them "ooh, ahh pictures" because of the reactions

This trade ad spread from 1936 shows the studio's output at the time. Despite the popularity of Popeye, Betty Boop was still important. Note the mention of both Grampy and Pudgy.

of the audiences. Pudgy could also put over a gag, and wound up being the real star of a good number of the post-1934 cartoons. One of the best was "Not Now," in which Pudgy fights a cat who scratches him. Pudgy touches his wound, looks at the camera and says, "He pulled a knife on me!"

While Grampy and Pudgy could be amusing, another character who periodically made visits to the Boop series was simply odd. Wiffle Piffle was a bug-eyed little guy with an amusing flapping arm walk that looked like he was trying to fly. Jack Mercer provided the voice, and the only characterization one could determine about Wiffle is that he had a habit of screwing things up. Wiffle Piffle also made frequent appearances in the Screen Song series. Animator Tom Johnson created him.

The late animator and historian Michael Sporn noted in his blog about Wiffle Piffle – which is still up online and is a treasure of information – "He seems to have been an Egghead type character whose sole character trait was a silly walk. Needless to say, they couldn't find a job for him."

In 1938, there was another attempt to breathe in new life to the series with the introduction of Betty's young tomboy cousin Buzzy. "Buzzy Boop" is another pilot for the character and like Wiffle Piffle, there isn't much there. Buzzy is simply an obnoxious kid. She appeared in a second cartoon "Buzzy Boop at the Concert."

The Fleischers had taken the same road as Walt Disney had done when Mickey Mouse was running out of steam. Just like Disney added Goofy and Donald Duck to assist Mickey Mouse, the Fleischers had added Grampy and Pudgy. In some of the post-1934 Boop shorts, Betty is

This late model sheet shows how much the character had changed in order to attempt to stay current.

only marginally involved with the lion's share of the footage devoted to her co-stars. The issue of longevity was addressed in a "New York Times" piece from Feb. 13, 1936. Bosley Crowther, writing about the growing animation industry, interviewed Sam Buchwald of the studio's management team.

"But an interesting thing about it [the animation industry] says Mr. Buchwald is the way that the familiar cartoon characters rise, have their day of great popularity, and then wane just as real stars do. Although Disney doesn't say much about it, his lovable Mickey, greatest animated character of all time, is definitely on the way out. And where are Koko the Clown, Mutt and Jeff and other of those favorites of a bygone era?

"Popeye and Betty Boop (the latter an original film creation and the other a recruit from the newspaper comic strips) have been doing quite well for about six years, but it takes imagination to keep them alive. Betty Boop is constantly undergoing imperceptible changes in size, hair, dress and such and is paradoxically growing younger in appearance, Mr. Buchwald confesses. But after all why shouldn't she? The essence of the animated cartoon's charm – the universality of its appeal – undoubtedly lies in its accomplishment of the utterly impossible."

A cartoon such as "Sally Swing" (1938) shows the problems with the character and the series. Betty is some sort of student activity director at a college and she has to find someone to lead a swing band at a dance. By accident she discovers a young cleaning woman who can swing dance. Out of her janitorial clothes, she looks like Betty Grable and is the star of the show.

Sally Swing's singing voice was provided by singer and actress Rose Marie.

The short is wonderfully animated by Willard Bowsky and Gordon Sheehan and is in many ways a perfect Betty Boop musical cartoon, except Betty is not the star. She had become a straight man.

According to a Film Daily article on April 18, 1938 about Paramount's upcoming schedule of releases as revealed at a Paramount sales meeting, "Sally Swing," had been at least in someone's eyes, a pilot for a new series.

"A new character, Sally Swing, joins the Paramount short subjects groups, replacing Betty Boop in 12 cartoons."

The character made no other appearances.

During the end of her run, some exhibitors expressed their lack of support for the latter Boop cartoons. In the Motion Picture Herald (Jan. 27, 1940) one theater owner wrote about "Rhythm on the Reservation" "not so good. Betty Boop cartoons seem to lack something lately." Another theater owner wrote, "These Boops not so hot."

The next month in the same publication, another cartoon "The Scared Crows" received a similar review: "Nobody gave it any cheers, only sighed with relief after it was over."

The Boop cartoons still could receive good notices, such as the reviewer in the Motion Picture Daily in 1939 who called "So Does an Automobile" an "imaginative and all together delightful Betty Boop cartoon."

The last cartoon in the series, "Yip - Yip - Yippy," was reviewed in The Film Daily on

July 25, 1939. "The birth of a new cartoon character is seen with Max Fleischer introducing Vanilla, a gay little horse. Then the story gets going with a thrill-meller as a soda clerk is deputized by the sheriff just as the bad man hits the town. His trusty horse is Vanilla, whose comedy antics aid greatly in making the clerk a hero."

It should be noted that Betty doesn't make an appearance in the short, even though it was sold to theaters as part of her series. The Boop series had been used during its run to potentially launch other characters, but Vanilla the horse did not make a return to the screen.

Exit and Entrance

Buchwald's words were prophetic. The Boop cartoons were running out of gas, and the series was terminated in the summer of 1939. It was a new era at the Fleischer Studios with Max moving his operation to the Miami, Florida area and a brand-new studio, and perhaps Betty was just not part of it.

In 1956, UM&M closed a deal with Paramount for the rights to 1,600 shorts, which included the Boop cartoons with a reported asking price of $3.5 million, according to Motion Picture Daily. The shorts would be programming for local television stations. At about the same time, Max's fellow Bray alumni Paul Terry sold his cartoons and merchandising rights to CBS for $5 million.

When Paramount sold a number of its cartoons for television distribution in the mid-1950s, Max Fleischer's name was blocked out on the 16mm prints used by the television stations. According to the June 23, 1956 edition of Television and Electronic Reports, it was reported that Max had filed suit against Paramount Pictures, Dumont Broadcasting and others "alleging TV use of his cartoons 'without the proper credit and authority.' The story added, "He claimed his cartoons can't legally be presented in conjunction with commercials and that screen credits on his films have been doctored."

Max sued Paramount, and through the legal action was able to acquire the rights to the Betty Boop character. This did Fleischer little good during his lifetime as he died in 1972, a few years before the Betty Boop revival began.

In the mid-1970s, a film distributor named Sidney Tager put together two theatrical compilations of Betty Boop, Screen Song and Talkartoons shorts. Although booked only at art houses and revival theaters, the two features drew attention to the character and to the Fleischer Studio. A modest merchandising effort started in the late 1970s.

While the merchandising revival of Betty Boop began to soar in the early 1980s, an effort to revive the economic worth of the cartoons began. National Telefilm Associates, a long-time supplier of television programming, had bought the rights of a number of Fleischer productions from Paramount in the 1950s. The NTA holdings included both Fleischer features, a number of Screen Song cartoons and the Betty Boops.

NTA had successfully sold syndication packages of these shorts throughout the 1950s and

'60s, but in the late 1960s and early '70s, the bias against black and white programming was beginning to manifest itself at local stations. The solution? Colorize the Betty Boop shorts.

The Boop shorts were not among the first to undergo the transformation to color. Broadcast executive Eliot Hyman had been at Warner Brothers/Seven Arts when he oversaw the colorization of early Looney Tunes. He then colorized 18 Krazy Kat shorts for Columbia. His company, Feature House, then tackled converting 100 Boop cartoons to color in 1972.

Basically, Hyman had the Boop shorts re-animated with color cels. In Asian animation studios, artists would project the black and white cartoons onto a frosted glass drawing board, trace the action onto a new cel, paint it, and photograph it.

There were problems with the process. To save money, not every frame was re-animated resulting in less-than full animation, The marvelous black and white backgrounds, in such cartoons as "Minnie the Moocher," were not reproduced in color, and were eliminated in favor of less complex background. Finally, the color selection was often times poor. Granted the Fleischer shorts were often surreal, but one doubts anyone at the studio would have selected purple for the color of a cat.

These colorized cartoons became the basis for an odd compilation film released by New Line Cinema in 1980. Record producer and composer Dan Dalton was approached in 1976

Many of the Fleischer and Famous cartoons were available to TV in 1950s introducing them to new audiences.

by NTA to create a "new" animated feature from the colorized Boop shorts that would be released in August of that year. The idea was to create a new storyline that would be supported by classic Fleischer animation and a new voice and music track. The theme of the feature would capitalize on the 1976 presidential race.

Dalton spoke to me in 1982, and confessed that the selection of the cartoon sequences and the creation of a new story took him much longer than he had expected. "I knew I was going to start with 'Minnie the Moocher' [the scene in which Betty is admonished by her father] and would end with 'Betty Boop for President,'" said Dalton. His problem was finding a suitable middle for his narrative.

Dalton kept some of the classic Cab Calloway numbers, but junked the 1930s scores for his original songs that were recorded by Debbie Boone, The Association and the singer hired to be the new voice of Betty Boop, Victoria D'Orazi. Working with four other writers, Dalton took scenes from 35 shorts to create his story, which depended on a narrator. Tom Smothers did the honors as the voice of Pudgy.

Dalton missed his 1976 deadline. Apparently NTA was anxious to release the film as they advertised an "all singing, all dancing feature length production" called "Betty Baby" in the Oct. 19, 1977 edition of "Variety." That incarnation of the film was apparently not released in November of that year as promised.

"Hurray for Betty Boop" finally surfaced in 1980 at the Cannes Film Festival (not in competition) and had two trade screenings in the hopes of attracting worldwide sales.

According to Dalton, the production had a budget of $300,000 that included promotion

This trade ad announced the first idea of a Betty Boop feature film made from the original cartoons but colorized. It would later be released as "Hooray for Betty Boop."

The cover of the movie's press kit featured the final title of the film.

and a test marketing in the college town of Madison, WI. Dalton blamed the timing of the booking – Labor Day weekend– but what few fans saw the finished product weren't impressed.

"Everyone said I couldn't do it and keep the continuity; it was very difficult. You and I could notice things [changes in styles of drawing Betty, her costumes and size] but not others [general audiences]," said Dalton.

Despite the lack of critical acclaim, Dalton was very proud of his film. "It's a great children's movie, a great dopers' movie, a great midnight movie."

The film went to cable television and then to video. It has not yet been released on DVD. Dalton, at the time of our conversation, reported that NTA was then thinking about re-doing the Fleischer's second feature "Mr. Bug Goes to Town" by dumping the soundtrack and coming up with new dialogue and a rock and roll score. Those plans never came to completion thanks to the failure of "Hurray for Betty Boop."

Perhaps part of the problem with "Hurray for Betty Boop" was that people had seen the real Betty Boops on video and liked them. The Fleischer cartoons became very successful on the exploding home video market. NTA, and its corporate successor Republic Pictures, marketed a wide assortment of Fleischer shorts. Because a number of Fleischer cartoons had fallen into the public domain, there was a seemingly endless parade of "bargain" tapes featuring the same handful of Boop cartoons.

Another revival of the character that never got off the ground in the 1970s involved Sid and Marty Krofft – the then-hot producers of such children's fare as "H.R. Puffnstuff "and "Lidsville." Richard Fleischer told this writer the producers wanted to produce a live-action Boop show that would star Bette Midler. The project never happened.

In the early 1980s, the Columbia Broadcasting System (CBS) had formed a division to produce theatrical films and had optioned rights to Betty Boop. In a 1982 advertising supplement to "Variety," the company announced their slate of up-coming films and listed under "In Development" was a live-action Betty Boop to be produced by Norman Stephens, Barry Krost and Joan Scott. Nothing else was ever announced on the project.

In 1983, plans were announced that CBS would bankroll a Broadway musical based on the character, apparently in response to the success of "Annie." Those plans never progressed either.

CBS finally did use the character in a half-hour animated television special in 1985. The same team who animated the hugely popular "Peanuts" specials, Lee Mendelson and Bill Melendez, produced "The Romance of Betty Boop."

Melendez, interviewed by UPI's Vernon Scott, said, "I predict Betty will make a comeback like Tina Turner. She's a good representative of the women's movement today. Betty wants to settle down, but she wants a career, too. She's a female paradox."

In an interview this writer conducted with Melendez in 1982, he commented that he planned to animate the character better than the Fleischer artists ever had, and that unlike the original shorts, his half-hour would have a story. He told me that he had no plans to hire any of the original animators who had worked on the shorts, nor would he consider using Mae Questel, Betty's long-time voice.

When the half-hour aired over two years after that conversation, it was relatively easy to see that while the special was competently animated, there was little "feel" for the character. Set in 1939, the production used vintage photos of New York in many backgrounds, a Fleischer stylistic move.

The contempt Melendez exhibited in our discussion for the Fleischer shorts were quite apparent. Although he followed the traditional Betty model, the supporting characters were of a different design that clashed with Betty. And indeed there was a story, but it was unremarkable.

The fact that the special never was repeated and there was no sequel clearly indicated the program's lack of commercial success.

The failure of "Hurray for Betty Boop" and "The Romance of Betty Boop" didn't put a brake on the merchandising success of the character.

In an Associated Press story from 1986, King Features Syndicate, which administrates the licensing of the character for Richard Fleischer and his sister Ruth Kneitel, reported that in the fiscal year 1985-86 300 licensed Boop products grossed "about $100 million."

In 1984, King Features syndicated a new Betty Boop comic strip, which co-starred Felix the Cat written and was drawn by Brian, Morgan, Greg, and Neal Walker. According to an article in People magazine, the strip started out in 75 pages and co-starred Felix the Cat. The story noted for comparison, "Beetle Baily," created by their dad Mort Walker was in more than 1,700 papers. The strip was not a success and lasted just two years.

Betty did make a return to the big screen, though, in an appearance in "Who Framed Roger Rabbit" in 1988. The animation directed by Richard Williams perfectly captured the classic Fleischer look, and Betty is well cast as a cigarette girl in the nightclub where Jessica Rabbit is performing. Questel reprised her vocal characterization, and Boop was the only classic cartoon star in the film presented in black and white.

In the late 1980s, Betty began appearing in the annual Macy's Thanksgiving Day parade in the form of a huge balloon.

Broadway Star Bernadette Peters portrayed Betty Boop in an episode of Saturday Night Live

This trade ad was support to launch a whole new line of merchandise with Betty Boop as a baby.

Besides the comic strip by the Walker brothers, there was also an attempt to bring back the character in a comic book in 1978. (Authors' collection)

in 1984. She appears out of an oversized inkwell and sings a song dedicated to the troops: "For all you G.I. privates who are standing at attention, there is something personal I'd really like to mention. We think it's quite terrific that you're in the South Pacific; just be good and careful you don't fall into a trap. Don't come home to Betty with a nasty dose of [she claps]. Johnny, keep your gun clean."

With all of the interest in the character King Features commissioned a new animated television show in 1990. San Francisco-based Colossal Pictures produced a half-hour special entitled "Betty Boop's Hollywood Mystery." Unlike the Melendez special, Colossal wisely recreated much of the look and feel of the Fleischer originals. George Evelyn, the show's director, told this writer that the production company wanted to re-create the Fleischer look and did so in part with the help of Richard Fleischer who supplied materials from the family archives.

Evelyn had wanted to use Mae Questel for Betty's voice, but the actress was busy filming Woody Allen's segment of "New York Stories." Evelyn launched a series of auditions, and in true "Hollywood" fashion, the secretary at the recording studio that was producing copies of the audition tapes had the voice Evelyn wanted. Melissa Fahn performed the Boop voice.

Although originally intended for broadcast over CBS, the special was never aired, until it was picked up by the Disney cable channel. Evelyn explained that a new management team at the network decided to shelve the special. Most animation fans have never had the opportunity of seeing what is commonly agreed to be a production of which the Fleischers themselves would be proud.

Both "Betty Boop's Hollywood Mystery"

and "The Romance of Betty Boop" can be seen on YouTube.

In 1991, Ivy Classic Video released a semi-documentary titled, "Boop Oop A Doop." The film was a collection of Boop shorts narrated by comic superstar Steve Allen, who spoke about the studio's contributions to animation technology and pointed out the risqué elements of the early shorts. At one point Allen's narration includes the dubious fact that in scene Betty's labia can be seen!

In 1991 Mainframe Entertainment announced it would be producing a CGI Betty Boop TV series in conjunction with the Fleischer Studios. An additional push in licensing would accompany the series. The series never came about, as Mainframe underwent a corporate shake-up shortly after the announcement.

The interest in Betty has certainly continued. There were published reports about a Broadway Betty Boop musical in 2010. In 2012 Lancome used her to help sell mascara and in the commercial she applied the makeup to model Daria Werbowy.

In 2014, Betty and Bimbo were seen in a three-dimension animated commercial for a smart phone video game, "Betty Boop Bop." She was also animated that year to sell paper towels with her image in Turkey. In 2015, the character was featured in a series of scratch tickets for the New Mexico state lottery.

Betty's voice

Five singers and actresses – Margie Hines, Harriet Lee, Little Ann Little, Kate Wright and Bonnie Poe – were cast by Max and Dave with providing the voice of Betty Boop, although one – Mae Questel – is most associated with the character.

Hines is credited for the Betty Boop voice in "Dizzy Dishes." She was profiled in a Freeport, NY, newspaper in 1930: "Freeport Girl, With Deep Blue Eyes That Register, Even On Screen, Fame Bound.

"Until the movies record colors, theatre audiences are going to miss one of the most attractive features of Marjorie L. Hines, 19-year-old Freeport lass, who has made her debut into the cinema world.

"Miss Hines, for whom great things are predicted by her directors, has the

Margie Hines had a career as a singer outside of doing voices for animation. She was profiled in The American magazine in early 1930s. (Authors' collection)

bluest of blue eyes. But they are as expressive as they are blue and even on the black and white of silver screen, they "register" as they say in Hollywood with 100 per cent effectiveness.

"Petite, vivacious and strikingly pretty, Miss Hines is the perfect type for a comedienne, a role for which she was picked by Warner Brothers to play with Benny Rubin.

"With Benny Rubin, she has just finished making a Warners picture called 'The Perfect Suitor.' The little Freeport girl plays the leading feminine in the film. Which was made at Warner Brothers studios in Flatbush.

"A Helen Kane contest launched Miss Hines into a theatrical career. She won the competition hands down and out-booped all other contestants.

"That got her on the stage and her voice won her a six months contract doing recordings for the Betty Boop cartoons produced by Paramount.

"Her work as the voice for the little girl in the animated drawings attracted the attention of movie directors and she received an offer to play in the Benny Rubin picture.

With her voice, her good looks and her natural talent, her associates predict a brilliant future for the young actress.

"Marjorie lives with her mother at 197 North Grove Street, Freeport."

I've yet to find any record of "The Perfect Suitor," other than a still that shows Hines with Rubin. Rubin, best known as a prolific comedy character actor, had a series of short subjects in 1931 and several in 1932.

Another undated newspaper clipping reports, "It was while she was touring in vaudeville that she was heard by Billy Murray, a member of the Fleischer staff who found in Miss Hines' voice exactly what he has been seeking for Betty Boop."

Murray was the singer who provided vocal performances for the early sing Screen Songs. For a good look at Hines performing, see her Vitaphone short "Harry Warren: America's Foremost Composer." In the short she sings in the Boop voice. It's available on YouTube.

Hines provided voices at Van Buren studios as well and did not return to the Fleischer Studio until it moved to Miami in 1939 when Questel decided not to move. In 1939 Miami newspapers reported how she and Jack Mercer were married. Hines at that time was providing the voice of Olive Oyl for the studio. The two were married until 1950.

Once the studio returned to New York City – now known as the Famous Studios – the role of Olive went back to Questel.

Hines died in 1985 at the age of 81.

Harriet Lee provided the voice – and a very different one – for the cartoon "The Bum Bandit" in 1931.

Little Ann Little also provided the voice of the character but perhaps became better known for playing Betty in vaudeville and promotional appearances with artist Pauline Comanor. Comanor explained to me in 1986 that she met Max when she was 16 years-old and working at Gimbals Department Store in Philadelphia performing as a sketch artist. Max was making a publicity appearance and liked her, so he asked her to come to New York City.

Max had her spend time in every department of the studio and then sent her on the road, as "the country's one and only girl movie cartoonist," which, of course she was not. Comanor never animated nor worked at the studio. She told me he even suggested hair styles and make-up for her for her appearances.

Bonnie Poe appeared in a number of cartoons in 1933 and 1934, including providing the voice of Olive Oyl in the Popeye pilot. She played Betty in the "Hollywood on Parade" short with Bela Lugosi.

Kate Wright, another Kane impersonator, is credited with doing Betty's voice as well as her cousin Buzzy in the 1938 cartoon.

No one person has been associated as much with Betty Boop as the character's primary voice artist, Mae Questel. Although several performers voiced the character before Questel, her take is the rendition that stuck with the Fleischer Studios and with the public.

Questel attempted to begin her professional show business career at the age of nine when she auditioned for the Broadway show, "Daddy." Although the producers liked her, her grandparents didn't believe the theater was a proper career for a young woman, and Questel's show business aspirations were put on hold for a few years.

In 1930, her high school sorority sisters entered her name into a Helen Kane impersonation contest. Questel won the contest that meant four days booking into one of the leading vaudeville houses in New York, the RKO Fordham and $150 in prize money. Helen Kane even autographed a photo "To Another Helen Kane." Neither performer could imagine how ironic this inscription would become in just a few years.

Her four days at the Fordham resulted in bookings in the prestigious Palace Theater and then subsequent bookings from Boston to Baltimore. At the relatively tender age of 18, Questel began her show business career with an act consisting of impersonations of well-known performers such as Mae West, Marlene Dietrich, Eddie Cantor and Jimmy Durante.

Max hired her in 1931, an assignment she had through the end of the series in 1938. Questel told this writer that she didn't want to move to Florida with the rest of the Fleischer studio, and the final Boop cartoons made in Florida used Hines.

A short brunette with a round face and large eyes, Questel bore a resemblance to her cartoon character.

Questel's mimicry extended to her characterization of Olive Oyl in the Popeye cartoons. Although at first the Olive voice was a deeper voice, Questel's version was based on popular screen comedienne Zasu Pitts.

Unlike her frequent partner behind the microphone, Jack Mercer, Questel worked hard to have an acting career in front of the camera. She appeared in two Paramount musical two-reelers with Rudy Valle, "Musical Justice" (1931) and "The Musical Doctor' (1932) and in the film "Wayward" supporting Richard Arlen and Nancy Carroll (1932). She retired from show business in the late 1930s for three years after the birth of her son.

Questel did stage acts as the voice of Betty Boop as noted by The Hollywood Reporter in its Jan. 3 1933 edition. The reviewer thought seeing Mae doing Betty Boop on stage "spoils the illusion of Betty Boop on screen."

In 1933 she also a song for RCA Victor. Variety described it as "a brief doggerel preceded Miss Questel who in accentuated cute and piping voices, 'Don't Take my Boop-doop-a-doop Away' coupled with the clever lyrical 'Girl in Green Hat.'"

Questel returned to voice acting with numerous appearances on radio programs during the 1940s and essaying Olive Oyl and other cartoon voices when Paramount moved the Famous Studios operation back to New York in 1942. She worked on the Casper cartoons and was the voice of Little Audrey. According to Jackson Beck, who played Bluto at Famous, Questel even played Popeye in several shorts made during World War II when Mercer was unavailable.

Beck told me in a 1995 interview "she was a great artist and wonderful lady."

She provided the voice for the television character Winky Dink on the show "Winky Dink and You," and did scores of voice-overs for commercials. And at an age when performers worry about making the transition to older parts, Questel had no problem with character roles. In 1960, she was praised for her role in the Broadway hit "Majority of One," and encored her performance for the movie version starring Rosalind Russell. Other Broadway roles came in "Enter Laughing" with Alan Arkin, "Bajour" with Chita Rivera and "Come Blow Your Horn." She had prominent parts in Jerry Lewis' "It's Only Money," "Funny Girl" and "Move." Her television appearances included guest shots on series such as "Mrs. G Goes to College," "The Naked City" and "77 Sunset Strip."

Questel even starred on her own comedy record in the early 1970s. "Mrs. Portnoy's Retort" was a satiric response to Philip Roth's bestselling book "Portnoy's Complaint." Roth's book was lauded for its candid depiction of obsessive masturbation, and the album took full advantage of this theme for a series of cheap laughs with Questel playing the role of the fictional Portnoy's mother.

In the mid-1970s Questel was picked for the role of "Aunt Bluebell" in a series of commercials for Scott Towels, and was a fixture on television for years.

I talked to Questel several times since 1977 when I began my research at the Fleischer Studio and always found her to be bubbly, out-spoken, and self-confident. Her character of Aunt Bluebell, who would butt into other people's problems with her unsolicited but friendly advice about paper towels, never seemed to me to be too far from reality.

She wasn't too happy that she wasn't selected for Hanna-Barbera's revival of Popeye, and was quoted by her son in a 1977 article that she was always hoping to get a telephone call from someone making more Betty Boops. She finally did get a chance to do Betty again in "Who Framed Roger Rabbit."

One of her performances of note was in Woody Allen's segment, "Oedepus Wrecks," of the 1989 anthology film "New York Stories." Although the film as a whole received mixed notices, Questel's performance was singled out for praise.

In poor health for a number of her last years, Questel lived to see and benefit from the rediscovery of Betty Boop. She died at age 89 in 1998.

Mae Questel gave the author a copy of the promotional brochure she had created in the early mid-1960s showing many of her non-animated credits as an actress.

The "real" Betty Boop

Helen Kane, who died in 1966 at the age of 62, enjoys an ironic form of immortality. Her features and style of singing are definitely caricatured by the Boop character, but relatively few people alive today are aware of it. For any performer that kind of twisted anonymity is a mixed blessing.

At the time of Betty's birth in 1930, Kane was a highly successful stage and recording star. With her round face, spit curls and pouty little girl singing voice, she projected a curious blend of sexual knowingness and innocence. She was, like actresses Clara Bow and Joan Crawford, a "jazz baby."

She began her performing career at the age of 15, and eventually reached the top of the vaudeville ranks earning as much as $8,000 a week. She became known for the songs "That's My Weakness Now" and "I Wanna be Loved By You."

Her use of the refrain of "Boop Oop a Doop" became so popular that a 1929 review of a vaudeville act in a trade journal noted how a "boop boop a doop" number by singer Harriet Hutchens resulted in "the amusement of the audience."

At the time of the production of "Dizzy Dishes," Kane was well known for her distinctive kewpie doll looks and high-pitched singing voice. Ironically, Natwick's caricature of her in "Dizzy Dishes" is not all that apparent until the unnamed nightclub performer sings. Kane's trademark was a scat-sing chorus of "boop-oop-a-doop," which was included in the cartoon performance.

Kane appeared in seven early sound films for Paramount from 1929 to 1931, such as the campus musical "Sweetie" and starred in the musical short "A Lesson in Love." She was also featured in "Paramount on Parade" (1930), a revue film that featured all of the Paramount contract players in various skits. Kane plays a teacher who leads his class in a song with the refrain of "Boop Oop a Doop."

Considering how the Fleischer Studio took advantage of its business arrangement with Paramount, it's not surprising that a caricature of Kane turned up in their cartoons.

Comic strip historian Bill Blackbeard noted in his collection of the Betty Boop comic strips that Kane contacted King Features in 1933 when she learned that negotiations between the syndicate and Max for a Betty Boop comic strip were stalled. She proposed a strip called "Helen Kane, the Boop-Oop-A-Doop Girl," which the syndicate accepted and ran in several Hearst newspapers in 1933 and 1934. The strip with its short-term contract was used as a bargaining chip in talks with Max. Once the deal was struck for a Betty Boop strip, the Kane strip was dropped.

Kane was drawn for her strip in a way that closely resembled Betty Boop. Interestingly the Kane and Boop strips both presented a "behind the curtain" view of life in show business.

Kane's time in the spotlight was waning by the mid-1930s though, while Betty Boop's career was flying high. Perhaps that is what motivated her lawsuit against Max Fleischer and Paramount in 1934.

The idea that Kane had been the inspiration for Betty Boop was certainly no secret. The April 1932 edition of Photoplay placed a drawing of Betty next to a photo of Kane and added the caption, "Folks meet Betty Boop. You'll be seeing a lot of her because she is the new animated cartoon character who is trying to cut in on Mickey Mouse's popularity. Does she look familiar to you? Now look at little boop-a-dooper Helen Kane. Helen was the cartoonist's inspiration for Betty, the first time a real-life character has been used for the popular jumping comics."

On March 6, 1934, "The New York Times" reported that Kane "sails east to her trial in four weeks against Max Fleischer. Besides the previously known demands, Kane wants an accounting of the profits from the Paramount cartoon releases." Kane was suing for unfair competition and imitation and sought the amount of $250,000. The trial began in April and concluded in May.

At the heart of the argument was just how much of the success of the Betty Boop cartoons could be traced to the spit curls and singing style of Helen Kane. On April 18, the "Times"

Helen Kane as she appeared in the Paramount musical, "Sweetie" in 1929. (Authors' collection)

reported that Max took three young women to court with him who had performed the Betty Boop voice who testified that they had made "no effort to imitate Miss Kane."

In the April 20, 1934 "Times" story, Max "declared that his character is a figment of his imagination and that the hair dress of Betty Boop also was developed by himself and was not in imitation of Miss Kane." Fleischer had a lot to lose if Kane won the case, and his testimony, clearly a lie, was an effort to keep the lucrative Betty Boop character and to prevent further actions by Kane.

On April 23, Supreme Court Justice Edward S. McGoldrick viewed a Helen Kane sound film with two songs and then watched two Betty Boop cartoons. The "Times" reported McGoldrick was told that out of 46 Boop cartoons 66 songs were sung and of those only four had previously been performed by Kane. McGoldrick saw more footage of Kane on April 24.

"Lou Walton, a theatrical manager, testified that Baby Esther, a Negro girl under his management, had interpolated words like 'boo-boo-boo' and 'doo-doo-doo' in song at a cabaret here in 1928 and that Miss Kane and her manager had heard her there. Justice McGoldrick will hear a sound film of her to aid his decision," the "Times" reported on May 2, 1934. The implication was clear; Kane's trademark was not hers and hers alone.

The decision was handed down on May 5, 1934. Kane's suit was denied on the basis "the plaintiff had failed to sustain either cause of action by proof of sufficient probative action." Kane and her attorney vowed to file an appeal, but never did.

In a 1935 interview, Kane said she was quitting show business because she was tired. Kane had amassed a considerable fortune during the peak of her fame, and, after fading from the public eye, invested in several businesses. Unfortunately, her investments failed, and Kane tried staging a comeback several times. When Debbie Reynolds portrayed her in the MGM musical "Three Little Words" (1950), Kane's career was largely forgotten, although she dubbed Reynolds' singing voice for "I Wanna to be Loved by You."

In 1958, Kane was the subject of an episode of the show "This is Your Life." Host Ralph Edwards would surprise celebrities and then present a biography of their lives, complete with appearances by family members, co-stars and colleagues.

During her show, composer Harry Ruby appeared and played the piano and Kane performed "I Wanna to be Loved by You."

Edwards never mentioned Betty Boop, but did discuss Kane having a nervous breakdown in 1936. He also mentioned how Kane and her husband Dan Healey were having tough times financially, but a mention in a New York newspaper column solicited help.

At the end of the show, Edwards urged viewers to see her perform at the Moulin Rouge Night Club in Los Angeles.

The year before her death, she had appeared on the Ed Sullivan's long-running variety show in her last comeback effort. She had suffered from cancer for ten years prior to her passing according to her obituary in "Variety."

Today, performers have greater legal protection over their features and trademark mannerisms and appearances. What Kane endured could not happen again.

Inaccurate origin story

In 2021, PBS issued an apology concerning statements made about the inspiration of the character. From the PBS website, "On a star-studded broadcast this summer, acclaimed actress Taraji P. Henson accented her role as host of the BET Awards by changing into a number of costumes throughout the show, each celebrating an iconic Black entertainer.

"One of the outfits was a black mini dress and a Jazz-Age bob of a hairdo, the signature look of Betty Boop, the cartoon character famous for her childlike "boo-boop-see-doo" vocabulary. "In her monologue, she said, 'In New York during the Harlem renaissance, Black women like myself dressed up like her [motioning with pointer toward short black skirt and garter belt], 'Baby Esther' Jones, aka Betty Boop – she was Black! Y'all didn't know that, did ya? Yes!" … and Josephine Baker were recorded shakin' a little somethin' somethin'. Later this evolved into the 'Harlem Shake.'

"Betty Boop's origin story is not that cut-and-dry.

"But this alternative Betty Boop history may have come to Henson's attention because of months of social media trafficking of an item on a web page promoting Black History Month programming by the Public Broadcasting Service.

"Here's the item:

"Esther Jones Was the Real Betty Boop!

"The iconic cartoon character Betty Boop was inspired by a Black jazz singer in Harlem. Introduced by cartoonist Max Fleischer in 1930, the caricature of the jazz age flapper was the first and most famous sex symbol in animation. Betty Boop is best known for her revealing dress, curvaceous figure, and signature vocals 'Boop Oop A Doop!' While there has been controversy over the years, the inspiration has been traced back to Esther Jones who was known as 'Baby Esther' and performed regularly in the Cotton Club during the 1920s.

"Baby Esther's trademark vocal style of using 'boops' and other childlike scat sounds attracted the attention of actress Helen Kane during a performance in the late 1920s. After seeing Baby Esther, Helen Kane adopted her style and began using 'boops' in her songs as well. Finding fame early on, Helen Kane often included this 'baby style' into her music. When Betty Boop was introduced, Kane promptly sued Fleischer and Paramount Publix Corporation stating they were using her image and style. However video evidence came to light of Baby Esther performing in a nightclub and the courts ruled against Helen Kane stating she did not have exclusive rights to the "booping" style or image, and that the style, in fact, pre-dated her.

"Baby Esther's "baby style" did little to bring her mainstream fame and she died in relative obscurity but a piece of her lives on in the iconic character Betty Boop.

"Here's the problem: In February, an observer pointed out a problem with the image accompanying the 3-paragraph item, which was part of a 10-item promotional "listicle" – a portmanteau combining a list and an article – on the PBS Black Culture Connections web page.

"The image was a photograph with a 1920s patina, showing a stylish Black woman. The header beside it said, 'Esther Jones was the real Betty Boop!' PBS digital editors received an email in February saying that the picture in all likelihood was not that of 'Baby Esther' Jones, who died at a young age (no one seems to be completely sure when) and may never have been photographed as an adult. The image was simply removed from the item about Betty Boop, but everything else, notably the text, was left intact.

"Hindsight being what it is, the email questioning the accuracy of the illustration image should have given pause to PBS executives about the overall accuracy of the item, which actually had been written almost six years before by a staffer who was no longer with the service.

"The Betty Boop item, which should have been either corrected or removed with an explanation, went on to be posted and reposted online, sometimes as confirmation of white appropriation of a Black persona. As the item was passed around on social media, PBS became the quoted source for the news that Betty Boop was based on a real-life Black performer.

"The grandson of Betty Boop's creator Max Fleischer became concerned that PBS had started a social media snowball, spreading an inaccurate version of Betty Boop's origins and yielding unfair criticism of the illustrator. The grandson is Mark Fleischer. He wrote a letter to PBS in June asking for help from PBS in straightening out the beloved cartoon character's origins. Mark Fleischer is president and CEO of a company that holds the rights to Betty Boop.

"'I've been aware for some time of inaccurate theories circulating on social media and elsewhere concerning Betty's origins, but didn't know their source,' Fleischer said in a written statement to the PBS Public Editor's office, after his June letter to PBS. "When I started to see some of these inaccurate theories appearing online saying that they had been confirmed by PBS, which PBS actually did, I became very concerned. It really troubled me that a source as trusted as PBS would repeat and assert conclusions without first ensuring that there was a factual foundation to support those conclusions. In this case, no such foundation existed."

"After the June letter from Mark Fleischer and an inquiry from the Public Editor's office, PBS web editors took down the article, but left nothing in its place.

"PBS Digital managers recently said they were not aware of the item's replication on social media, and that they had initially treated the item as promotional copy, not journalism. But that distinction means nothing to average readers and audiences. If PBS Digital had followed established protocol for retracting or clarifying dubious content, Internet audiences would have found an explanation that the item had been taken down because of doubts about its accuracy.

Correct steps finally were taken after PBS' Standards and Practices team stepped into the picture.

"PBS Editorial Standards & Practices 'are the cornerstone of our commitment to preserving the credibility and integrity of all content that PBS distributes,' said Talia Rosen, PBS Assistant General Counsel and Senior Director for Standards and Practices. 'Editorial content should generally not be deleted without explanation, and the editor's note or correction is tailored to each instance.'

"The spot where the problematic item once stood now features the following editor's note: Retired: Ten Little Known Black History Facts

"Editor's Note (July 26, 2021): The post titled "Ten Little Known Black History Facts" originally published in February of 2015 has been removed from this site because we are unable to verify the contents of the post.

"That explanation does help clean up the PBS process.

"'(The Betty Boop item) is a contested narrative that has been publicly debated for some time," said Amy Wigler, PBS vice president for multiplatform marketing and content. "However, we acknowledged that the Black Culture Connection listicle from years ago was not properly sourced, and we replaced the post with an editor's note explaining the issue."

'But PBS' belated action has not completely quieted concerns that a stronger action is needed to eliminate the notion that Betty Boop's creator appropriated the stage persona of a Black singer. A studio representative suggested PBS should at least contact sites like Black History.com, which attribute the new take on Betty Boop's history to the PBS item.

"This column is an attempt to explain what went wrong after PBS published the item, and establish a more thorough retelling of Betty Boop's history for Internet search engines to deliver when someone looks her up on the web.

"The correct history: Fashion and music trends used by a number of Jazz Age performers, Black and white, influenced for the cartoon's evolution.

"'The concept that Betty Boop grew out of and reflected the Jazz Age culture of her time is absolutely true, yet, as history shows, she was not modeled after any single performer,' Mark Fleischer said. 'It's important to distinguish the collective creativity of the Jazz Age and its style from the many individual Jazz Age artists who contributed to it. And the number of amazing artists and performers who created that great era and who are embodied in Betty Boop is so large that it's impossible to single out any one great talent as her inspiration."

"Betty Boop debuted on August 9, 1930, in the Fleischer Studio's cartoon short 'Dizzy Dishes,' where she appeared as an anthropomorphic dog performing onstage at a jazz club full of other anthropomorphic animals. In that debut, she didn't say anything, but her high-pitched scat-singing style and scandalous little black dress and a visible garter stole the show. Audiences demanded that she appear in more cartoons. Her puppy-dog eyes became smaller and rounder, and her floppy dog ears were replaced by hoop earrings. By 1932 she was starring in her own series of Betty Boop cartoons, produced by Fleischer.

"That year, Helen Kane, a popular jazz performer, sued Fleischer and Paramount Pictures, then known as Paramount Publix Corp., claiming Betty Boop was a 'deliberate caricature' of her 'baby vamp' persona. Kane, who was white, said her voice, looks, and mannerisms were uniquely hers, and copied by Betty Boop. She added that Betty Boop's appearance and her style of scat-singing — including the word "boop" — were also originally hers, even though scat-singing had been popularized by artists like Clara Bow, Little Ann Little and the Duncan Sisters.

"By 1930, scat-singing had long been a staple for some Black performers. Clarence Williams, a Black musician, producer and performer testified in the Kane v. Fleischer trial that he'd been scat-singing since 1915. Throughout the 1920s, Black performers including Gertrude Saunders, Florence Mills, and Baby Esther Jones used the technique and mannerisms.

"Baby Esther, who often had been billed as a 'miniature Florence Mills,' was a popular child singer and did not testify in the trial. But her manager did, and alleged that not only had Esther been performing that style since 1928, but that he had seen Kane at a club in Manhattan that same year while Baby Esther performed. According to History.com, this claim was corroborated by Kane's manager, Lou Bolton, who also provided sound recordings of Baby Esther's singing during the trial.

"The court ruled that Kane could not claim ownership of Betty Boop or her characteristics, since none were unique enough to her that they could be deemed her intellectual property.

"Later in the 1930s a rigid enforcement of the Hays Code, a set of moral guidelines for film productions, triggered changes in Betty Boop's character. Her dresses became more conservative to hide her famous garter, and her attitude and antics were adjusted to seem more demure and what was deemed "appropriate" for a single young lady.

"Betty Boop remains an icon in American pop culture — her signature look and voice have evolved to fit with styles and standards of each passing decade, but she's never lost the traits that made her so recognizable.

"Lesson learned: "Esther Jones was a truly talented young performer," Mark Fleischer said. "What is so problematic here is that to mistakenly single her out — or anyone else – as the sole source of Betty Boop's Jazz Age inspiration creates an untrue narrative that distracts from and potentially eclipses our appreciation and enjoyment of the very real contributions that those involved have made to our culture. ... This would include Esther Jones ... Esther Jones was a real person with her own real story that deserves to be heard."

"This more complete history shows us two things: Max Fleischer did not whitewash a Black character when he created Betty Boop. But Betty Boop was, partially, influenced by fashion and music whose origins can indeed be traced to Black performers.

"If the original PBS item on that Black History Month listicle had been even a bit more nuanced and complete, it likely would not have become a viral source for the blunt assertion that Betty Boop was Black. We could have thus avoided this teachable moment.

"'PBS.org is meant to serve as a curator of content, not a place for unique editorials,' added Amy Wigler, the PBS multiplatform marketing and content chief. 'We gather relevant content from across PBS and the public media system and present it to our audience in an accessible way across our site. Moving forward, all editorial-style content will be reviewed to ensure it aligns with PBS Standards and Practices.'"

"Every bit of public affairs information that PBS puts on screen or publishes on the Internet, from promotional content to what its news anchors say, is a form of journalism; it must be factual and clear. To offer less than that undermines PBS' standing as a trustworthy source of information."

Betty's animators

Of the 120 Betty Boop cartoons, several head animators stand out as having repeated contact with Betty Boop. Willard Bowsky worked on 11, Roland Crandall on 12 and Tom Johnson on 17. No one at the studio matched Myron Waldman's association with the series. Waldman worked on 29 of them, more than any other animator at the Fleischer Studios.

The Fleischer Studio did not assign animators and their units to particular characters or series. So, unlike directors such as Chuck Jones, Tex Avery and the team of Bill Hanna and Joe Barbara, few people at Fleischer's ever became identified with a single character. Waldman's track record with Betty Boop stands out, though. Waldman, who created Betty's pet dog Pudgy for the series, was very self-effacing about his career in animation, despite the fact that he was the director of two of the four Fleischer shorts to be nominated for an Academy Award ("Hunky and Spunky" and "Educated Fish"). He did outstanding work on the Fleischer Superman series ("Billion Dollar Limited," "Magnetic Telescope") and directed the two-reel "Raggedy Ann and Raggedy Andy" short.

Waldman told me that much of Betty's success could be traced to the work of animator Roland "Doc" Crandall. Crandall, born in 1892, left the studio in 1941 and was a commercial artist. He died in 1972.

Crandall's biographical sketch in the studio newsletter reported "he had an early ambition to be a cartoonist and contributed political cartoons to the 'Stamford Advocate' when he was only 13 years-old and still living on the farm [in New Canaan, CT].

"Doc received his school in New Canaan and at the Yale Art School in New Haven, CT. His first job was in New York City with an engraving company. A few years later he decided to go west. He staked out a homestead in Montana sold it, and then went to Los Angeles, CA where he opened a commercial art studio. A year or so later he tried gold mining in Alaska. His next adventure was with the Yale Battalion Field Artillery during the Mexican border trouble.

After this he decided to try animating and after a few minutes instruction was put to work animating 'Foxy Grandpa' and 'The Katzenjammer Kids [two popular Hearst comic strips of the era]. During the World War, Doc went overseas with the 11th Engineers. He was in the Battle of Cambrai and later promoted to sergeant-major. He was then transferred to General Headquarters where he was put in charge of secret maps. At the close of the war he made a 13-reel animated history of war for the War College.

"Upon his return to New York he worked at the Bray Studios. When Max and Dave went into business, Doc was one of their first employees, some 16 years ago. Ten years after the war, Doc returned to Paris and did a picture for the Paris Auto Show. He returned to the studio in 1929 and a couple of years later animated 'Snow White,' a Betty Boop picture alone. It took him six months to do it.

"Doc is a genial person well liked by those who know him. He is five feet eight inches tall and weighs 145 pounds. He has brown hair, not very much of it. He keeps his blue eyes half shut because of the smoke coming from a cigarette that is always in his mouth. His most favored food is lima beans or clams. In the line of strong drinks give him gin. Demands that the coffee he drinks be good.

"Doc's hobbies are stone fireplace building, digging lakes and landscaping. He owns a speedboat named 'Rose Marie.' His pet peeve is to get free advice.

"In 1923 he married Julia Hoffman; their son Davenport was born the following year. Doc is very fond of dogs and has a Welsh terrier named Paddy.

"Doc is a sound sleeper, once he falls asleep, but he usually resorts to counting sheep. Blue is his favorite color and 13 is his lucky number. Doc is now in charge of a new group [and] their first picture will be a Screen Song starring Wiffle Piffle. Max was the first person to call him 'Doc' and the name stuck. Someone we just can't picture calling him anything else."

Bowsky, according to animation historian Joe Campana, was a native New Yorker born in 1907. He began working at the studio in the late 1920s and was one of the young group of artists who were promoted to animators when a number of senior artists left in 1930.

Bowsky, according to Waldman, was one of the members of the Fleischer inner circle and was well liked by Max and Dave, despite complaints that he was anti-Semitic.

Bowsky is the artist who added spooky elements to the Boop shorts, Waldman added.

After the Fleischers lost their studio in a take-over by Paramount in the spring of 1942, Bowsky enlisted in the army and became a platoon leader in the 94th Calvary Reconnaissance Squadron. Campana wrote, "The 14th Armored Division arrived at Marseille, France on Oct. 30, 1944. Within a couple weeks Bowsky's unit was among those mobilized to join the Seventh Army in the Southern Vosges Mountains (due east of Paris, near the German border.) Willard's was among the squadrons that comprised The Division's Combat Command A (CCA). They were soon ordered to advance into an area southwest of Strasbourg, just west of the Rhine. CCA's mission was to clear German forces from the area and fight its way south to the town of Selestat. Cavalry squadrons were used for reconnaissance and were deployed in front of and along the flanks of advancing armored columns. Bowsky's unit encountered a German column withdrawing eastward to cross the Rhine. A nighttime firefight erupted and Second Lieutenant Willard Bowsky was killed in action on Nov. 27, 1944. Willard and the men of his platoon were good soldiers who fought bravely. In the end the fight was won. Willard was a genuine war hero. He was awarded the Silver Star and the Purple Heart and is interred at the Lorraine American Cemetery in St. Alvold, France."

Johnson was also a native New Yorker, born in 1907. According to his short biography in the studio newsletter, he had both an interest in drawing – he had his own comic strip at one point in school – and in motion pictures. Although going to school to become a teacher, his artistic bent made itself known through a side job as a sign painter.

He joined the studio as a writer in the story department and then switched to the animation department where he was eventually made the head of a group or unit. He stayed with the Fleischers and then with Famous Studios literally his entire career working on some of the last theatrical cartoons produced by Paramount in the late 1950s. Some of his last work was on the Felix the Cat television series produced by fellow Fleischer alumni Joe Oriolo. Johnson died in 1960.

Born in 1908, Waldman joined the Fleischer Studio in 1930 after graduating from the Fine and Applied Arts Program at the Pratt Institute. At the studio, he started as an opaquer and then moved into the inking department. After winning a studio competition, Waldman was promoted to the in-betweening department and was given his own animation unit in 1933. Waldman's strength was with sentimental themes and softer gags, although he worked on several Popeye shorts and proved his abilities with the taxing Superman cartoons.

One Betty Boop cartoon of which Waldman was particularly proud is "A Language All My Own" (1935). Betty Boop was very popular in Japan, and this short was designed to appeal to the Japanese market. In the short, Betty travels to Japan and performs there. Waldman wanted to make sure that none of her gestures and movements would offend the Japanese, so he asked a number of Japanese exchange students in New York to check his work.

Waldman was also the creator of Betty's dog, Pudgy, who was the star of many of the later Betty Boop cartoons.

Waldman was in a unique position at the Fleischer Studio. On one hand he was a talented and loyal team player, but on the other, he was an iconoclast who wasn't afraid to speak his mind. Waldman championed the cause of Lillian Friedman,

Myron Waldman had a very long career in animation. This photo is from 1968. (Author's collection)

the studio's first woman animator when others gave her a rough time. He also attempted to persuade Max to talk with striking artists in the lengthy 1937 strike.

Waldman returned to animation after serving in the Army during World War II. He worked at Famous Studios on Screen Songs, Popeye. Little Lulu, and Casper shorts. He wasn't content just with a career in animation, though. He branched out to create a "novel without words," "Eve," that was a critical and financial success when it was published in 1943. He was the artist on the postwar Sunday comic strip "Happy the Humbug." He appeared on television shows during the 1950s with his "Try A Line" drawing act.

In the 1960s and '70s, he worked on a number of Saturday morning series, and was the director of the pilot for the "Out of the Inkwell"

A late in life rendition of Betty and Pudgy by Myron Waldman. (Author's collection).

series produced by Hal Seeger. Seeger, a former Fleischer Studio employee, had convinced Max not only to sell him the rights to do the series, but to appear in the pilot as well. For his final appearance with his silent screen co-star, Waldman recalled that Fleischer had his hair dyed for the occasion. Waldman quit from the series when the budgets would not permit him to do Ko-Ko justice.

He continued to work with Seeger on subsequent series such as "Milton the Monster."

Waldman stayed very active up to his death in 2006 with providing original artwork for collectors as well as creating limited edition cels. He was the last surviving head animator from the studio.

Betty's musical directors

Sammy Timberg was the most important of the several tunesmiths used by the Fleischer Studio to compose music and songs for the Popeye and Betty Boop cartoons, and other productions. Thanks to the efforts of his daughter Pat, he is beginning to receive the attention being afforded to fellow cartoon composers Carl Stalling and Scott Brady.

Sammy's contributions to the Fleischer Studio productions reads like a cartoon Top Forty list. His works included the "Sweet Betty" theme song heard to introduce the Betty Boop shorts; the biggest hit from Gulliver's Travels, "It's a Hap Hap Happy Day"; "Don't Take my Boop-Oop-A-Doop Away"; "I'm Sinbad the Sailor"; "Boy Oh Boy" from "Mr. Bug Goes to Town" and many others.

Sammy received an opportunity that fellow composers Carl Stalling and Scott Brady never got at Warner Brothers and MGM. He composed all the music for the Fleischer Superman cartoons, which enabled him to show a wider and more dramatic range of his musical abilities.

In a brief interview in 1977, Timberg told this writer that his favorite assignment at the studio was composing for the Betty Boop shorts. His contributions to the shorts were integral to their success. Since many of the Betty Boop shorts have show biz settings or references, Sammy's classic Tin Pan Alley pop compositions were always on target. He also contributed greatly to the incidental music of the shorts as revealed by the cartoons musical cue sheets maintained by ASCAP.

Sammy obviously understood the intent of the animators and knew his characters. Some of his music provides a structure for the short, such as the great "I Want A Clean Shaven Man" in the Popeye cartoon of the same name. Other songs set the stage for the action of the short such as the song Popeye sings about looking for his father at the beginning of "Goonland."

Composer Sammy Timberg had a successful career in vaudeville, as well as a song writer. (Courtesy of Patricia Timberg).

"The music had to be synchronized with the action, and I worked with the artists from the first drawings up to the end," Sammy told one interviewer.

His compositions for the Superman shorts perfectly match the animation as being one of the true highpoints in American animation. The Superman shorts easily prove that Sammy had the talent to score dramatic films.

Sammy with Sammy Lerner (who composed the Popeye theme song) wrote two live-action shorts "Musical Justice" (1931) and "Musical Doctor" (1932). The two shorts starred Rudy Vallee and Mae Questel and the first short features Questel as Betty Boop.

Sammy had aspirations beyond his success in cartoons. His daughter Pat told me that her father never saw the value in that work and instead sought fame as a composer of hit popular songs and "serious" music. Considering that he had a classical music education with a teacher whose students included Aaron Copeland and George Gershwin and the lack of critical attention animated cartoons received in the 1930s and '40s, it's little wonder Sammy favored other projects.

One only has to look at what Sammy was doing prior to his start at the Fleischer Studio. In 1930, he led a 100-piece orchestra at New York's Capital Theater in performing his jazz rhapsody.

Listening to Pat speak about her father and his life is not unlike reading the plot of an old "behind-the-scenes of a show" musical.

Timberg was born in New York City on May 21, 1903, the youngest of seven children of Austrian immigrants. The death of his father forced the 15-year-old to abandon his training as a concert pianist and join his brother Herman in vaudeville.

Herman Timberg was an up-and-coming comedian, and Sammy was his straight man. A legend in vaudeville, Herman wrote one of the Marx Brothers' early acts while Sammy provided the music for it, and their sister Hattie performed with them and acted as the business manager for the Marx Brothers.

After 14 years on the vaudeville circuit, Sammy decided to devote himself to his music. He wrote songs for several Broadway shows, and then found work with the Fleischer Studios. His music can be heard on dozens of Fleischer shorts and in several of the live-action musical comedy shorts produced by Paramount in New York featuring singer Rudy Valle. His association with animation lasted through the end of the Fleischer Studios and continued with the Famous Studios where he composed music for Little Lulu and Casper cartoons.

While essentially a New Yorker, Sammy ventured out to Hollywood on several memorable occasions. In the 1940s, the great dramatic actor Lionel Barrymore chose Timberg to compose the score for a recording of Dickens's "A Christmas Carol."

Sammy collaborated with lyricists Buddy Kaye and Sammy Cahn on a number of popular songs. The song, "Help Yourself to My Heart," written by Timberg and Cahn, was recorded by Frank Sinatra and included in a Sinatra retrospective released in the mid-1980s. Pat Timberg has discovered dozens of unreleased compositions among her father's papers, including four other songs co-written by Cahn.

Later in his career, Timberg produced shows and managed performers such as Don Adams, Jackie Gleason and Edie Gorme. Pat remembers going to show business restaurants with her father and having people such as Milton Berle come to their table to greet Sammy. The Timbergs were truly a show business family as Pat's mother and Sammy's first wife, the late Rosemarie Sinnott, was a former Ziegfeld Follies dancer and magazine cover model.

His second marriage to a native of Scranton, PA eventually drew Sammy to that city where he spent the last years of his life. Full of old-fashioned show biz charm, Sammy was a well-known figure in the capital city, and just months before his death in 1992, Sammy was honored by the city with a "Sammy Timberg Day."

"I did everything – managed people, conducted, wrote music, did everything in all ends of show business," Timberg said in a 1984 interview. "It's been a busy life."

In late 1990s Pat released a CD of her father's music that included new recordings of many of his songs for the Betty Boop and Popeye cartoons as well as an archival recording of Sammy Timberg performing one of his tunes and his theme from the Superman cartoons.

***

Lou Fleischer headed the music and sound department and came into the studio and helped make the process that produced the "Bouncing Ball" silent song cartoons possible.

The studio newsletter profile of him noted "he can not remember having any childhood ambitions around the house, which would indicate that his musical talent began to blossom early.

"He studied violin and piano and mastered them both. He is also an expert mathematician and knows the dope, all the way from zero to square root to the fifth power of the fourth dimension. Or whatever you call the higher mathematics."

"…After the early period of his musical career had passed, he became associated with his brothers-in-law in the jewelry business. Things were going fine until 'sound' was introduced into the picture business. Max and Dave, his brothers, wanted him in the studio; his brothers-in-law wanted him in the jewelry business. Lou had helped out in the studio before, on the 'bouncing ball' feature. It was a hard decision to make, with two opposing forces pulling him from opposite directions. Max and Dave won, thus making it a twofold honor – that of having their brother with them and at the same time securing one of the best soundmen in the business.

"Lou's tastes in music are what might be called broad. He likes all good music whether it is classical or popular. This ability to appreciate the best in all grades of music is a valuable asset to him in his present duties as music director of the Fleischer Studios."

In a 1936 studio newsletter essay, Lou wrote about the music department: "In shooting actual motion pictures, a microphone takes the sounds while the camera takes the picture. The difference and difficulty in the production of cartoons is that the characters are imaginary in the sounds must be produced to watch this task of synchronization is the main duty of the music department.

"This is accomplished in one of two ways:

"The sounds are first recorded on film and the cartoon is then made to match. This is called pre-synchronization. The cartoon is produced in the sounds are recorded to match this is called post synchronization.

"In pre-synchronization The music and the other sounds are recorded on film. This film is analyzed and the location of every music beat, every note, every syllable, accent, expression, is indicated on exposure sheets. These, when followed by the animator, produces a cartoon that matches the recorded sound.

"In post synchronization, the music department must give the animators exposure sheets in order that the animation will be of the correct timing to permit the sounds to be recorded in the exact tempo contemplated. We must also provide a musical score, if followed by the musicians' vocalist and the effects men, (noise makers to you) will match to the fraction of a second. We prepare the first print of the cartoon called a work print by punching a series of holes which, when projected on the screen in the recording, becomes an automatic conductor. The musicians reading the score while following the conductor through the corner of the eye synchronize accurately every beat in every affect without following the picture.

"All our calculations are based on the principle that 90 feet of film passed through the projector in one minute in other words one and a half feet of film per second one for the film has 16 frames or exposures. So in one second 24 frames pass by. Thus, our calculations are figured to be correct to 1/24 of a second. Darn close, eh? Durn tootin' !!!"

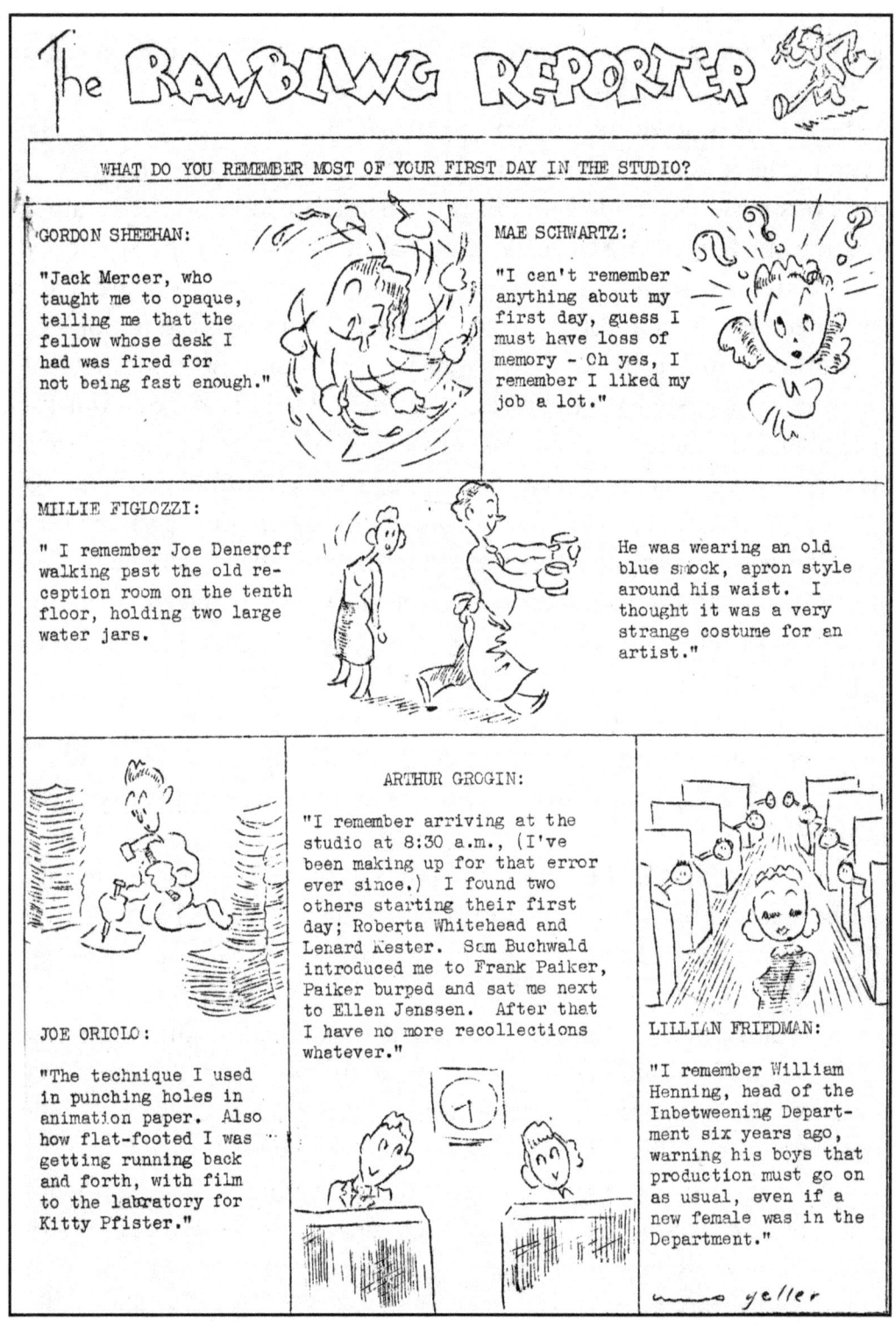

From the studio's newsletter, are recollections about employee's first day in the studio. (Author's collection)

Chapter Four

As detailed in Chapter 2, the Screen Songs series gave the studio an identity in the early sound era, before Bimbo was developed and before Betty Boop gave the studio a new star.

Initially in 1929 through 1931, the Screen Songs carried on a format established by the Song Cartunes of the silent era: there was a loose narrative which framed the performance of the song and the song itself was presented with multiple lyrics.

The success of the Screen Cartunes was based in less expensive animation, using most frequently songs in the public domain and the pop cultural tradition of people singing in a group. The first Screen Songs carried on that format but with sound.

A 1929 trade ad claimed, "No short subject in sound during the current season leaped to more universal popularity than Paramount Screen Songs. Scores of theatres of all classes voluntarily wrote wires and letters of enthusiastic praise for these novelties. The words of the songs appear in unique and humorous style on the screen with the celebrated 'bouncing ball' to keep time. With instrumental and vocal accompaniment. The entire audience joins in singing and signifies its approval at the end with thunderous applause. Prove this for yourself."

Another trade ad from Paramount proclaimed "Move Broadway into your Theater!" with its talking films that included the "Paramount Screen Songs."

In many ways the Screen Song was a product for its time. Once the success of the "The Jazz Singer" convinced theater owners that was now time to embrace sound technology, one could see the sound-crazy movie public would want sound cartoons as well, especially cartoons that featured music.

One might theorize the Screen Songs provided the studio with a valuable niche in this early period. The Fleischers did not have a character at that time to truly challenge Mickey Mouse and his ascendancy into stardom.

A 1930 Paramount trade ad seems to confirm that theory. It emphasizes the Screen Songs over the Talkartoons.

Look at "Bedelia" (1929). There is a male character that some people have mistaken for Bimbo, but it isn't. The plot revolves around this male character going to Bedelia's house, his girlfriend who then gets ready for their date. The girlfriend looks like the earliest Bimbo and there's some funny business, as she gets ready. The song, played with a dirge-like rhythm, then starts.

So why not make Bimbo the male character? Why not build his character up to audiences?

It's been my thought the decision to essentially do away with Ko-Ko created a vacuum at the studio the Fleischers were apparently unable to fill with another star character.

Take "Yes! We Have No Bananas Today (1930) for instance. Two mice steal bananas from a street vendor who catches them and beats them up. In fact, he wads one of them up and plays handball with him, while the other mouse eats the remainder of the fruit. The vendor chases them, slips on a peel they've thrown at him and the song begins.

The animation for the framing sequence is crude, while the animation for the lyrics is actually clever. The short ends with the conclusion of the song.

The problem with the short is that it has no other elements by which it could be sold. There is no recurring character.

In late 1930, though, Bimbo – or characters that approximated Bimbo – started turning up more in the series. In "My Gal Sal," Bimbo is singing the song in a deep baritone in a tenement neighborhood much to the consternation of the residents who thrown a variety of things out their windows to discourage him. By the end he has the furniture he needs to set up housekeeping.

The song then commences with a voice-over emphasizing the nostalgic aspect of the tune. Identifying the title song has being from another era is also a hallmark of many of these early cartoons.

During the sing-along part, Bimbo returns to perform. He is depressed about Sal – the song expresses loss and love – and attempts to commit suicide – a questionable subject for gags.

In an odd ending, a female character who appears during the final set of lyrics takes off nearly all her clothes and dances a topless hula. The hand of the animator appears to bring down the curtain.

When animators have told this writer many cartoons were made up as they went along, one could easily see this assertion was true. The result seems to be almost a stream of consciousness.

A male character – who looks more like Fitz from the Ko-Ko cartoons – appears in "Alexander's Rag Time Band" (1931), which the titles herald as Irving Berlin's famous song. He is learning music from a teacher who selects the well-known song.

There seems to be greater care with the animation, although once again the central character doesn't look exactly like Bimbo. The closing lyrics sequence has instruments playing themselves followed by a parade.

Even with greater care in the animation, there is still something lacking in this short.

The evolution to the Screen Song format many people know started in 1930 with singer Rudy Vallee appearing in a college football-themed cartoon "The Stein Song," one of his hit college songs.

Vallee in many ways was the first pop star who directly appealed to younger audiences through his performances of college songs. It may be difficult to understand his appeal today, but Vallee was popular then as any pop star is today.

His 1929 musical "The Vagabond Lover" had been at hit for the newly formed RKO in 1929, although Valle had little love for it. He told TV host Mike Douglas in 1980, " They're still fumigating the theaters where it was shown. Almost ruined me. In fact, I think it's only shown in penitentiaries and comfort stations."

Valle was a huge name at the time, regardless of his feature film debut, and it was a great coup to have him in "The Stein Song." He appears briefly on screen introducing the song for the sing-along sequence.

MADE OF PEN & INK: FLEISCHER STUDIOS

In an edition of the Paramount Pep-O-Gram from 1930 – an inter-studio newsletter – there is a profile of Lou Diamond, the Paramount executive in charge of short subjects. The anonymous writer recounted, "Rudy Vallee and Lou met over a dish of borscht at Sardi's one early morning. Funny place to meet, over a dish of borscht."

It was apparently at this meeting that Diamond suggested putting Valle into "a very successful Screen Song quickie." The story then speaks about how Diamond was planning "another quickie presentation of the boy from Maine, this time under the title of 'Betty Co-Ed.'"

It has along been thought the Fleischers were able to use music from Famous Music, Paramount's music publishing company, because of the business arrangement with the studio. It has also been generally accepted the studio was able to bring in the popular singers and bands at the time for its Screen Sings because of its connections to Paramount and because the studio was in New York City, a center for stage, vaudeville, radio and recording activities.

Nowhere in the Pep-O-Gram story is Max or Dave Fleischer mentioned. Considering this was a house organ for Paramount and Diamond's position in the company, it's no surprise that he is seen as the star here.

The result is a well done short with a red-hot pop singer with a song that was not from the turn of the century.

In 1931, the legendary vaudeville team Gallagher and Shean were the subject of a Screen Song that featured the song the team made famous on stage. Gallagher had died the year before and only Shean appears in the film.

This was the start of a format that would be carried on in the next Screen Song release. In 1931's "Betty Co-Ed," the formula that would characterize the best Screen Songs was introduced. The studio used a song that was popularized by Vallee. A college student comes to woo Betty Co-Ed and is removed from her house by upper classmen. A proto-Betty Boop is featured in this short, as is a live action sequence with Vallee singing.

Vallee appeared again in 1931's "Kitty From Kansas City," a Screen Song that featured Betty Boop. Betty is a country girl waiting for a train. She has several pets with her and when her parrot grabs her behind, she accuses the ticket agent of pinching her. The mail hook of passing train grabs her and she stops at the next stop marked "Rudy Valley." The song begins and Betty exclaims, "That's my Rudy."

The live action sequence with Valle is actually funny and charming with more production value that any of his two other previous short.

The second sing-along features a heavy Betty Boop acting out gags to the song.

***

An interesting side-note to the Screen Songs are two live-action shorts: the 1931 all live action short "Musical Justice" with story and songs written by Samuel Lerner and Samuel Timberg and the 1932 short "Musical Doctor."

The first short was directed by Aubrey Scotto, an editor who later directed shorts and then worked at Republic Pictures as a director of features.

The premise is that Valle presides as judge over a courtroom insuring "musical justice." For instance, a couple seeking a divorce because one enjoys classical music while others enjoys "syncopation."

Betty Boop is charged with upsetting the musical peace and the actress is Mae Questel. Although not appearing in Betty's standard black short skirt, Questel plays the part to the hilt.

Judge Valle proclaims her "boop-boop-a-doing" must stop, to which Betty proclaim, "Anything but that!" The band – which doubles as the jury – starts in with "Don't take my Boop-boop-a-doop Away" and Questel sings as her defense.

Valle ultimately decides not to punish her with a not guilty decision from the jury. There is a few seconds of animation as the short's closing image of a statute of blind justice dancing along to the music and dropping her robes.

The next year, "Musical Doctor," was released with Questel receiving billing with Valle. Once again Lerner and Timburg have written the script and music. This time Vallee is curing people with music and Questel is a nurse who is also manning the telephone switchboard. The director was Ray Cozine, who had helmed several shorts featuring George Burns and Gracie Allen.

There are a few moments of animation in the film. Neither short acknowledges any connection to the Fleischer Studios, but these are fairly close to what I think a live action Fleischer two-reeler at that time would have looked like.

***

Broadway star Eddie Cantor appeared in "My Baby Just Cares for Me," a 1931 Screen Song showcasing Cantor's huge hit from the show "Whoopee," while radio and recording star Arthur Tracy, known as the "Street Singer," performed in "Russian Lullaby."

The format for the series was now established for the next two years: the Fleischer Studio featured a number of popular performers. A trade ad from 1932 in the Film Daily said declared the shorts were "more than program fillers" and noted all of the performers who were to appear in upcoming Screen Songs: Vallee, the Boswell Sisters, Lillian Roth, Ethel Merman and Irene Bordoni.

Once again, there was a clear distinction between the Fleischers were doing and their competitors.

I think it would be fair to say that Max and Dave saw the advantage to having these kind of appearances in the cartoons, the guest performers appeared in Betty Boop's series such as Cab Calloway in "Minnie the Moocher," "Snow White" and "The Old Man of the Mountain;" Don Redman and his orchestra in "I Heard;" famed violinist Rubinoff in two shorts, "Morning, Noon and Night" and "Parade of the Wooden Soldiers."

The cartoons benefitted from featuring a radio, Broadway and recording star and the performers received additional national attention.

In the case of Redman and Rubinoff, both men supplied the entire musical soundtrack for the shorts, something the Mills Brothers also did in the Screen Songs "Dinah," (1933) and "I Ain't Got Nobody" (1932). The Mills Bothers did more than just play and sing in these two shorts – they also supplied all of the sounds made by musical instruments other than the guitar.

It didn't almost matter there was an animated story about a lion with hypnotism/magic skills. The shorts are a showcase for the vocal talents of the group.

Clearly someone at Paramount publicity thought the addition of the Mills Brothers to Screen Songs was worthy of note. A trade ad in 1931 is dedicated just to the brothers. "Everywhere they're asking, 'Have you heard the Mills Brothers?' Without a doubt the greatest broadcast on the air today! Signed to make three Screen Songs the first of which will be 'I Ain't Got Nobody.' The outstanding popularity of these boys combined with the clever showmanship of Max Fleischer Cartoons give you a series of single reel attractions that can't be beaten for audience appeal. Short features that command large space in your newspaper advertising!" The animated story was a series of gags around the loading of a merchant ship, but again "Dinah" comes alive when the performance starts.

The final Screen Song for the group was "When Yuba Plays the Rumba on the Tuba" (1933). The first animated story revolved around an airship voyage, while the second was about train gags.

Another repeat performer was recording and radio star Lillian Roth who appeared in "Down in the Sugar Cane," (1932) with a plethora of sugar gags and "Ain't She Sweet?" in 1933.

Radio comedians Stoopnagle and Budd weren't know for their singing skills, but they starred in "Stoopnocracy" in 1933. The short opens with an ambulance from an insane asylum collecting potential patients, including an animator working on a Betty Boop cartoon.

We meet the two comics as residents of the asylum. Budd is a reporter interviewing Col. Stoopnagle about his latest inventions. After several gags, he asks if Stoopnagle has any inventions that would make people sing in a theater. He has the Crosby cigar, which is designed to make anyone who smokes it sound like Bing Crosby. Budd smokes it and leads the audience in a near perfect Bing Crosby impersonation of "Please."

The next invention involves a questionable gag in which Stoopnagle produces a bottle of "Cab Calloway milk" that he promises "would make a baby sing." An African-American boy dressed as a baby materializes, drinks the milk and sings "Minnie the Moocher" with Stoopnagle and Budd as the chorus.

With the conclusion of the songs comes more insane asylum gags. The short is perhaps the oddest of the Screen Songs, but it is very entertaining.

In 1933, "The Peanut Vendor" offered the song in both English and in Spanish by the Mexican singer and actress Armida. It was a real showcase for her as her footage included three costume changes. Appropriately enough the cartoon framing features gags at a zoo where peanuts played a significant part.

"Boilesk" (1933) is a Screen Song that would probably never been made after the Production Code came into effect in 1934. The short has the elements of a 1930's burlesque show: a tinny live band, chorus girls, a blackout skit about a wife's infidelity, a strip tease, an eccentric dancer and a singer. The live performers were the Watson Sisters who were actually a comedy and music act.

It's a very funny short.

Myron Waldman, one of the animators of this cartoon, told me they had censorship problems when the cartoon was released. The scene in which a chorus line of hippos kicked off their garters was actually cut from prints shown in Philadelphia. Waldman added they weren't allowed to show cows with udders in cartoons at that time. When the compilation film, "The Betty Boop Follies" was released in the 1970s, this cartoon was among the 14 in the collection. It was not complete, however, and had the Watson Sisters footage removed and footage from another cartoon added.

1933 marked the pinnacle of the Screen Song with 15 releases, the following year with the series decreasing to eight cartoons and then only two in 1935 with a different format. Instead of individual performers or groups, the musical part of the shorts featured big bands.

The first of these new formats featured Abe Lyman and his Californians and the song "I Wished on the Moon." The cartoon framing involved an airship that built theaters by dropping the components from the air. The last building was one that got pretty mixed up in the process. Naturally that doesn't prevent audiences from flocking to it. The gags revolve around the theater's crazed design.

The musical sequence is framed as a short projected at the theater. Unlike the other Screen Songs that had the song performed more than once, in the new format, it was once and done. The short is notable as well for its animated star, Wiffle Piffle. The late animator and historian Michael Sporn detailed in his blog how the character came out of Betty Boop cartoons and the studio then tried to make him a standalone star. Developed by animator Tom Johnson, the egghead character had a very funny walk but did not seem to have too many of characteristics on which a writer or artist could capitalize. Jack Mercer contributed the voice.

Yet in the remaining 18 Screen Songs from 1935 through 1938, Wiffle Piffle appears in six of them.

Wiffle Piffle appeared as well in 1936 "I Don't Want to Make History" with the Vincent Lopez orchestra. Also set in a movie theater, the gags come from a newsreel being shown. The musical was once again part of the show the audience was watching.

The theater and the newsreel format were repeated in another 1936 cartoon "I Can't Escape from You" with Joe Reiechman and his orchestra. While some of the gags were funny, the format seemed lazy. There was no effort to integrate the music with the animation.

Jack Denny and his orchestra was featured in 1936's "I Feel like a Feather in the Breeze," another Wiffle Piffle outing, this time in a nightclub. Wiffle is a waiter delivering mugs of beer and meals. Once again there is no real effort to give the character a personality. The musical number is the act at the club.

A 1936 trade ad noted there were six Screen Songs scheduled for release and were described: "The 'Bouncing Ball' returns by popular demand, in a cartoon series featuring only the latest and most popular songs sung by leading radio personalities." I think the fact that no performers were identified indicated the fact the time for these shorts had passed.

A 1937 trade ad described the series as "A standby for any theater manager who wants to play safe with is fans and give 'em popularity tested shorts."

"You Leave me Breathless," one of the final Screen Songs in 1938 repeats the theater/newsreel format but frames it as broadcasts seen on a television set.

It would appear that both the studio and Paramount was simply tired of the feature. It may have been the costs associated with hiring and filming the musical talent.

At the very least, the Screen Songs provide an interesting insight into American popular music of the 1930s.

***

During this early 1930s, while the country's economy struggled, there was a boom in animation. A front page story in the Film Daily (June 26, 1934) carried the headline "Wanted 5,000 cartoonists; No Kiddin'."

The story read, " Wanted 5,000 animated cartoonists. Salary $100 to $300 a week. Apply to Max Fleischer.

"Sounds like a gag but it's gospel according to the film creator of Betty Boop, Popeye, etc. Fleischer would hire 5,000 men tomorrow if he could lay hands on them. In his words, "there ain't no such animal." Meaning of course outside of the 3,000 artists now employed at cartooning in the film business.

"Film cartooning is a highly specialized art and to be entrusted only to those few who understand motion and timing. A man may be an excellent artist but unless knack of those requisites he'd be useless to the studio.

"Fleischer, who represented the cartooning industry on the NRA [National Recovery Administration]. One of the few who made General Johnson reverse a ruling. The keeper of the Blue Eagle ordered shorter hours for the cartoon men so that more artists could get employment. Fleischer was willing to but when it was pointed out that animated cartoonists were scarcer than blondes in Africa the general reneged."

The story concluded there was a demand for short subjects and that a shortage of artists was holding back production.

***

Color Classics

Starting in 1934, the Color Classics were supposed to be the all-color high-end competition to Disney's acclaimed "Silly Symphonies" and while the series has many good entries, it also had some spectacular clunkers. This was one of the first times the Fleischer Studio attempted to compete head-to-head with a Disney product.

With a title of the series being Color Classics, the Fleischers started out of the gate somewhat hobbled. "The Silly Symphonies" were known for its exclusive of three-strip Technicolor and the Fleischers were at a disadvantage because they were restricted to use Cinecolor at first and then two-strip Technicolor until 1936.

Cinecolor and two-strip Technicolor both used a two-color method with one strip registering red and the other registering blues and greens. This meant the color palette of the finished product was muted.

Looking at the series, now one can see – at least in this writer's opinion – the strongest entries in the series are those that continue the more off-center approach for which the studio was known.

"The Cobweb Hotel," "The Fresh Vegetable Mystery," "Poor Cinderella," "Dancing on the Moon," "Educated Fish," "Small Fry," "A Car-tune Portrait," and "Ants in the Plants," for example all have the Fleischer themes and style. They are among my personal favorites with strong imagery and gags.

The series' attempts to do something sentimental frequently succeeded as well. "Somewhere in Dreamland," "Christmas Comes But Once a Year" and "Hunky and Spunky" all pluck at the heartstrings successfully.

There is also a heavy-handed use of sentiment or melodrama in cartoons such as "The Song of the Birds," "The Little Stranger" and "Play Safe."

Part of the issue with re-assessing the Color Classics now is that contemporary viewers can't view them as they were intended. In the 1950s the copyright on most of the series was not renewed – similar to the fate of the Fleischer Superman cartoons. Falling into public domain, the Color Classics were introduced to a new generation through cheap VHS collections in varying levels of quality.

Thanks to animation historian Jerry Beck and Kit Parker Films, a collection was assembled using the best prints available to them. "Somewhere in Dreamland: the Max Fleischer Color Cartoons" was released in 2003 by VCI and is the best way to see these cartoons. The set is still in print from VIC, (https://www.vcientertainment.com/).

What the Color Classics featured though, and was played up in trade ads, was the Fleischer 3-D process.

A 1936 trade ad gushed, "So real they seem to walk out of the screen, these three-dimensional color classics – THE ONLY ONES OF THEIR KIND IN THE INDUSTRY – will be even more exciting this year than in the past. The Fleischer Studios have created and developed new trick effects both in color and dimensional treatment and exclusively own the patent rights to the three dimensional process and equipment. You cannot get these effects in shorts released by any other company.

"Tailored to known box office demand, guaranteed 100 percent box-office tested."

The series' first cartoon was "Poor Cinderella" (1934) featured Betty Boop in her only appearance in a color cartoon. Betty registered as a redhead in the short's color system.

Betty is Cinderella, the slave to her three evil stepsisters. The story sticks closely to the accepted fairy tale, but there is a scene in which Betty appears in her bra and panties, which is pure Fleischer.

The use of the 3-D sets is done very well in the short and there are some impressive background paintings. The dance scene with Betty and Prince Charming has some nice animation – some of it may have been rotoscoped – as well another effective 3-D set. A caricature of Rudy Valle makes a guest appearance in the short, a nice nod to his earlier involvement with the studio. The end gag is great with the stepsisters being squeezed by the gates. It was an auspicious start for the series.

The second film in the series, "A Little Dutch Mill" has some extremely effective use of the 3-D sets. The film, set in a fantasy version of Holland tells a very simple story of a dirty, mean spirited tramp who comes into the neat and orderly Dutch village to recover this cache of gold he has hidden in a windmill. Two children and their pet duck discover his secret.

The tramp kidnaps the children and threatens to burn their tongues out, an amazingly grotesque image. The pet duck brings the villagers who punish the tramp by cleaning him and his windmill. The cleaning reforms him and he gives the villagers his gold coins.

There are two wonderful uses of the 3-D effect. To show the children are missing the camera pans through a set showing the doorways of the homes. On the top step are neat lines of wooden shoes. The children's shoes are missing.

An elaborate set of the cleaned interior of the windmill is also a highlight of the film.

"Little Dutch Mill" sets the bar pretty high in terms of the 3-D sets, something that is not carried forward to the next cartoon in the series "An Elephant Never Forgets." Essentially a string of school kid gags; the short is anchored by the song "An Elephant Never Forgets." While "A Dutch Mill" reminded viewers they were watching something technically different, this cartoon did not.

"The Song of the Birds," the first release of 1935, opens with the use of a 3-D background of a bucolic countryside. The short focuses on a baby bird being taught by his parents to fly. The baby birds rests on a windowsill of a home where a little boy is plying with a B-B gun. He shoots and apparently kills the little bird. The parents discover the baby and try to revive him to no avail.

There is an elaborate funeral service by the bird flock and the little boy clearly feels guilty. During the burial it begins raining and the rain revives the baby bird. The little boy breaks up the gun and feeds the birds.

The harm to children – or baby animals – is an on-going theme to the series. It's particularly jarring to see the little boy take aim at the bird.

"Dancing on the Moon" has been a fan favorite. Again built around a song, "Dancing on the Moon," the slender plot has a rocket ship carrying a variety of animal couples to the moon for a post-wedding trip. The cat couple is accidentally separated.

This is a hearty slice of Fleischer fantasy. There is really no story to speak off and yes, the animal couples actually dance on the moon. The couples go the moon, have a good time and return to Earth.

There are some very nice 3-D sets on the moon and the one of the rocket is very memorable.

"Somewhere in Dreamland," (1936) is perhaps the ultimate harm to children short in the series, because the harm was so relatable, especially in the Depression. The short features two children who are walking through a town during winter looking for firewood. They are in tattered clothing and shoeless. A group of merchants see them and devise a plan to help.

Their mother can't provide for them and the children's only real escape is through the dreams of being in a place where everything they don't have is provided in abundance. When they awake the merchants have given them food and clothing.

Considering the level of poverty caused by the Great Depression one wonders how audiences responded. A child going hungry was reality for many. This cartoon just doesn't pull at heartstrings, it rips your heart out of your chest.

The 3-D sets are reserved for the children's trip to Dreamland where they can get clothes and food.

"The Little Stranger" (1936) continues the efforts in sentiment. A hen secretly puts one of her eggs in the nest of a duck, creating confusion for the mother duck. When a hungry hawk attacks the ducks the chick saves his siblings. A chase into an old mill results is the defeat of the hawk and the acceptance of the chick by the ducks.

"Cobweb Hotel" (1936) is pure Fleischer with a spider running a "hotel" for insects – actually an old roll-top desk. The spider introduces his business by singing a song about the hotel. As he sings the camera pans across the desk to reveal insects trapped in their "rooms."

Enter a newly wed fly couple – the husband is a "flyweight" boxing champion – and while the spider prepares the room by laying out a new web, the couple rides a dial telephone and a blotter. Once in the room, they hear the cries of the caught fly next door and look into the camera with horror.

The spider then approaches them and the husband escapes to fight the spider. His wife then frees the other insects that join into the fight.

The cartoon is inventive, funny and actually quite scary at times. Jack Mercer provides a memorably creepy voice for the spider. The use of a 3-D set is limited to the opening scene, unfortunately. Like several of the others in the series, this cartoon features an original song by Sammy Timberg and Bob Rothberg.

"Greedy Humpty Dumpty" (1936) has a certain element of horror as well in the form of "human" greed. King Humpty Dumpty is obsessed with gold and commands the members of his fairy tale kingdom to build the tower on his castle high enough for him to take the gold he believes is in the sun. He is even seen snapping a whip! Reaching the sun (!) his tower topples and he falls to the ground and breaks into many pieces.

"Hawaiian Birds" (1936) has a wonderful set that figures prominently in the beginning of the cartoon. The cartoon deals with a theme that was seen in quite of number of Fleischer shorts: a character being seduced away from love and home to find out their choice was not a good one and they return to their true life.

In this case a bird from Hawaii joins the traveling show of "Big City Orioles" and her sweetheart travels "north" to find her. The short has a second 3-D set – a big city in winter – that provides a visual counterpoint to the set in the opening. This short also has a climatic scene involving a suicide attempt.

"Play Safe" (1936) is another child in peril cartoon with a young boy in love with trains escaping the safety of his yard and the protection of the family dog to go to a parked train. He falls from the train car and onto the tracks where he has a vivid dream.

In this dream/nightmare one of the best 3-D sets was used: a train going through a mountainous landscape. It's very impressive. Again, horror elements are used in the nightmare with anthropomorphized train engines about to collide and whistle and scream at each other.

Orphans who receive defective gifts for Christmas is the theme for "Christmas Comes But Once a Year" (1936) setting stage for Betty Boop's Grampy, known for his inventions, to bring some holiday happiness. This is essentially a color Boop spin-off short and the Grampy character is entertaining.

"Little Lambkins (1937), directed by Dave Tendlar, tells the story of family moving from the country to the city with the child of family bitterly protesting as he has to leave his playmates, a racoon and a squirrel, behind. The apartment has many "modern" – think science fiction-like – amenities which the kid manages to sabotage so the family would move back.

Although it has a fun cartoony style, it features an obnoxious main character.

One of the features of the Motion Picture Herald in 1930s and '40s was brief reviews from exhibitors, which give something of a sense of the how audiences accepted or rejected films. The theater owners and managers who contributed the reviews were from all around the country in both big and small markets.

In the Jan. 9, 1937 edition several Color Classics are mentioned. The manager of the Palace Theater in Pemacook, NH called "Greedy Humpty Dumpty" "a very good color cartoon," while the representative of the Princess Theater in Lincoln, KS, wrote, "very pretty coloring in this cartoon and worth a spot on any program."

"Musical Moments" was reviewed in the Film Daily on Nov. 1, 1935. "Presenting a group of old time songs, with appropriate scenic accompaniment, this color cartoon contains an entertaining concoction of melody, sentiment and comedy. The 'memories' unfurl as an old couple sit before the fireplace and go through their album, recalling earlier days."

This review that was printed in the December 1937 edition of World Film News reflects an interesting perspective: "Most people number among their acquaintances the human approximation to a Donald or a Pluto, and the lion conductor in Mr. Max Fleischer's 'Car-tune Portrait,' is a familiar type. He is earnest, he is sincere, he is a lion with a purpose. He addresses the audience in a manner that is a mixture of commercial showmanship and moral 'uplift.'

"The orchestra is one with the conductor's baton and them something goes wrong, a false note creeps in, a joke is made and the concert collapses into an uproarious free-fight. There is something in these animal creations which is charmingly reminiscent of the moods of childhood. At one solemn moment intensely and self-righteously solemn; the next throwing all restraint to the winds and thinking it the best joke in the world to break a violin over a neighbour's head. Mr. Fleischer's animals are not as highly individualized, as are those of Mr. Walt Disney, though it will take a long time to forget those hippopotami blowing away through their instruments as though their lives depended on it.

"Critical summary: The Max Fleischer cartoons have never received their just recognition for, alike all other cartoon pictures, they have been hopelessly over-shadowed by the works of Walt Disney. Certainly Disney has always been a long way ahead of his rivals in his ability to create strongly individualized characters in his composition and colouring and above all in his fantasy, revealed just recently at its exquisite bets in "The Old Mill.' But the Fleischer cartoons have been frequently outstanding – one remembers with pleasure 'The Elephant Never

Forgets,' '[Poor] Cinderella,' 'Time for Love,' and 'Dancing on the Moon' with their engaging theme songs and most noticeable stereoscopic effects – and besides this series of Color Classic there is also, of, course the inimitable Popeye to prove that Disney is not the only person who can create forceful characters.

"Popeye has recently appeared in colour, following Mickey mouse's lead in 'The Band Concert,' and his spinach is almost as well known as Donald Duck's 'Wanna fight?' Fleischer, no doubt, will never make anything like 'Water Babies,' "Lullaby Land' or "The Old Mill,' but has yet the art of working in a happy word of unreality and make-believe and his little pictures should be given the praise they merit."

"The Fresh Vegetable Mystery" (1939) seems in many ways a stereotypical Fleischer cartoon: a fun concept playing with the tropes of a police mystery with some outrageous action. It's overnight in a kitchen and all the vegetables are asleep with the exception of the police – all (root) beer-swilling Irish potatoes.

A mysterious kidnapper is at work, though, abducting some baby carrots. The police round up the wrong suspects and torture them for a confession – yes, that's pretty dark even by the standards at the time.

The short was directed by Myron Waldman who told me that he gave long-time studio employee Edith Vernick an opportunity to animate for the first time. Waldman had championed the career of Lillian Friedman as an animator and he tried to do the same for Vernick. Unfortunately, he explained that while her work was good, she could not keep up the pace to animate at the studio.

1940's "Ants in the Plants, directed by Waldman, is also thoroughly a Fleischer cartoon with a level of grotesquery that is part of the studio's DNA. The short goes back to series' roots by using the studio's 3-D process at the opening of the cartoons.

An anteater is going to attack an ant colony and the short revolves around the acceptance of the threat and their preparations to fight him. The anteater design is truly horrifying and Sammy Timberg provides a jaunty yet vaguely militaristic song.

***

Many of the Color Classics had beautiful backgrounds and in a 1937 essay Erich Schenk who headed up the department contributed an essay on background for the studio's newsletter:

"Outside of the artistic side of the work in this department, it is undoubtedly the one that offers the greatest variety jobs. Just where it fits into work of the other departments has never been explained. I have a suspicion that it will always start with the animation and end up with the cameras.

"The most interesting part and probably the most attractive one is that the scenery used in the various pictures takes us into every possible and impossible surrounding.

"In the old days the animator made his own backgrounds just as he made his own in between him, inking, and so forth. Those first backgrounds consisted, for the most part of only a horizontal line or two and perhaps a tree trunk in the foreground. That was the time when the audience got a thrill out of merely seeing a drawn figure move on the screen.

"Some five years ago the Fleischer studios started to develop a background department and today we have a regular art department consisting of 12 members and we are still growing.

"The work which is done in the background department is of course mainly the painting of backgrounds and setbacks but there is other work such as retouching photographs and cells, posters, titles and various kinds of lettering jobs.

"Until recent times the animator made a rough sketch which was often a puzzle to the background workers today. Whenever it is possible a background artist works with a group of animators making careful layouts of the backgrounds and setbacks. The sketches for flat backgrounds or than traced on Bristol board or any other suitable paper and then the sketch is rendered or washed in. Making a wash means to apply a tone or tent of watercolor to the paper. Most of our backgrounds are rendered in sepia, a water color which has a brown tone, but sometimes they are done partly or even wholly in opaque colors the same that is used for coloring the cels. They have now added oil colors to above mentioned mediums.

"Perhaps some of you think that all we do is paint pretty pictures, or at least try to, but in reality, it is a different matter. First of all, we are not painting a whole picture, but only a half and that half is the second half, which has to be fitted to the first half, which is the animation. Animation is of course the most important part in a scene.

"What we really paint is only the surroundings or environment for the characters and that has to be done in such a way as to show all the objects necessary to the scene. At the same time they should not require attention or in themselves unless the story requires it. The audience should not be in doubt as to the place of action but merely assisted and in understanding the action itself. The best background artist is the one who can sacrifice his own artistic conception of the work, to the benefit of that first half of the picture which he is not doing. Of course we are acquainted with the first half of the picture by the sample cells. These are cells taken out of a scene, ink and colored for that purpose. The cels tell the artist where to put his lights and darks and where they keep the background free from unnecessary detail and someone. There is no definite rule of how much a background should carry or far it should be worked out it depends on the story the characters and the action, the length of the scene and the continuity and so forth.

"If a few lines will be enough for a background it is all that should be used and one whatever it is it should be made to fit the characters in the story just a running board and a naked wall can be made interesting and a good artist can with a few washes suggest the distance between the character and the wall. If on the other hand, there is too much detail in the background we can use the elimination process and do away with as many lines as possible, pulling the groups of objects together and working more from the suggestive side.

"A very powerful and picturesque means of expression is the silhouette, which is quite frequently used on backgrounds and occasionally in the animation, but I would like to see a change of colors on the characters by entering or leaving a shadow. It is not with the idea of making the business more complex than it is, it would only mean one single line of animation more; the one that suggests the beginning and the end of the shadow. It could also be used to indicate distance and speed and panoramas, where repeated action is used. I believe that this addition would result in a closer tie between the characters and backgrounds and perhaps would add a third dimension appearance to our pictures.

"This article is not meant to be a complete view of the background department and I would be glad to explain in detail any ambiguous details that may have had be omitted owing to the lack of space just come up and see me sometime. WHEN I'M NOT BUSY.

"I want to thank the writers for their interesting stories and explanations about animation timing and so forth which of appeared in the Fleischer Animated News."

***

Interestingly enough, the Color Classics provided the studio with half of its Academy Award nominations. The studio had received a nomination for "Popeye the Sailor Meets Sinbad the Sailor" in 1936.

The Color Classic "Educated Fish" was nominated in 1937. "Hunky and Spunky" received the nomination in 1938. The last Fleischer short to be nominated was "Superman" in 1941.

From the first nomination in 1931-1932 to 1939 the Disney Studio won every award in the animated short category.

"Educated Fish" features a young fish who isn't interested in learning about the dangers of fishing hooks, poles and bait until of course he encounters them. It also has a fun song by Sammy Timburg, but no 3-D sets.

In 1939, the studio made a semi-sequel, "Small Fry" featuring the same wise guy young fish. Again there was a clever song and no 3-D sets, and the same character design was used for the youthful delinquent fish. This time he is cutting school to hang out in the pool room where he wants to be a "big fry." The older fish decide to pay him a lesson and there is a marvelous sequence in which they frighten him through an initiation process.

Myron Waldman developed the Hunky and Spunky characters and format. The two burros – a mother and child – wander through the American West. The first one was

Original promotional art for the Hunky and Spunky series. (Author's collection).

MADE OF PEN & INK: FLEISCHER STUDIOS

deemed enough of a success there were seven more cartoons produced in the series. Generally in the eight-cartoon series, the story lines revolved around the youngster getting into trouble and mom rescuing him. In many of the shorts they are roaming wild, but in "Vitamin Hay," they are clearly domesticated.

Waldman told me he much preferred doing cartoons with sentiment than with violent gags and there was plenty of sentiment in this series.

The end of the Color Classic series came in 1941 with the release of "Vitamin Hay," the last cartoon in the Hunky and Spunky series.

By that time, the studio was busy with the Animated Antics series, the Stone Age cartoons, and the series featuring Gabby from "Gulliver's Travels." None of these series enjoyed the lasting popularity of the Color Classics.

***

Model sheet for Hunky and Spunky. (Author's collection).

In the October 1938 edition of the National Board of Review magazine published a transcript of "an instructional talk" about the medium by Fleischer animator Thomas Moore and voice and story artist Jack Mercer, described as the studio's "director of dialog," to the listeners of WNYC in New York City.

In an industry where generally the only people who received press attention were the producers, it's refreshing to see these two talented men have a bit of the spotlight, even if it reads like a comedy routine at times. What is fascinating to me is this was carefully scripted and yet there was no mention of Max or Dave Fleischer, especially Dave's role in the creative process. The other glaring note is at no time is it revealed that Mercer is the voice of Popeye.

The announcer prefaced the interview by saying, "If any of you imagine that an animator is an instrument for registering electrical discharges, Mr. Moore will put you right and give a real account of the importance of an animator's work in the drawing and painting of a cartoon. Mr. Mercer hasn't much to say about this side of cartoon making, but he's going to show you who behind the strange sounds and chatter that accompany the characters in a cartoon."

Mercer: Mr. Announcer, this might be a little irregular, but I wonder if you would do me a favor by allowing me to be the interviewer this evening. I've always wanted to put Mr. Moore on the spot.

Announcer: Surely, go ahead, the mic is yours.

Mercer: Good evening, Mr. Moore.

Moore: Hello Jack, what are you doing here?

Mercer: I'm going to be the interviewer so just assume that I know nothing at all about the making of cartoons.

Moore: What do you mean – assume?

Mercer: I walked into that. Well, on with the interview. I'm sure everyone is interested in animated cartoons. Will you give us something of a history?

Moore: Thomas Edison experimented with the idea of animated drawings as early as 1900, but the first man to make an animated cartoon film was the great cartoonist Windsor (sic) McCay. The idea struck him as he observed his young son flipping the pages of a book of 'Magic Pictures.' After many months of extensive study, he made an animated version of his cartoon strip, 'Little Nemo in Slumberland.' But he considered this film only an experiment and in 1909, two years after his first attempt, he made the first film for exhibition, 'Gertie the Dinosaur." Prior to 1922 most animated cartoons were made with paper cutouts and were pretty crude.

Mercer: You mean sorta like cutting out paper dolls, eh?

Moore: Yes exactly, you should know. The drawings of the characters in different positions were cut out and pasted over a simple background and then photographed in sequence. But since that time many improvements have been made so that today we have the full-length cartoon.

Mercer: A great many people seem to think that the full-length cartoon involves a different and more complicated process of production.

Moore: The only real difference is a matter of length, the feature being much longer permits the story to be told with more finesse and detail. The average short requires about 10,000 drawings and takes approximately seven minutes to be shown on the screen, while the full-length feature requires more than a quarter-million drawings and runs over an hour.

Mercer: There certainly has been a great advance made in the industry. Why don't you tell our listeners how the work on a modern cartoon begins?

Moore: Gladly, the modern studio is a beehive of activity, highly systemized.

Mercer: In simple language you mean they do a lot of work.

Moore: It takes over 230 artists and technicians at least 10 weeks to prepare the drawings, which make up an animated movie cartoon. Work on the cartoon begins when the musical director and the scenario writers call into conference a few of the head artist animators (Mercer, ad lib: Tell 'em I'm in the Story Department). They discuss the general lines of the plot and principal gags. The music which is to be adapted to the plot is selected. By the way Jack you are in the Story Department. I'm sure you could explain just how your department functions.

Mercer: Huh? Oh. To be sure. To be sure. Well the first thing we do is try to get an idea or facsimile –

Moore: (taking up) And after getting the idea of a synopsis, the story men write a script in complete form for the animators. In order to do this they must know all of the cartoon characters intimately – how they think and how they react. They must know the limitations imposed upon them by the censors by the audiences and by the technicalities of production. In other words, a certain subject might be condoned by one country and barred by another. One community might be flattered by an incident that would insult the next. You may like picture that I thought dull and boring. So if the script can please some of the people part of the time then the job is well done.

Mercer: Then the story goes to the Animation Department and that's how we write stories.

Moore: Very good Jack. The head animator upon receiving the new story visualizes the picture and roughly lays it out illustrating each scene. He then calls his group together for a conference when through analysis and discussion they try to get into the mood of the story. The scenes are then divided amongst the group and they start to work. And that is where the fun begins. If you unexpectedly walked into a group of animators at work you would probably be amazed at what you saw. For the chances are, you would find one chap standing in front of a full-size mirror gesticulating wildly and making horrible faces at himself. Another on roller skates in the center of the room would be trying to act like Olive Oyl while a couple of his colleagues offer helpful suggestions such as: 'Tom try that fall again, only this time throw your feet higher so that when you land your weight is more concentrated in one spot. We want to see how high you bounce.'

The survivors then sit at their desks and attempt to draw on paper what they saw. An animator never knows what he may be called on to draw next. It might range from a pygmy wedding ceremony to a Giant baseball game.

Mercer: Personally I'm a Brooklyn fan.

Moore: You would be.

Mercer I resemble that remark!

Moore: At this point I'd like to make an observation. In order to be an animator one must be slightly wacky.

Mercer: You should make a very successful animator Mr. Moore.

Moore: Thank you so much. But drawing is not the only phase of the animator's work, for he must give complete instructions to each department as to the handling of his scene. He is director, actor, technician.

Mercer: And wacky.

Moore: The animator does not make ever drawing, for that would take up too much of his time. He only makes the extremes or key drawings and then an assist or 'in-betweener,' completes the scene. For instance, if he wants to animate an apple falling from a tree, he makes one drawing of the apple as it starts to fall and another at the end of the fall. The in-betweeners then make the drawings that will carry the apple from one position to the other. The animator regulates the speed of the fall by indicating the number of drawings that must be made between the two positions. When the animator starts his scene of the apple falling, he first makes a rough drawing or layout to serve as a guide to the Background Department for every action has to take place in a proper setting or location. With this guide the background artists make a detailed and carefully rendered watercolor drawing of the scene.

Mercer: And that completes the work on the picture.

Moore: No, the picture is far from being completed after the animators have done their job and an enormous volume of technical work is necessary before the shooting or photography can take place. In the Inking Department, each drawing is traced on transparent celluloids. This work plays a very important part in the general scheme of preparing for the camera.

Mercer: Oh, then the drawings are ready for photographing?

Moore: No the Coloring Department now receives the celluloids together with the corresponding animator's drawings. The colorers or opaquers fill in all the blank spaces between the ink lines with paint of various shades. All colors and shades are sued for the purpose. This process is highly technical and the task is very arduous, but very important, as only a perfectly colored set of drawings will result in clear and perfect photography.

Mercer: Well how do you photograph these individual drawings so that they will appear to move?

Moore: The photographing process or cartoons is essentially the same as in regular moving pictures. The same type of camera catches the progressive movements of the cartoon character recording each successive movement. The difference between the regular and the cartoon camera is only in the speed of the operation. When filming a regular moving picture the camera runs 90 feet of film per minute. Not so the cartoon camera where individual drawings are be photographed. The work here proceeds very slowly because of the time spent by the operator for removing the photographed drawing and then assembling and adjusting the celluloids for the next photograph. One foot of film may take a whole hour to photograph and the camera instead of photographing 90 feet a minute as in the case of the regular moving picture may take a whole day to photograph 30 feet of cartoon film.

Mercer: Now we come to the process, which plays so great a part in making moving pictures today and especially cartoons. The application of sound is called "Sound Synchronization."

Moore: That's right. In the spacious projection room the sound director, vocal artists and the effects men face the screen. They watch the running film harmonizing the voices and the sound effects while the picture is being projected. Microphones in effective positions in the recording room pick up and carry the sound over wires to a soundproof room, where wax and film records are made. The recording thus made is called a 'take' and the film record is called a 'sound track.' The picture is projected in the screen a second time while the wax record is 'played back.' The directors now get the result of their first synchronized effort pick the flaws and make the necessary corrections for the second take to follow. This procedure may be repeated again and again until a perfect or satisfactory 'take' is accomplished, after which the played back wax record is discarded. The film "sound track" is then developed and transferred to the picture film. This is called the finished negative from which the prints are made. Any number of prints can be made from a single negative. The animated cartoon is now ready for distribution. (Pause) Jack, Jack, oh Jack, wake up!

Mercer (adlib) Where am I?

Moore: Now suppose I ask you a few questions for a change.

Mercer: Why, for sure, for sure.

Moore: Inasmuch as you are in the Sound Department as well as the Story Department, perhaps you will demonstrate for us how you make some of the sounds.

Mercer: I'd be glad to.

Moore: Then suppose you give us your interpretation of a chick.

Mercer: Chicken? Mm-mm (gives imitation)

Moore: I think that one laid an egg.

Mercer: How's this for a cow? (gives imitation)

Moore: Mm – Strictly off the cob.

Mercer: Well, you should enjoy this one. It's a pig that gets caught in the fence. The farmer saw into the fence and the pig is freed. (gives imitation)

Moore: The pig is very natural.

Mercer: If you don't like those imitations, let us see what you can do.

Moore: Oh, it's easy. Why I can imitate three different dogs.

Mercer: All right, go ahead.

Moore: This one is the Mexican Chu-wa-wa [sic]. (gives imitation)

Mercer: Uh-huh.

Moore: Next, the whippet (repeats same imitation)

Mercer: Oh. That's the whippet, eh?

Moore: And this one will be the Dalmatian Bloodhound. (repeats same imitation)

Mercer: Oh, those were three different dogs, eh? I must admit that was pretty good. Suppose we team up and do a cat and dog fight. You do the three dogs and I'll do the cat.

Mercer and Moore: Ad lib.

Here is a trade ad for the 1935 - 1936 season of Color Classics.

This trade ad emphasizes the Color Classics are no other cartoon series in the market.

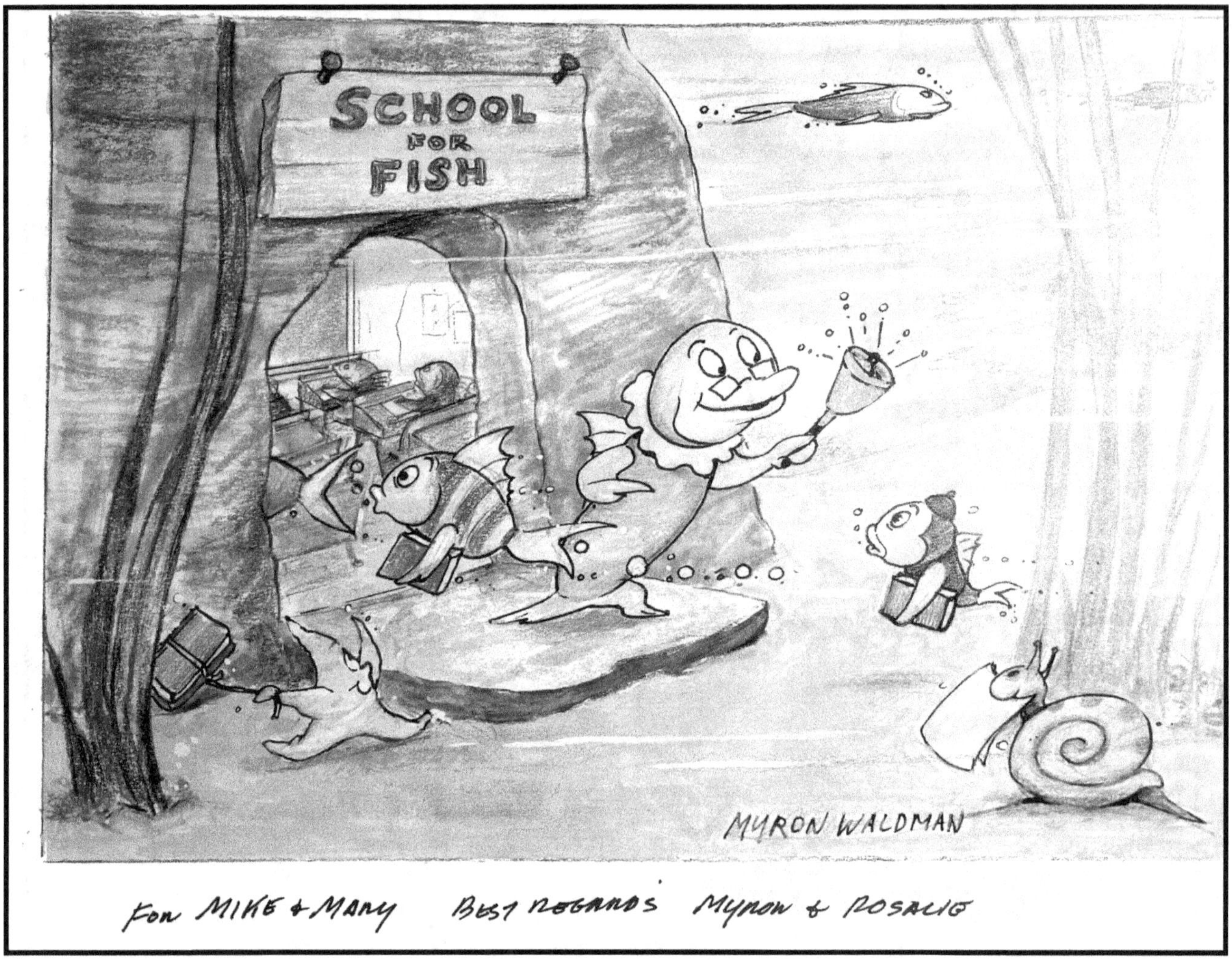
SCHOOL
FOR
FISH
MYRON WALDMAN
For MIKE & MARY Best Regards Myron & Rosalie

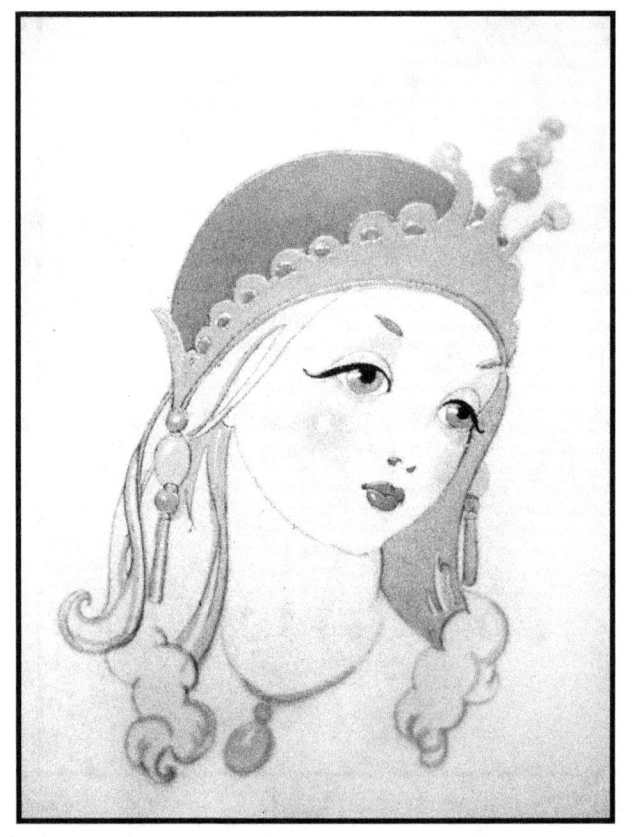

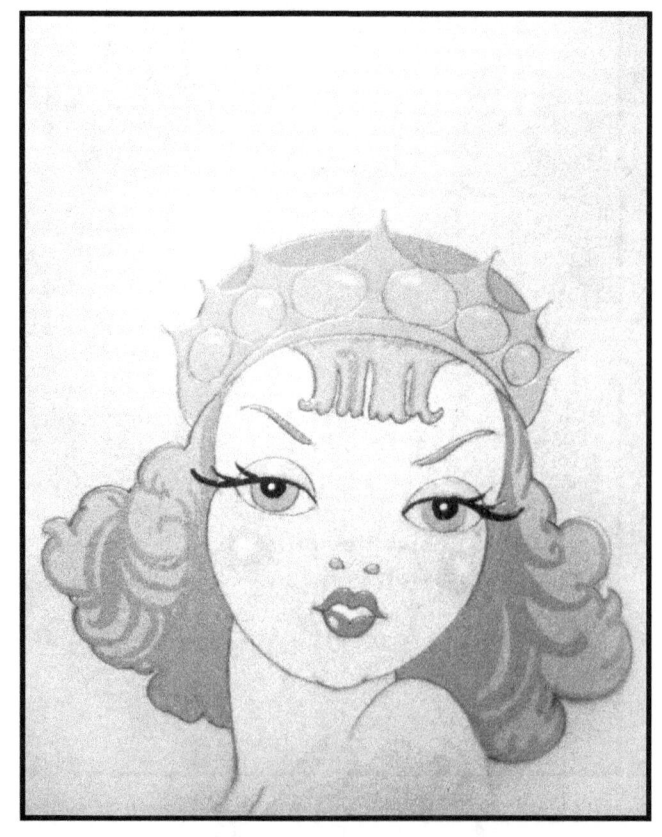

Animator and director Myron Waldman re-created a scene from the Color Classic "Educated Fish" in the 1990s. Author's collection.

When I met Ruth Kneitel in the 1970s, she allowed me to photograph several original drawings that had been completed as part of an effort to launch a cartoon about mermaids. She did not know what series the cartoon would have been part of, and I wondered if drawings might have been for a Color Classic. The originals are quite striking and she said they were displayed in the studio. The final drawing showing an Olive Oyl-like character was added anonymously to the others as a gag and she thought Willard Bowsky had done that drawing. Along with the images was a story treatment with many notes on the side in red pencil.

She told me those notes were from Max. That is all she knew, but she wanted me to see that Max maintained an interest in the content of the shorts. (Author's collection).

A Popeye Animated Cartoon begins its existence at a story conference in the New York offices of the Fleischer Studios. William Turner, in the center, is the story chief.

LIFE CYCLE OF POPEYE

Willard Bowsky is one of six head animators who do the basic drawings. They often add gags of their own invention.

Elzie Segar originally created Popeye as a comic strip character. Hearst's King Features exploited his talents.

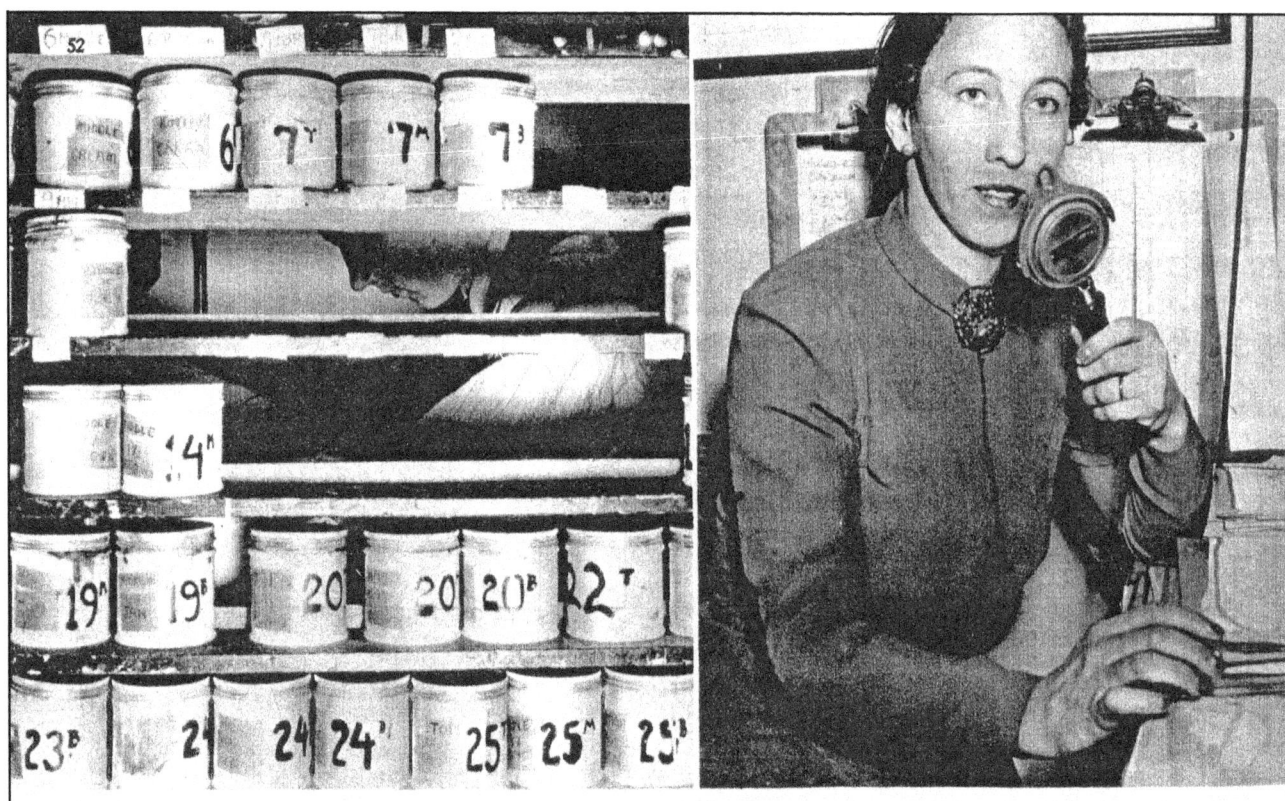

Fifty young artists use between 1,000 and 1,500 shades of paint to color the cells. Each section of a cell is marked with the number of the shade desired by the color experts.

Shayne Miller of the background department is painting a scene for a pan shot. Fleischer Studios require 180 gallons of paint every year in the production of their thirty-six animated cartoons.

Liesel Howsen is in charge of the coloring department. Through the mike she is telling her assistants that their fifteen minute afternoon rest is finished. She is German.

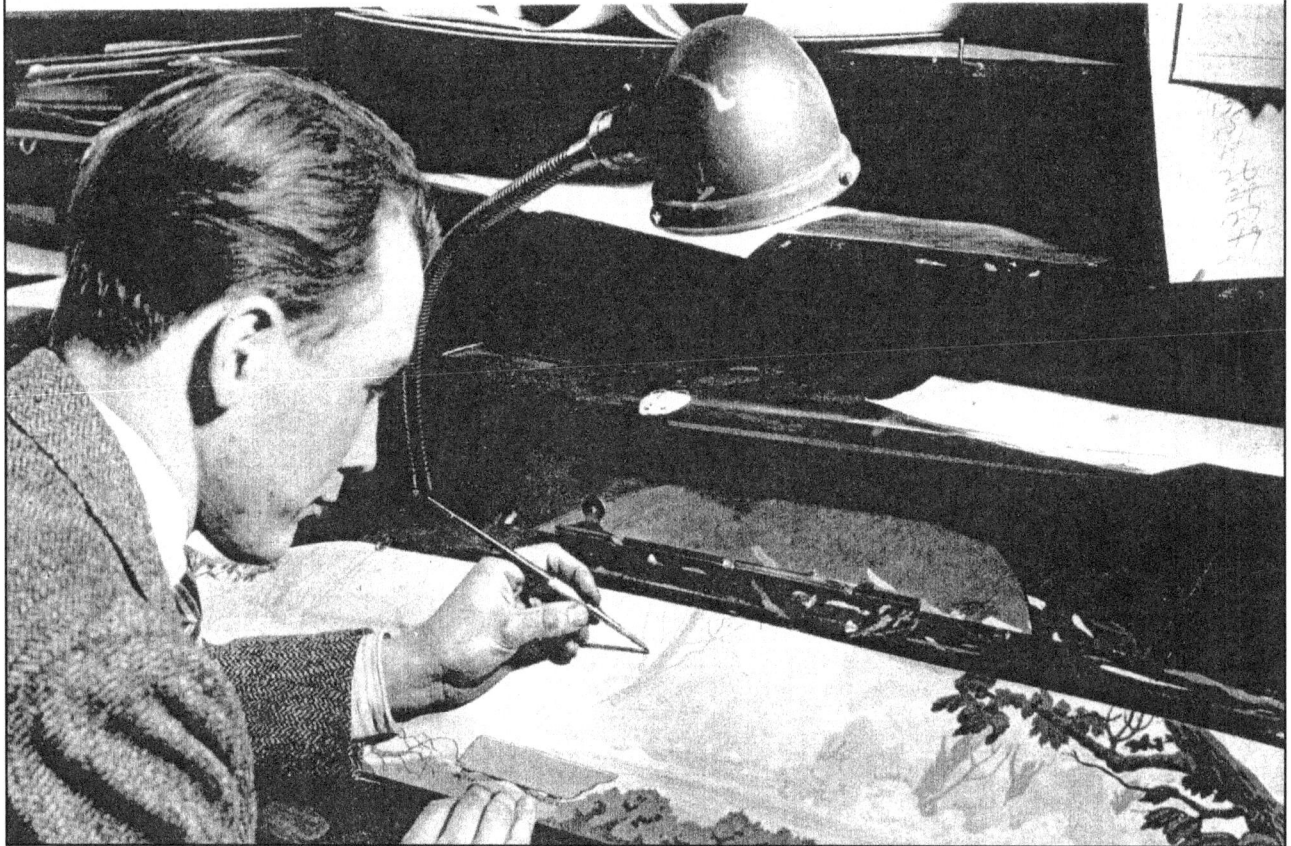

Thirty "in-betweeners" take the head animators' work and fill in to give an impression of smooth action. To show a character taking one step, twenty-four drawings may be needed.

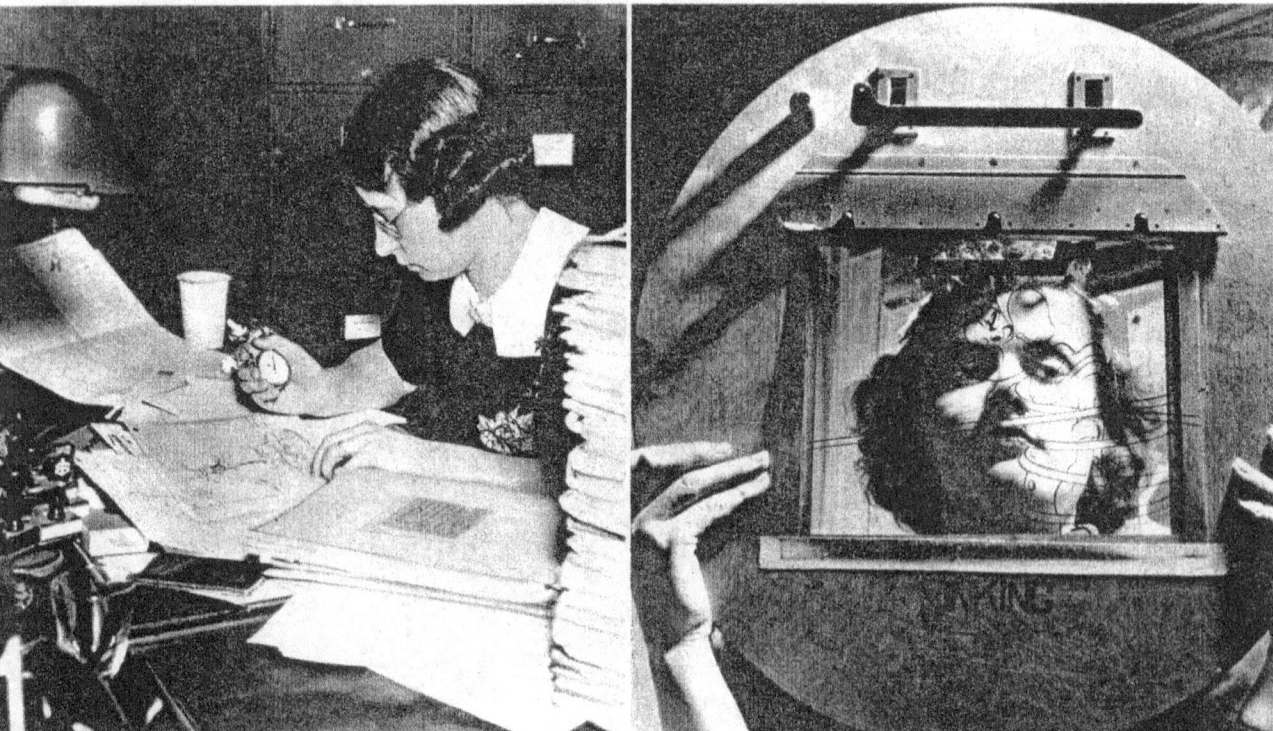

Nelly Sanborn heads the timing and general check-up department. She leafs through the drawings to see that the animation is realistic. In the business for more than twenty years, she rarely needs her stop watch.

Eighteen-year-old Marion White is one of thirty members of the inking department whose job it is to transfer the pencilled drawings of the animators to celluloid panels or "cells" with pen and India ink.

MADE OF PEN & INK: FLEISCHER STUDIOS

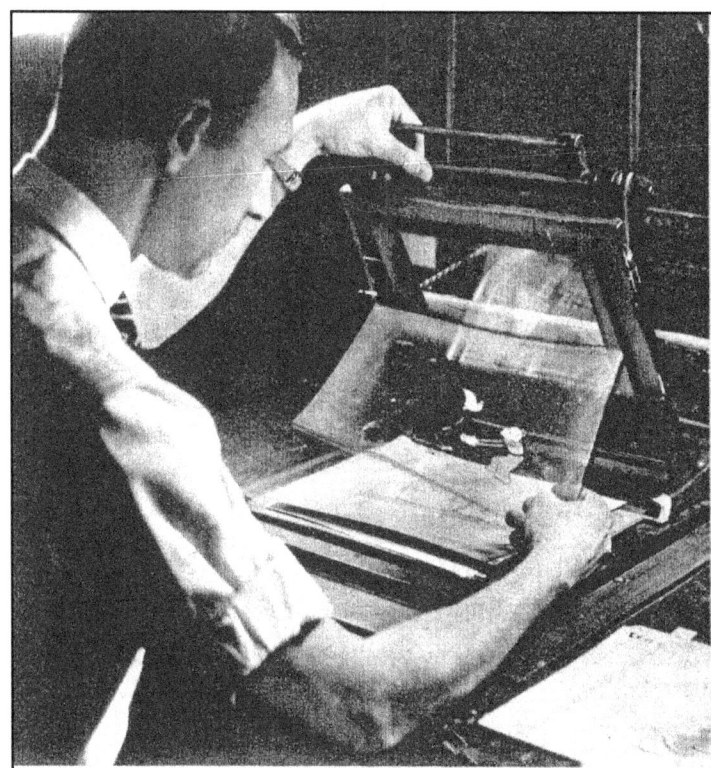

Charles Schettler, head technician, pulls down the glass plate of a flat background camera and automatically records a shot; 12,000 shots make up a complete cartoon.

Max Fleischer, Popeye's boss, observes a miniature set built for the special tri-dimensional camera developed by him. The stage is a revolving one and helps give an impression of motion and depth.

The technicolor camera takes a red, blue and green shot of each cell placed before it. These are then superimposed. A revolving stage has also been placed behind the camera frame.

In the mid-1930s, a New York newspaper did the following photo essay of the Fleischer Studio. You will see Dave Fleischer, Sammy Timburg and Lou Fleischer hamming for the camera at the piano as well as two photos of Timburg conducting the band and Dave working with Jack Mercer and Mae Questel.

When the directors are satisfied with the quality of the reproduction, it is then transferred to a regulation sound track. Sound effects men are expected to produce any known effect at a moment's notice. They employ a large variety of horns and gourds.

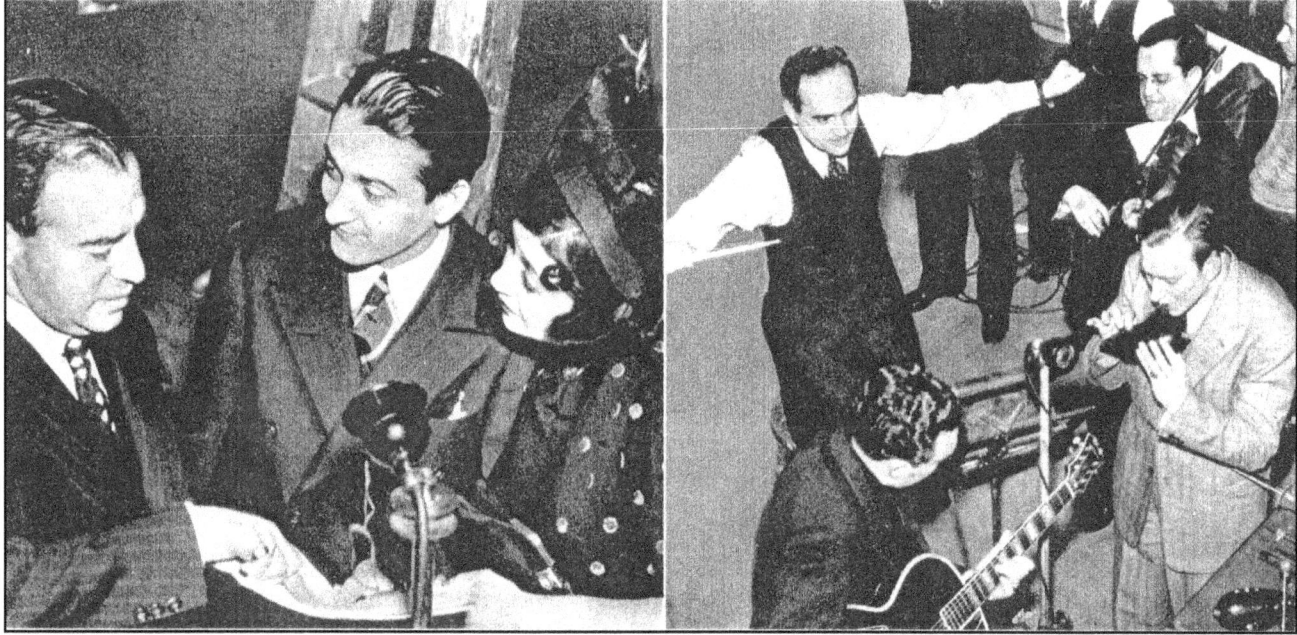

Sound recording for a Popeye cartoon takes place at the Paramount News Building in New York. During actual recording, the room is dark while performers watch the silent film being run off.

Vice-president Dave Fleischer here gives last minute instructions to Jack Mercer, the voice of Popeye, and May Questel, the original Betty Boop girl, who also pinch-hits for Olive Oyl.

Sam Timberg arranges the music for the animated cartoon and directs the crew of musicians, who are forced to perform on instruments which as a rule are used only by hill billy orchestras.

The Fleischer Popeye shorts soon became a big hit with exhibitors and audiences after their introduction.

Chapter Five

Until the release of the Fleischer Popeye cartoons by Warner Home Video in 2008, the only ways to assess the long-running series was generally by contemporary written accounts, memories or what titles had lapsed into the public domain.

One of the great injustices in animation scholarship was it took decades of prerecorded home video to finally see the Popeye shorts produced by the Fleischers released in a way that invited a new look.

Certainly hardcore animation fans and scholars understood the place the Popeye series has in animation history, but due to several factors the more casual fan had a stunted perspective due to what was available to see.

The irony was the Popeye cartoons in many ways were staples of TV once released to the medium in the 1950s. Baby Boomers grew up watching the shorts on the kid shows that were produced by many local TV stations. Those shorts stayed on-air until the prejudice against black and white production manifested itself among TV programmers in the 1970s.

It's difficult to understand what the Popeye series meant to the Fleischer Studio and what it meant to audiences when it debuted in 1933. This was the first time Max had licensed a comic strip character, a common practice in the silent era during which the funny pages were regularly raided for content. William Randolph Hearst even established an animation studio to make animated versions of some of the strips syndicated by his King Features company.

George Herriman's Krazy Kat had been the subject of many cartoons, although few, if any of them, truly reflected George Herriman's brilliant drawing style or narrative. Bud Fisher had been reportedly more involved in several series of Mutt and Jeff shorts.

While licensing a comic strip may not have been an oddity for the industry as whole, it was new to Max and his staff. The decision certainly pushed the studio away from its animal/human universe of the Betty Boop series and kept it largely away from the funny animals that dominated animation at the time.

The decision also meant that, for better or worse, Max was involved with a pre-sold property. E.C. Segar's creation of "Thimble Theater," Popeye's newsprint home, was enormously popular. While any cartoon Max would produce would find a ready audience, the question was whether or not the results would satisfy the fans.

Popeye had made his debut in E.C. Segar's "Thimble Theater" in 1929. The strip was popular but Popeye's introduction as a secondary character changed the story trajectory as well as the comic strip's popularity.

"Thimble Theater" told the misadventures of the Oyl family: the scheming Castor, his sister Olive and Olive's boyfriend Ham Gravy. In a story line that started Sept. 10, 1928, Castor has obtained Bernice the Wiffle Hen, a bird with miraculous powers originally from Africa. Castor finds out that Bernice is also known as "Luck Hen." Stroke her feathers and you can win any game of chance, he explained. Castor decides to buy a boat to go to a remote island off the coast of Africa, but needs a crew.

He sees a sailor and asks, "Hey there, are you a sailor?" The reply is "Ja think I'm a cowboy?" A few strips later we find out his name: Popeye.

Popeye slowly but surely become the center of the strip.

Segar populated his strip with eccentric and often dark characters. If you have not discovered it, you might be surprised at the sophistication of the writing.

With the decline of newspapers today, it may be difficult to understand that newspapers relied on comic strips on a selling point. Newspapers actually promoted their selections of strips. "Thimble Theater," especially after the introduction of Popeye, expertly blended humor with adventure.

Segar told stories that lasted weeks, months and his readers loved it.

Certainly in the last few years – when the name "Popeye" conjured up thoughts of animation – more and more efforts have been made to shine the spotlight deservedly so on Segar as a master storyteller and cartoonist. At the same time there has been criticism of the Fleischer/Famous shorts, especially from some comic strip scholars.

In his essay introducing the first volume of Segar comic strips published by Fantagraphics Books in 2006, cartoonist and writer Jules Feiffer wrote, "The animated Popeyes didn't bother with character, wit or nuance. There was but one story, repeated thousands of times in endless versions: Popeye fighting Bluto over Olive Oyl and able to win the end only because he was lucky enough to find a can of spinach. Jeez!

"It was a wildly successful animated series moving from Paramount to Famous Studios to TV and most of it, 60 years-worth dates badly. Its one lasting charm remains the voices of the actors who played Popeye and Olive Oyl, Jack Mercer and Mae Questel," Feiffer noted.

While I respect and admire Feiffer's work – yes I even liked the "Popeye" feature he wrote that was directed by Robert Altman – he falls into the trap of putting all of the Popeye shorts into the same barrel, a move that is both unfair and indicates a lack of scholarship.

The bottom line to a series of anything in popular culture is there are highs and lows. There are Popeye cartoons produced by Max that aren't very funny or charming, but overall the series shows how the studio successfully brought forth a Popeye I'm willing to bet that Segar recognized and liked.

Segar did do several promotional drawings to publicize the cartoons, but that appears to be the extent of his involvement.

And Segar received screen credit for his creation, something that not every cartoonist of his era was able to achieve.

Segar's original Popeye stories are wonderful: funny, yet cynical and a vehicle for social commentary at times. The comic strip Popeye himself evolved from a crusty old sailor into truly a role model for humanity. For instance, in December of 1933, Segar started a story called "Plunder Island," that ran eight months. The story details how Popeye eventually wins a fortune from the Sea Hag and returns a multi-millionaire.

He's not satisfied, though, and gives all of his money away to deserving people. He realizes he is now as poverty-stricken as he was when he first started his adventure. Popeye said, "It took munts to find that treasure an' now two days after I gets home with it I yam broke – that's funny! – I gived away me money, but I got millings of dollars worth of good feelins under me chest an' tha's why I yam happy."

Popeye is a true literary character. Readers could relate to the comic strip Popeye on a level similar to a character in a novel. Although it was not evident in the first five or six Fleischer cartoons, the studio began to understand the character and who he was.

The humor was character-based. Popeye operates under a set of rules for his character. While critics may be right about the repetition of the love triangle formula – especially in the Famous shorts – the Fleischer Popeyes presented a nuanced one-eyed sailor as well. He was loyal to his friends, wouldn't throw the first punch, was kind to children and animals and loved Olive despite the fact the Fleischers had carried over her fickleness from the comic strip.

Popeye's slogan, authored by Segar, was also carried into the cartoons. "I yam what I yam, and that's all that I yam" is both an admission of modesty and a declaration of self-esteem.

The studio also recognized the sailor's language and thanks to the wonderful talents of Jack Mercer – whose performance as Popeye was much more nuanced than that of Billy Costello, the character's first voice actor – Segar's language came through.

Despite what some animation critics have written, the Fleischer Popeyes do present a character from which comedy can emerge. The series at its best is character-driven, not just a series of gags.

What the Fleischers could not do within the convention of the seven-minute animated theatrical short was to replicate the serial format of Segar's great stories. One could argue that perhaps if the studio had treated the shorts as a serial with each cartoon a chapter of a longer story the series would have reflected the comic strip more. That is pure speculation.

Doing something such as that could have limited the sales potential of the shorts in a marketplace in which cartoons were rented at differing times by theaters. A connected story would have thrown a monkey wrench into how the cartoons were sold to theaters.

The criticism that too many of the cartoons relied on the Bluto-Popeye rivalry over Olive is valid – especially for the shorts were produced by Famous Studios. During the Fleischer period, though, even when this device was used, the shorts frequently transcended its limitation and showed why more than half a century later they still entertain audiences.

Two-time Fleischer animator James "Shamus" Culhane wrote in his memoir "Talking Animals and Other People" that he had approached Max about producing a short starring Wimpy that would portray him closer to Segar's creation: a morally compromised greedy person who none-the-less can do the right thing. The studio brass didn't care for the suggestion and Culhane presented it as an example of a lack of Max's sophistication.

Segar's strip was ripe with great supporting characters and it took several years before the Fleischers used some of them. Wimpy, Swee' Pea, the Jeep, the Goon and Poopdeck Pappy all made it the screen. It is a shame they were not used more frequently and the cartoons could have been much richer with them.

Regardless of the series' imperfections, the simple fact is many of the Popeyes represented a height in the Fleischer Studio style and of 1930s animation. They were extremely popular cartoons and undoubtedly helped drive the comic strip's popularity as well as the massive merchandising effort by King Features. Their long life on television reaching new generations of fans underscored their appeal and the cartoons' release on DVD was much heralded.

Despite what Jules Feiffer might say many of them did have charm and nuance.

In the 1930s, the gold standard for cartoons were, of course, the Disney Mickey Mouse shorts. I think it's fair to say the sunny tone that typified the Disney shorts was not replicated by the Popeye shorts. The Popeye cartoons were urban, which mirrored the Segar strips. The comic strip Popeye lives in a world of dangerous adventures and imperfect characters (Wimpy was morally compromised, Olive was a fickle flirt) set on waterfronts, wildernesses and towns.

The addition of Popeye and its subsequent huge success meant many changes to the studio and in 1935 Bill Turner, a writer for the studio, posted a nostalgic essay in the studio newsletter. He wrote, "Before becoming troubled with astigmatism at the studio Christmas dinner party I looked over the surprisingly large crows of 160 people – later I would count 320 – and the main thought that struck me was the great strides the business has taken in a comparatively short space of time.

"As an example: there was a dinner party held 12 years ago attended by members from every studio in the business and the crowd numbered less than 100. Less than two-thirds the number of the people working in one studio today.

"After making a few more comparisons I felt and still feel that a few facts on conditions as they were in the old days might prove both interesting and surprising to the addicts of recent years. So here 'tis and let anyone who remembers more than I do expose their age.

"All that was needed to go into business in those days was a Parker pen and pencil set. There were no separate departments everyone working in one room about as large as a good sized doll house. Such departments such as Music, Story, Timing and Backgrounds were unheard of. (Who hears of them now, even?)

"Secretaries, clerks and switchboard operators were something you read about, and the total number of girls in the business could be counted on a three-fingered guy's bum hand.

"It used to be a very difficult business to crash. Everyone knew each other, either personally or by reputation, and when one studio closed it was easy to connect with another. Studios would close quite frequently, sometimes throwing out of work an entire staff of seven or eight people.

"Animators were as scarce as hair on a bald-headed guy and it took about 10 years of apprenticeship before you could hope to be one. Today Fleischers develop animators in about five years in spite of the fact that an animator must know much more today than in former years.

"Of all the old time studios producing pictures as 'Happy Hooligan,' 'Katzenjammer Kids,' 'Little Nemo,' 'Ko-Ko the Clown (Fleischers's), 'Bobby Bumps,' 'Mutt and Jeff,' 'Felix the Cat' 'Col, Heezaliar,' and "The Laughing Cat,' Fleischer's studio is the only one going strong today.

"The place where I saw my first light under a drawing board – Felix the Cat Studio – had a staff of four people. Two animators and two assistants who did the work. By that I mean the assistants inked, traced, colored and photographed and in their spare time washed cels and swept the floor. Later we expanded and hired another fellow.

"The animators animated straight-ahead, leaving no in-between. (How you've been Edith [Vernick]?) We had no cutting room, splicing film by hand. Matching the sprocket holes was like threading a needle. The pictures were run on a portable projector against the wall. In place of a dark room, the camera magazines were loaded in a black bag or overcoat.

"Despite these primeval methods, we still turned out a picture in less than three weeks, photographing it in two days. And here's how: everything was done in black and white with no tone being used. In place of the all cel system the cut and tear system invented by Max and Dave (all paper) or the combination system (paper and cels) were used.

"In the combination system when a figure was held, it was traced onto a cel and the other action was on paper drawings, was photographed underneath it.

"When a character talked, he didn't. He was held still with a titles pasted over his head.

"Most of the actions were repeats. A six drawing repeat sometimes being good for 10 feet [of film.] Pat Sullivan, my old boss, once gave me a 12 drawing repeat of cats going into a theater and said, 'Photograph this until I tell you to stop.' He then went out to lunch. It was all used."

"No exposure sheets were required. There was usually a celebration on the completion of each picture and then the assistants would sit around waiting for the animators to get to work on the next one, The pictures didn't have to be too good or too funny, which they weren't. But to prove that the boys loved their work on those days, I knew an animator who actually married a girl named Anna Mason. Honest."

Max wrote a reaction to Turner's essay and said, "In spite of the humorous and light vein in which Bill handled his article, it is nevertheless quite authentic and true to the facts."

The next year this noting of the changes in the studio were continued by Sydol Sherman in the studio's newsletter. He wrote, "Turning the click backward brings to light the many changes since my first day at the studio [1931].

"Most our animators were opaquers then and these were but a handful or two. There were about 75 people in the organization, occupying three rooms on the tenth floor [of 1600 Broadway in New York City]. In those days, promotions did not necessarily mean going to another room or floor.

"With the addition of Popeye and his party and the color cartoons to the Betty and bouncing ball pictures, lack of necessary space sent us first to the fourth and then to the eighth and fifth floors.

"The complete absence of individual departments, public announcer, newer systems, messengers, studio magazine, relief fund, convenience club, hospital and nurse did not prove much of a drawback. Since we all occupied the one floor, we ran our own errands. Unfortunate cases always received sympathy from everyone and our illnesses were generally cured by aspirin or eyewash. For means of proving talent, there was the gentle act of leaving drawings on the back of one another's desk.

"Studio weddings were as popular then as they are now. Many a week brought to light two to three coming weddings.

"We were banded close together and one man's party was every man's party. Frequent luncheons and outings gave us the opportunity to become better acquainted. Numerous lasting friendships were the results. The annual Christmas dinner proved to be successful not only as a get-together, but in bringing out the talent to be had in our organization.

"It would make an interesting pictorial review, could we re-enact before the camera those changes as they have taken place."

The legend is that Max wondered what was making the elevator attendant in his apartment building laugh so much. When he found out the young man was reading "Thimble Theater," he obtained the rights to the Popeye, despite officials at King Features believing the comic strip sailor was too ugly to be a cartoon star.

Max reportedly closed a deal in November 1932 and interestingly enough Universal announced in February 1933 – as noted in The New Movie Magazine – it was pairing lanky character actor Slim Summerville with Zasu Pitts as Popeye and Olive in a live action comedy based on the comic strip. That film never went into production, although the two were paired in a series of comedies.

It's also interesting that eventually Pitts' distinctive fluttery voice would eventually become the basis for the cartoon Olive's voice.

Rather than launch Popeye into his own series, the studio essentially created a pilot in the guise of a Betty Boop cartoon, entitled "Popeye The Sailor."

According to Richard Fleischer's memoir of his father "Out of the Inkwell: Max Fleischer and the Animation Revolution," the film opened at the Paramount Theater in Manhattan on July 14, 1933.

Richard wrote that his father paid $500 to King Features as a licensing fee and then 17.5 percent of the gross for a 12 cartoon-series.

The short opens with Gus Wickie – better known as Bluto's voice – energetically singing "Strike Up the Band for Popeye the Sailor." The studio took no chance to identify the character on the screen with the one in the comic strip with having a scene in which newspapers are rolling off a printer with the headline that Popeye is now in movies.

Now comes a truly iconic moment in the history of American animation, our first chance to see Popeye, singing his theme song for the first time. The lyrics set the tone for the character:

"I'm Popeye the Sailor Man,
I'm Popeye the Sailor Man.
I'm strong to the finich
Cause I eats me spinach.
I'm Popeye the Sailor Man.

*I'm one tough Gazookus
Which hates all Palookas
Wot ain't on the up and square.
I biffs 'em and buffs 'em
And always out roughs 'em
But none of 'em gets nowhere.
If anyone dares to risk my 'Fisk,'
It's 'Boff' an' it's 'Wham' un'erstan'?
So keep 'Good Be-hav-or'
That's your one life saver
With Popeye the Sailor Man.
I'm Popeye the Sailor Man,
I'm Popeye the Sailor Man.
I'm strong to the finich
Cause I eats me spinach.
I'm Popeye the Sailor Man."*

The song was written in a reported two hours by Sammy Lerner and, despite his other successes in songwriting, was probably his best-known work. It may be argued it became the most recognizable cartoon theme from its era.

The first short set up much of the elements we associate with the Popeye cartoons. The Fleischers appropriated Bluto, a villain Segar created for the story "The Eighth Sea" that appeared in 1932.

Although Popeye was almost from the beginning of his appearance in 1929 in Segar's "Thimble Theater" as something of a superhero – he could give and take quite a licking – additional power was given to him by stroking the head of Bernice, the rare African Wiffle hen.

By 1932, although Segar had introduced the use of spinach, although it was not as prevalent as used in the cartoons.

It was clear with the repeated use of Bluto and spinach, the studio wanted to establish a format from which a story and gags could be hung.

Betty Boop makes a guest appearance in her own cartoon, appearing as a hula dancer with animation that was recycled at least in part from "Bamboo Isle." She and Popeye appeared together dancing.

The cartoon sets up Bluto's rivalry for Olive's affections, his abduction of her and, an undoubtedly parody of 19th century melodrama, her being tied to a train track. Popeye, with the aid of spinach, has the strength to stop both Bluto and the oncoming locomotive in short order.

I think it is safe to say there hadn't been any sound cartoon to that date quite like it.

Although there was a mix of styles in the short – Segar characters and Fleischer funny animals – it was apparent the studio animators tried to keep as "on model" as possible with

Popeye, although there was a certain stiffness in his facial expressions that would change with time.

The reviews for the pilot were good. "Popeye gets as many laughs as do any of a number of established stars of the stage, screen and radio," the Milwaukee News wrote. "Hard-hitting gob makes striking impression in his first movie," the Oakland (CA) Inquirer trumpeted. The Minneapolis Tribune declared, "Popeye The Sailor Man has stepped into a new role. He's a movie star, as the first release proves."

It's fascinating to watch the Popeye cartoons in order as they show a progression in both characterization and storytelling. It's also interesting to compare how Betty Boop evolved. Betty was an organic kind of creation the studio had to nurture. Popeye came to them ready for the screen.

That readiness had its down side. As mentioned above, the great stories Segar created that took weeks to unfold could not be duplicated in a seven-minute short and the animated Popeye had to be authentic to his comic strip version.

If the initial Boop cartoons were loose in their story construction, the Popeye shorts could not be and yet the first several Popeye shorts clearly illustrate the studio trying to find their way.

The second short "I Yam what I Yam," introduces Wimpy but is mired in a near plotless narrative about Native Americans. Despite not being the tightest story, the reviewer at the Film Daily wrote, "Popeye of cartoon fame bids fair to become one of the most popular cartoon comedy favorites as well. The Max Fleischer studio has done a swell job in putting the super strong sailor on the screen."

The third cartoon, "Blow Me Down" does have some inspiration from Segar with Olive as a saloon girl in a Mexican cantina. The short features the first apparent ad-lib and has a great gag with Popeye hitting Bluto – a Mexican bandit – so hard he flies around the word.

There is a gag that illustrates the super powers Popeye has. Someone shoots him and the bullet bounces off of Popeye's head and kills the would-be assailant.

Audiences liked these early Popeye shorts. The manager of the Orpheum Theater in Oxford, NC, wrote to Motion Picture Herald in its May 12, 1934 edition, "Blow Me Down – here is one of the best cartoons I have ever had the pleasure of screening for my patrons. They all like these cartoons and they are fast becoming more popular than Mickey Mouse and personally I think they are much more entertaining."

The next short, "I Eats My Spinach," is the first with the distinctive urban setting, obviously something from Segar's strip with which the Fleischer crew felt comfortable. This short, though, is a bit of a throwback as it has the mixed animal universe of the Betty Boop shorts.

"Season's Greetinks" is a Christmas cartoon that none-the-less had Popeye beating the crap out of Bluto.

"Wild Elephinks" is the last time the use of animal characters as in the Betty Boop shorts is seen in a Popeye short.

In "Sock a Bye Baby," Popeye is tasked to keeping a baby asleep – not Swee'Pea – and is the first short in which Popeye sings, which is largely in Costello's own voice, although he does switch to Popeye's voice at some moments. Everywhere Popeye goes he has to keep people quiet by pummeling them into submission. He even sinks a ship that is blowing its steam whistle and knocks down a building under construction.

More of the Segar feel was in "Let's You and Him Fight," a Wimpy-esque title in which Popeye is seen as a boxer getting ready for a fight against Bluto. In the comic strips, Popeye was initially seen in the ring against more opposing opponents.

Olive has a great scene in which she is crying as she listens to the fight between them on the radio. She runs down the arena with a can of spinach and the admonition "Fight you palooka, fight!"

Everything works in this short and for me it is the start of the studio being comfortable with the character.

"The Man of the Flying Trapeze" represents another true break-through. It mixes some of the Segar elements – a guest appearance by Olive's mom Nana Oyl – and Olive's fickle nature with the studio's musical strength. The cartoon is basically an operetta built around the vintage song "The Man on the Flying Trapeze."

This short also illustrates the animators were now at ease with putting more emotion into Popeye's face. Earlier shorts seemed to show the studio was so concerned to reflect how Segar drew the character there was little change in his expressions.

The Fleischers had shown a real talent in combining music with animation and with this short music played a significant role in the Popeye series.

"Can You Take It" is an absolute delight and revels in the kind of violence that was a staple in the Segar strip – and which got Segar in trouble from time to time. Olive is a nurse at the Bruiser Boys Club, an organization whose members regularly beat the crap out of one another. The initiation is brutal – Popeye has to walk through buzz saws and is beaten by automatic devices – but passes. He is only done in when they fire a cannon at his stomach. The spinach emerges when he finds out he is not a member.

It was clear the Popeye series was imposing some artistic restrictions that allowed the studio to improve its animation and its storytelling. Watching the Popeye cartoons showed the growth of the Fleischer Studio.

"Shoein' Horses" was the first appearance of the Olive Oyl voice most people remember. It was based on the popular comic actress Zasu Pitts and performed by Mae Questel. Pitts, who has a very long career as a character actress primarily in comedies was known for her fluttering voice and her despondent phrase, "Oh, dear!"

A Paramount trade ad heralded the connection between newspapers running the comic strip and how they were cross-promoting the character. "Newspapers all over the country tie-up with theatres as Popeye popeyelarity [sic] sweeps the nation."

"Shiver Me Timbers" also reflects a successful combination of Fleischer themes with the Segar characters. Animator and the co-director of Willard Bowsky was well known for his use of haunted locales and ghosts and uses these devices to create a gag-driven short that works well.

Popeye, Olive and Wimpy happen upon a beached and haunted ship and the ghosts raise havoc with them, with Popeye discovering his strength almost useless. The cartoon's backgrounds of the haunted ship and its construction with overhead shots reflect an increasingly sophisticated approach to the character.

Bluto makes a reappearance in "Axe Me Another" in which he is the evil lumberjack "Pierre Bluto" who tosses Olive into a river because he doesn't like Olive's spinach. The short is an example of using an original song – more of a ditty – than a complete song. "I'll Do Anything You'll Do" is used to frame the action of a contest between the two characters – something that will become a fixture in the cartoons.

Exhibitors tended to love the Popeye shorts. The Motion Picture Herald in is Dec. 7 1935 edition ran several reports from theater owners about the shorts. "For Better or Worser: Popeye the Sailor Man – We have yet to show a Popeye cartoon that was not pleasing to the audience."

In the same edition: "The Hyp-nut-tist: Popeye the Sailor – This is the first Popeye we've played but you can rest assured it will not be the last, for the general verdict was the same one that old Popeye has won from cost to coat, the kingpin of the cartoons!"

The next short in the series is undoubtedly one of the best Popeye cartoons made and could be argued it's one of the best animated short subjects ever. In "A Dream Walking," (1934) Olive, Popeye and Bluto all live in an apartment building near the construction site of a new building. The boys are awakened when Olive begins sleepwalking and follow her to the site where the girders of the building stand.

She begins walking on the girders and cranes are activated in order to attempt to keep her safe by moving girders to create a path for her.

Popeye tells the guard, played by Wimpy, "Hey there's a sleepwalker up there." Wimpy replies in cold logic, "She'll awaken when she falls."

The rest of the short involves Popeye and Bluto trying to manipulate hanging girders to keep Olive from falling and, naturally, beating each other in their effort to be the one who rescues her.

The timing and inventiveness of the short is impressive and Olive's movements are perfectly times to a rendition of the popular song " I Saw A Dream Walking." Interestingly enough, the song had appeared in the motion picture "Sitting Pretty," a Paramount feature film released in 1933.

The conclusion of the short has Olive returning to her bedroom safely and waking up to see Popeye apparently as a Peeping Tom. She is outraged and begins throwing things at Popeye in anger. Popeye is philosophical, though and said, "I saw my duty and done it."

"The Dance Contest" certainly emphasized Popeye's humanity. He and Olive go to a dance contest and he is awful, stepping on her feet. He is easily replaced by a suave and cleaned-up Bluto, who can dance.

"I guess I have no sex appeal," Popeye moans.

Spinach comes to the rescue by putting rhythm in Popeye's step. To see the perfectly timed dance sequence that follows is proof of the proficiency of the Fleischer animators.

"Beware of Barnacle Bill" is a very sly joke by the studio and one I'm surprised the Hays

Office allowed. The cartoon is based on the bawdy drinking song and certainly any adult who knew the song who watched the cartoon understood what was going on.

The cartoon is a testament to Olive's fickle nature and Popeye's rejection of her behavior, all told by nearly written lyrics to the song.

In the July 1, 1935 edition of the Motion Picture Daily, an article discussing the finances of the film industry noted, "how it goes in some cases: Business on the Popeye cartoon, which Max Fleischer makes for Paramount, increased 39 ½ percent for the first 39 weeks of this year."

"The Hyp-Nut-Tist" carries over a convention from the early Thimble Theater comic strip. Segar often framed his stories as if they were plays and listed his characters as actors. In this short the villain is a stage magician and hypnotist which Popeye and Olive go to see. It's clearly Bluto "playing" character. The best gag in the short is the magician hypnotizes Olive to make her believe that she is a chick and she lays an egg!

"Choose Yer Weppins" has a villain with the Bluto voice but does not look like the character. The short involves an escaped criminal who comes into Popeye's pawn shop and winds up in a sword fight with the sailor. The fight is coordinated to a Sousa march with the swords keeping time to the music.

"For Better or Worser" (1935) has bachelor Popeye reassessing his situation after burning his dinner and deciding he needs to have a wife. A trip to a matrimonial agency naturally means he and Bluto will pick the same woman – Olive – and the contest ensues.

This is the first Popeye short in which the Fleischer three-dimensional technique was used.

"Dizzy Divers" returns Popeye to a maritime adventure, this time trying to race to a sunken treasure before Bluto gets there. There is a very unusual shot with Bluto, having stolen the treasure map,, waving good bye to Popeye who is in the background. It appears almost the two animated characters were married in the shot by an optical printer.

There are two elements that added to the enjoyment of "You Gotta Be a Football Hero." First, it was the song was a successful pop tune, written in 1933 and recorded by both Fred Waring and Ben Bernie. The Popeye shorts to date (1935) had used original music and this is the second time the Fleischers had used a current pop tune in a Popeye cartoon. The practice was, of course, normal for the Betty Boop series, but not Popeye.

A one-sheet for "Let's Celebrake."

At the end of the short, Popeye scats sings Betty Boop's "boop de doop" signature.

"The Adventures of Popeye" is essentially a cheater, using clips from previously produced cartoons. What is charming is the live-action framework. A little boy is bullied by an older kid and Popeye emerges from a book to show the younger boy how to handle bullies. Naturally, spinach is involved. The live action footage was shot silent, with the dialog dubbed later and there is photo that shows Dave Fleischer directing the young actor.

"Vim, Vigor and Vitality" gives us the nightmare fuel of Bluto in drag as a woman. He infiltrates Pope's gym for women and proceeds to beat up Popeye in the disguise. "Ya knows I can't be rough with a woman," Popeye tells Bluto. Luckily Bluto's wig falls off and justice is served.

This is another example of the depiction of Popeye's world. His gym has cracked walls and shoddy equipment. Popeye is a definitely working class hero.

A caricature of fellow Paramount star Mae West is featured in "Never Kick a Woman." The character is a shapely gym instructor at a sporting goods store who says to Popeye, "You're not an oil painting but you're a fascinating monster."

The Trouble with Wimpy

As noted previously Segar's J. Wellington Wimpy was a complex, frequently dark character. Originally in the comic strip he was a coward and a scam artist. He was always trying to cheat Rough House, the owner of a greasy spoon, out of food, particularly hamburgers.

Wimpy was so hated by one of the strip's supporting characters, George Geezil, that Geezil poisoned him to death. Wimpy only came back when there was a hamburger involved.

His catch phrase became very well know: "I would gladly pay you Tuesday for a hamburger today."

Shamus Culhane's assertion that Max and the others at the studio didn't understand Wimpy is a difficult statement to assess. The challenge for the studio was how to translate Segar's character into seven-minute-long narratives. Afterall, Segar had the advantage of a daily comic strip that allowed him to build lengthy stories and characterizations.

Wimpy in the Fleischer cartoons is far less complex. Yes, he is a mooch, a coward and lazy but he doesn't usually have the dark side of his comic strip origins. He is often relegated as a background player whose activities are centered around getting something to eat.

Wimpy and his baser instincts are featured though in "What – No Spinach?" he employed as the wait staff at Bluto's short order restaurant. He is constantly trying to cheat Bluto out of food. Popeye comes in and orders a duck dinner, which Wimpy proceeds to try to steal and ruin. Popeye leaves without paying and Bluto knowing none of this tries to beat Popeye up. The short ends with Wimpy getting more than what he wants, waddling out of eatery with a lot of stolen food.

This is close to the Wimpy of the strip. He is duplicitous and is determined to cheat both his employer and a customer and has no conscience.

Other Supporting Characters

It took years for the studio to add another character from the comic strip and in 1936, Swee'Pea was added. In the comic strip, the infant was left on Popeye's doorstep and he became his adopted son. Considering the rules and regulations of the Production Code, it's amazing that the studio was able to make Popeye and Olive as non-married parents of a child of undetermined origins.

The young character, though, allowed both Segar and studio to show a softer side of the sailor. Segar turned the Swee'Pea into a major character in the strip.

In "Little Swee'Pea," (1936) the infant lives with Olive and Popeye is charged with taking him not the zoo. There is no explanation of who he is. The film has an elaborate 3-D set, which takes the viewer from Olive's neighborhood to inside the zoo. As the innocent, Swee'Pea naturally interacts with dangerous animals with no harm as Popeyes tries to "save" him.

"The Jeep" (1938) is another introduction of a favorite character from the comic strip and this cartoon assumes Popeye audiences knew the Jeep, so it is not an origin story. Instead, we get a modest but amusing little story about Swee'Pea disappearing from his crib from Olive's apartment. Popeye has brought the Jeep over to play with the child but instead asks the Jeep to find Swee-Pea.

If Popeye can be seen as a proto superhero, then certainly Eugene the Jeep, as he is known in the comic strip, with his various powers is definitely a superhero. He can go through solid walls, float through the air, among other feats.

Segar introduced the dog-like animals in 1936 and a scientist in the strip explained to Popeye just what the Jeep can do: "A Jeep is an animal living in a three dimensional world—in this case our world—but really belonging to a fourth dimensional world. Here's what happened. A number of Jeep life cells were somehow forced through the dimensional barrier into our world. They combined at a favorable time with free life cells of the African Hooey Hound. The electrical vibrations of the Hooey Hound cell and the foreign cell were the same. They were kindred cells. In fact, all things are, to some extent, relative, whether they be of this or some other world, now you see. The extremely favorable conditions of germination in Africa caused a fusion of these life cells. So, the uniting of kindred cells caused a transmutation. The result, a mysterious strange animal."

Naturally Popeye is a little confused.

In this short the Jeep gets no introduction, but he sort of gets one in his next short (1940). In "Popeye Presents Eugene the Jeep," the Jeep is a gift from Olive, who instructs Popeye that he must sleep outdoors at night. Popeye is unaware of the Jeep's abilities, and all Eugene wants is to sleep with Popeye.

It's an odd short as audiences have already seen Eugene in the early cartoon and one wonders why the studio chose this kind of story as opposed to Eugene joining Popeye on an adventure.

Popeye's father, Poopdeck Pappy, made his debut in "Goonland, (1938), one of very best Popeye shorts, which introduced two characters from the comic strip, the other being The Goons.

In the comic strip Pappy was introduced in 1936. Popeye goes on an expedition to finds his long-last father who lives on an island and flirts with mermaids. Looking at his son, he declares "I don't like relatives."

Alice the Goon was another creation of Segar's that is totally original. A humanoid figure, she was originally the slave to the Sea Hag in the comic strip, but Popeye helped liberate both her and her people.

Alice doesn't make an appearance in the short, but her tribe certainly does and in "Goonland" they are holding Poopdeck Pappy. Popeye sets the story up through song at the beginning and when he discovers his father, Pappy delivers that line about relatives straight from the comic strip.

Popeye is captured by the goons and Pappy feeling sentimental rescues his boy but not before such a horrendous battle that the film (!) is broken. A live action pair of hands uses a safety pin to mend the film the cartoon continues.

The short is funny and sentimental. Pappy subsequently appeared in a number of shorts where he played his irascible self.

The Specials

In the 1930s many critics viewed any cartoon that didn't come from the Disney studio as second rate. The Disney shorts were frequently seen as "art", while the animation from Fleischer, Warner Bros. and MGM were also-rans.

Of course, today one can see strengths from the work of other studios. Animation in the 1930s didn't start and stop with Disney.

If there was ever proof of that it would be with the three Popeye specials. With the running time of nearly 20 minutes, the Fleischer studio was able to base a longer story not only on the characters but come closer to the type of stories told in the comic strip.

Once again, the Fleischer Studio was producing something that ran counter to the work from other studios. No one had decided to go longer than seven minutes with an animated cartoon format.

As indicated by trade reports all three were successful at the box office and with audiences. More modern evaluation had been hampered by the fact the specials had fallen into the public domain and for years inferior murky prints on both VHS and DVD collections. The first special was "Popeye the Sailor Meets Sinbad the Sailor."

Thankfully all three have been restored and it's obvious they are in a class of their own.

It was not the first time the story of Sinbad was animated. Hugh Harmon and Rudy Ising did a version in 1924, while Ub Iwerks did a color short in 1935. There was at least one silent live action film based on the story as well.

In the April 13, 1936, edition Film Daily announced the cartoon would be on 1936-1937 schedule with no indication it was a two-reeler and in Technicolor.

With the first special, the studio was able to use Technicolor and designed a film that took full advantage of it. The use of the 3-D sets was also a key component of several sequences. The color design was both vivid primary colors as well as softer pastels.

The studio followed the conventions of Segar original Thimble Theater comic strip in that the characters were billed as playing particular parts.

In many ways the two-reeler was indeed structured like a legitimate musical. Bluto as Sinbad sings a song to introduce himself as he walks through a 3-D set of his island hideout. He is a classic blow-hard giving viewers a tour of his island and his many victories. Sinbad's song about himself is interrupted by Popeye singing his own song.

Popeye, Olive and Wimpy are on a nearby ship minding their own business until Sinbad spots Olive through his telescope. "Wreak that ship, but bring me the woman," he snarls to his captured Roc, a giant bird, winks in response.

The introductory song is reprised between the Popeye and Sinbad with Sinbad increasingly frustrated that Popeye doesn't know who he is. There is almost a comic opera effect here.

With Popeye taking care of two of Sinbad's effort to kill him, then the short presents the climatic battle. Naturally the main event is between Sinbad and Popeye, and it is a well-staged battle.

The effort paid off with the studio's first of four Academy Award nominations. Disney won the statue with the Silly Symphony, "The Country Cousin." The other nominee was Harman-Ising's "The Old Mill Pond."

The Academy voters had been voting for Disney for the previous awards the past four times the award had been offered. Disney would continue the win the Oscar every year until 1940 when MGM's "The Milky Way," directed by Rudy Ising broke the streak.

What makes this first two-reeler from Fleischer is that the studio pulled out all the stops. Technicolor, fun music, great vocal performances from Jack Mercer, Mae Questel and Gus Wickie and a tight story were used to make a ground-breaking cartoon.

The Film Daily wrote on Nov. 4, 1936, about "Popeye the Sailor meets Sinbad the Sailor, "All in fun and all in color is this rollicking chapter of the adventures of Popeye the Sailor, his spindly spouse [sic] Olive Oyl, and the redoubtable Wimpy. Their craft cruises near the island retreat of the might Sinbad with the accent on the last syllable of this gent's name – for he is bad, though and tyrannical. He sends the super-giant bird the roc, to destroy Popeye's ship and carry off the fair Olive Oyl. But Popeye swims to the rescue and after beset with dragons, lions, gorillas and other fearful creatures he comes to grips with Sinbad himself. But a stout heart plus a handy can of spinach bring Popeye out on top Olive is rescued and the beasts capitulate to the visiting conqueror. Kids and grown-ups alike with love this episode. It's top-notch."

In the Motion Picture Herald on Nov. 14, 1936, the reviewer called it "tops" and continued, "By far the best Popeye to date, this latest edition of the adventures of our nautical friend rates the special classification given to it. The running time has been extended to the length of two-reels. Added merit is some splendid coloring which makes more real and appetizing that particular diet of spinach favored by Popeye. Action and humor have not been neglected, but if possible for this series have been even more increased and bettered. The exhibitor may be assured that any extra exploitation he may give this subject will amply repay him in return of the enthusiastic audience response."

The manager of a theater in Maine wrote the Motion Picture Herald in 1937, "Popeye the Sailor Meets Sinbad the Sailor: Popeye the Sailor, Step on it. It's a feature in itself."

In a story about the best shorts of the year, The National Board of Review magazine chose "Popeye the Sailor Meets Sinbad the Sailor" as number one of the best two-reelers of 1937.

The Motion Picture Herald in its review advised, "The exhibitor may be assured that any extra exploitation he may give to this subject will amply repay him in returns of enthusiastic audience response."

Naturally there were some opposing viewpoints. Also in a 1937 edition of The Motion Picture Herald was this remark from a theater owner in Oregon, "This much ballyhooed, two-reel, all color, third dimensional cartoon failed to come up to the entertainment value of the single reel, black and white Popeye series."

The British magazine Picturegoer Feb. 1938 published in an open letter from its editor to Walt Disney concerning the British film censor board's refusal to give "Snow White and the Seven Dwarfs" a universal rating. The editor noted, "You are of course by no means the only offender in this respect. The tendency to aim at terrifying as well as amusing is so universal among American screen animators that the phenomenon has puzzled us. Frequently 'Popeye the Sailor versus Sinbad the Sailor' [not the correct title] for instance was more like an inexpensive attack of delirium tremens than a suitable bedtime fairy tale for children."

Despite the possibility of frightening British children in the future, the success of the first special was followed up by a second.

"Popeye the Sailor meets Ali Baba's Forty Thieves" was released on Nov. 26, 1937, several weeks ahead of Disney "Snow White and the Seven Dwarves."

It's important to understand that releasing a film today is radically different than it was in the 1930. Today, we are used to national releases that target the entire country. Digital releasing, which has eliminated film prints, has made that kind to strategy more affordable.

Looking at trade publications and the reviews sent in by theater owners, one can see the finite number of film prints resulted in films being made available to theaters over a much longer period of time. The first Popeye special was being shown into 1937 as theaters got an opportunity for a print.

Like the first film, the thieves' leader Abu Hassan introduces himself through song and a great 3-D background. Popeye and Wimpy are members of the Coast Guard and when they hear on the radio the Forty Thieves are active and they take off to meet them in a seaplane.

Crashing in the desert, they make their way to a desert oasis. There is a wonderful moment in this march across the desert when the day shifts to night and the sun is replaced by a large crescent moon. It's fleeting but lovely.

They make it to the village where the Forty Thieves rush in stealing everything they can.

The film is filled with great ad libs from Mercer and funny lines such as when Popeye reaches down into Hassan's shirt and pulls out a pair of long johns. "Abu Hassan got them anymore," he quips.

This two-page trade ad highlights the first color special.

The thieves strip the village clean, but Popeye is able to follow them, rescue Olive and Wimpy and bring them all to justice. The final shot is a wonder 3-D model of a huge cart laden with the thieves' spoils.

Interestingly enough, Hassan shows no lust towards Olive and instead is more interested in having her do the thieves' laundry.

The final Popeye two-reeler was based on the story of Aladdin and the story was framed by a clever concept. Olive is a screen writer at Surprise Pictures and she is writing a script in which she will play the role of the princess, while Popeye is the hero Aladdin. The film than goes to Olive's story.

This is the only one of the three specials in which the Bluto character does not appear as the villain.

Instead, the evil magician is a new character who dupes Aladdin into getting the lamp. Aladdin secures the lamp though, becomes a prince and courts the princess. Naturally the magician winds up with the lamp, vanquishing Aladdin and carrying off the princess.

The climax of the story centers around what the magician can conjure with the lamp against a spinach defense.

A beautifully realized cartoon, it has many moments that impress. For contemporary audiences they may not realize the voice of genie of the lamp is an imitation of a popular radio and film comic Lew Lehr.

It is this cartoon on which Popeye admits, "I've never made love in Technicolor before."

The film was released in April 1939 and the reviews were solid in approval Showman's Trade Review (April 29 1939) noted, "Dave Fleischer, who directed this cartoon, hit the bell with it for a sock. The smart showman will devote plenty of space in his ads to this subject."

The Exhibitor (April 19, 1939, wrote, "Probably the best of the annual two-reel Popeyes, this should be hilarious entertainment where

The Popeye version of Aladdin was released in 1939.

Popeye fans dwell ... Excellent."

The Flm Daily in its May 11, 1939, ediion called it "Classy fun," while Boxoffice (April 22, 1939) called it "by far the best short subject the Fleischers have turned out... the laugh provoking situation had a Paramount Theatre in unusually fine spirits. It's not only a short for children but it makes for top entertainment for adults... don't hesitate to book it and hold it over."

While the studio made two more two-reel features in following years, neither featured Popeye.

Popeye's Music

It should be noted the importance of music in the Popeye shorts. Popeye was not portrayed as a singer in the comic strips and music was clearly a Fleischer invention.

The result are some absolutely delightful and memorable moments.

With the special music composed for the Betty Boop cartoons, as well as the Screen Song series that featured contemporary artist and pop songs, it's easy to see how much music meant to the character of the studio.

The Popeye shorts were no exception and the importance of music was evident early on.

Two musical elements were used often. The theme song was often used to close out a cartoon with special lyrics demoting the plot of the short.

The other was the use of John Philip Sousa's rousing "The Stars and Stripes Forever" in fight scenes. "Columbia the Gem of the Ocean" was also used for the same purpose.

As the series progressed, music was used to advance the plot or to tell something about a character, not unlike musical theater.

"The Spinach Overture" is built on music with Popeye was the struggling leader of a little band. Bluto in this cartoon is the leader of an orchestra.

Perhaps the most recognizable cartoon theme song ever composed.

The Popeye music was so popular this folio of sheet music was released.

This song was a collaboration between Sammy Timberg and Dave Fleischer.

He shows up Popeye and brings Olive, Wimpy and the rest of the band to join him. Spinach gives Popeye the musical talent he lacks and there is an outstanding animation and musical performance on the piano, highlighted by a wonderful bit of scat singing by Jack Mercer.

This a cartoon that shows the influence of Thimble Theater – Bluto is playing a different character – as well as an example of a short without the love triangle of the three main characters.

In "Clean Shaven Man," the song performed by Olive sets up the cartoon. She sings that she wants a clean shaven man, which sends Popeye and Bluto to the barber. The barber isn't there so they agree to shave each other. You know what follows. The punchline is Olive walks by them and is accompanied by a character from the Segar strip, George Geezil, who sports a huge beard.

"Brotherly Love" has the same format Olive heads the Women's Brotherly Love Association and sings a song that inspires Popeye to do a series of good deeds. He comes upon a street fight between gangs at the same time Olive is marching with her fellow members and is unsuccessful in stopping it as is Olive. Spinach changes the situation.

"I-Ski Love-Ski You-ski" also has a charming song that Popeye sings to invite Olive to ski with him. The vocal skills of Jack Mercer are never to be underestimated as this cartoon points out. It's one thing to perform lines of dialog in character, it's another to sing and in this short to yodel.

In this cartoon Gus Wickie, the voice of Bluto through most of the 1930s, also shows his singing talents. A bass singer, Wickie played Bluto until 1938 and the short "Big Chief Ugh-Amugh-Ugh" in which he played the title character. Before and after his time at Fleischer, he performed in nightclubs and Broadway shows, according to research done by Davis Gerstein. He passed in 1947.

Although it hasn't been documented, one could assume like his colleague Mae Questel, Wickie decided not to go to Florida when the studio moved there in 1938. He stayed in show business, though and Variety noted his death years later.

"I-Ski Love-Ski You-ski" also has an opening sequence with a 3-D model. It's a short sequence that is almost a throw-away scene as is a bridge set in "Bridge Ahoy."

Sammy Lerner wrote the Popeye Theme as well as Betty Boop's "Made of Pen and Ink" theme. Among his other compositions were "Falling in Love Again," sung by Marlene Dietrich in "The Blue Angel."

Gus Wickie, a memorable Bluto voice.

Timberg teamed up with lyricist Bob Rothberg on many of his Popeye songs. The two wrote "Moving Man," "I Wanna be a Life Guard," "I'm King of the Mardi Gras," "Brotherly Love," "Hamburger Mine," and Won't You Climb a Mountain with Me."

Rothberg worked a great deal with Timberg on songs for the Betty Boop series as well as tunes for the Color Classics. He was educated in accounting and had a degree in law, but clearly loved music.

His non-Fleischer songs were recorded by such performers as Fats Waller, Ella Fitzgerald, and Guy Lombardo and his Royal Canadians.

Rothberg died at the age of 37 in 1938.

Dave Fleischer is credited for the lyrics of "I Want a Clean-Shaven Man" with Timberg's music. This is an interesting credit as Richard Fleischer wrote me about Dave's interest in composing music for the cartoons, which apparently created tension between him and Max.

Many of the Timberg-Rothberg songs are available on a CD with new recordings produced by Sammy's daughter Pat and performed by Sammy's granddaughter Shannon Cullem and Richard Halpern with Dean Mora and his Modern Rhythmists. The CD also includes a recording of Sammy singing one of his compositions. It's a great CD and available through www.timbergalley.com.

With Popeye's success, someone at Famous Music decided a sheet music collection of the Popeye compositions was in order. Published in 1936, the "Popeye Song Folio" has 24 songs with great illustrations. Because at the time, there were not enough Timberg songs to fill a 24-song collection, Famous Music hired one of its song-writing teams to compose more songs of a Popeye theme. Tot Seymour and Vee Lawnhurst were hired for additional songs. Active composing for Broadway and radio, Famous Music described them as "the first successful team of girl song writers in popular music history."

The Voice

The voice of Popeye was initially provided by musician and singer William "Billy" Costello, who had toured as a comic scat singer, as well as being a drummer in Fred Waring's orchestra. There are two stories about how Costello came to Max's attention. One is that he played "Gus the Gorilla" on the Betty Boop radio show, while the other is his recording of "I'm Nobody's Sweetheart Now" was used in "Berry Boop M.D." (1932).

Costello's performance in that short was a combination of a light baritone singing voice mixed with scat singing and some gravelly sound effects.

In "Sock a Bye Baby," (1934) a moment of Costello's regular singing voice can be heard during a yodeling number.

Costello did start the murmuring Popeye does that added post-animated dialogue to the shorts, but he did not do it to the comic effect his successor Jack Mercer did.

During his time as Popeye, Costello rode the wave of the cartoon's popularity by touring with the emphasis that he was the sailor's voice. Variety reviewed his performance at a Chicago theater in its June 26, 1934 edition, "Billy Costello, voice of the Popeye cartoons, is here for a short six-minute turn. After singing 'I'm Popeye the Sailor Man," he then turns into a second Ukulele Ike [Cliff Edwards, the recording star who eventually became the voice for Disney's Jiminy Cricket in "Pinocchio"] and does Cliff Edwards better than Cliff Edwards. He's the Ukulele Ike of five years ago. Besides that Costello goes bass voice like McClintock of Fred Waring's band for some laughs. But there was no 'Asleep in the Deep.'"

An ad for Costello's act stressed his connection to Popeye and noted he made his entrance

Jack Mercer as a variety performer.

Jack Mercer while he worked on the Popeye series produced by Hanna-Barbera.

Back in New York at Famous Studio can be seen the Popeye voice cast: Jack Mercer, Mae Questel and Jackson Beck.

wearing a "false face and bulging muscles."

Numerous sources have characterized Costello as more difficult with whom to work as the success of the series increased. His last short was "You Gotta be A Football Hero" (1935).

Although he appeared to have continued performing, Costello never achieved the prominence he had achieved through his work at Fleischer's. He died in 1971 as the manager of a trailer park. Like Mercer and any other voice actor working on the Fleischer shorts, he never received on-screen credit.

Costello was succeeded by a man who was already working at the studio, Jack Mercer. Born in 1910, Mercer had a background of performing onstage and he described how he received the role after Costello had departed.

Few people in show business lasted with a role longer than Mercer. He performed Popeye until his death in 1984, a period of nearly 50 years. Unlike Mel Blanc, who received credit at Warner Bros. for his work, Mercer, like Costello, never received on-screen credit for the vocal performance of the character until 1980 when he received credit on Robert Altman's "Popeye."

Unlike Questel and Blanc who both had active careers before the camera, Mercer seemed content to be in the writer unit at the studio as well as behind the mic.

Mercer proved his versatility at the studio by supply a great number of secondary voices in Fleischer and Famous cartoons, and actually received screen credit of his work in both Fleischer features.

He played King Little in "Gulliver's Travels" and Mr. Bumble and Swat the Fly in "Mr. Bug Goes to Town."

Mercer continued doing Popeye through the made-for-TV cartoons produced by King Features in 1960 as well as the Hanna-Barbara Popeye series in 1978.

Another prominent credit came with the Felix the Cat cartoons made by former Fleischer animator Joe Oriolo starting in 1958. Mercer supplied most of the voices from the high pitch voice of Felix to gravely villain Rock Bottom. He said he didn't particularly enjoy the Felix shorts as he had to switch between the characters. Oriolo also used Mercer on his subsequent series "The Mighty Hercules" in 1963.

In 1963 he also worked on a Casper the Friendly Ghost show for TV.

In the early 1960s, Mercer wrote episodes of "Deputy Dawg" and in 1965 wrote episodes of "Milton the Monster," a series produced by another Fleischer alumni Hal Seeger.

Fellow vocal artist Jackson Beck, who played Bluto in the Famous cartoons, among other roles, had nothing but praise for his co-stars Mercer and Questel. He told me in 1996, "Mercer was the most versatile voice man that I knew" and he put him in the same league as Mel Blanc. He explained that while Mercer didn't have the dramatic range of Blanc, he could create sound effects that Blanc couldn't.

"If you were short of a sound effect, he'd do it with his voice," said Beck, who characterized Mercer as "self-effacing and brilliant."

Mercer's relative anonymity in show business was underscored with a 1974 appearance on the TV game show "To Tell the Truth." The format of the show was to have three people claim to a person of interest. One of them is the person in question while the others are imposters. The celebrity panel is supposed to figure out who is real and who is just pretending.

On Mercer's show, the panel was actress Peggy Cass, TV hosts Bill Cullen and Gene Rayburn, singer Kitty Carlise. Despite Mercer's long tenure in the role, only one of the four panelists accurately guessed who he was. The clip of his appearance is on YouTube.

I met Jack Mercer in 1977 when I conducted the following interview in his apartment in the Woodside section of Queens in New York City. He was at first reluctant to meet with me as there had been an increasingly steady flow of interview requests from animation fans. Once he realized I was working on a Max Fleischer book with the blessing of the family, he set up an appointment. He and his wife Virginia were wonderfully hospitable, and Jack was very gracious in answering my questions, some of which he had heard hundreds of times before.

I had been told that Jack was one of the most modest people who worked in animation. Despite his accomplishments, he had never received the type of personal publicity his colleague Mae Questel gathered. The biggest difference between the two vocal performers was that Questel actively worked as an actress on television, the Broadway stage and in films. Jack, whose other main contribution to the animation was his story work at Fleischer and Famous, didn't seek a career outside of animation in the way Mae had. The result was an unfortunate anonymity.

For years, there were a number of people who asserted to have performed the voice in the cartoons, and these untrue claims were painful to Jack. Years later I still can't get over the injustice of the situation. This very talented man had never been given the recognition his career deserved.

At the end of the interview, I asked Jack for an audio autograph, and he performed the "Popeye" theme song. It was a fulfillment of a childhood dream, and interestingly enough I couldn't watch him as he leaned towards the microphone of my recorder and sang. I just sat listening. When I think of the opportunity of meeting the man whose supplied the voice to my favorite cartoon character, I still get choked up.

Jack Mercer: *I was in show business, of course, my whole family was in show business, and they wanted me to do something else. I could draw a little bit, and my mother had an agent who booked her vaudeville act, and he was acquainted with someone at Paramount who suggested I go to the Fleischer Studios, and see if I could get some type of work drawing. When I first started I was* in the opaque department. I went through all the various departments, the inking department, the in-betweening department.

Did you like it?

I enjoyed it, yes. I hadn't done any professional drawing before that. It was just on my own.

How did the job as Popeye's voice come about?

I was imitating various characters in the inking department just out of my own amusement, and everybody seemed to get a laugh out of it. And a lot of the people I try out for it [the Popeye voice]. I didn't know they were looking for anyone. So I eventually went home, and tried to improve the voice I was doing. So I finally got the voice after I practiced a while. I thought I could really do the voice, and got the quality I was after. I gave an audition over the phone to someone at Paramount. They heard it and from then on, they said, "Why don't you come over and so some voices." Which I did. Sort of a breaking-in period, I guess. They told me I was going to do the Popeye voice. That's how it started. You know, fooling around while I was working at the other jobs.

Was Max Fleischer make that final decision?

Well, there's the thing. I don't know whether it was Max because I was more involved with Dave and Lou [Fleischer] at that time. Whether he was informed about it, I don't know, but he never came around to see. [Jack later commented that Max believed he was too skinny when he started performing the voice and suggested he'd eat spaghetti and drink Guinness Stout!]

What type of a guy was Dave Fleischer to work with?

He was always kidding around. Very jolly. I had no conflict with him at all as far as I can remember. It was always sort of a happy family.

How about Max?

As far as I was concerned I was working for Dave and Lou Fleischer and the animators. Max was always in the front office. I very seldom saw him. He was always engaged in some innovation for the studio, the technical end of things, inventing machines like the turntable for dimensional effects, things like that. Every once in a while I'd run into him and we'd say "hello." So as I say I knew very little about him. He invited me once out to dinner in Miami when he got his new home. I guess that's the only social event I could think of outside of appearing at the parties. Sometimes he'd come in and look at a picture or sit in on a recording session or something like that. Very seldom.

He was like the "Godfather," though. If you had any troubles, you'd go to him and he'd straighten them out.

After the 1938 strike was the studio still a happy family?

During the strike I was working in the story department, and that was sort of a section all by itself, you might say, and I didn't associate with the others. I didn't notice anything.

You see, with the story writers, we were just one big happy group. It was only the attitude of the opaquers and the inkers that might have been different. As far as I was concerned I didn't notice anything.

Other studio personnel were affected by the strike. Seymour Kneitel was injured by the strikers. Edith Vernick had to be escorted by the police through the picket line.

Well, I did have one incident. One day, of course, they asked everyone in there to pitch in and help anyway you could. If they needed someone to in-between I'd pitch in and help. The people out on the picket line used to take pictures of people going into the studio, and threaten you. One night I was going home on the subway, and some strange looking characters sat down on other side of me. There wasn't anyone else in the car at the time, so I felt perhaps they were trying to intimidate me in some way. It was very funny. These two fellows would come in and sit on either side of me. At the station before the one at which I usually got off, I got off the train real fast and left them sitting there! [laughing] The door closed, and the train went on. That's the way I got rid of them. Maybe it was just my imagination, I don't know. That and the fact they would harass you as you entered and left at work, and that they would take a photo of you going past their picket line.

What was the experience of Florida like?

They did increase a lot. A lot of people came in from the coast, and that did give us sort of a Disneyland atmosphere. All of those guys were crazy, and they brought a bit of Hollywood to Miami. I suppose that's why people thought it was all a party and I suppose there was, but I didn't get involved with it.

There was one fellow, Cal Howard; he did some crazy things. He had a car similar to mine, and he'd go around the neighborhoods screeching the tires. He sat up in the back of the car, and he had some arrangement by which he could reach the gas pedal. He'd sit in the back and steer the car. It was a convertible, and the cops were always after him.

I'd go out in my car, and they'd mistake me for him! I'd always have a siren blowing in back of me. I had a heck of time explaining it wasn't me. And he'd follow people around the studio: visitors, tourists. He'd make funny faces, all kinds of stuff and they would turn around because all the employees were laughing. He'd straighten right up, and act like he was one of them, and they couldn't figure it out.

Did it ever bother you that you didn't receive screen credit for your work as Popeye?

Yes it certainly did. I think it would bother anyone because of this situation where so many people claiming to have done it. That's the biggest thing I felt was bad. But that was just their policy. Mae [Questel, the primary actress for Olive Oyl's and Betty Boop's voice] couldn't do anything about it. They said something it took too much time in the credits. I don't know what their reason was whether they felt if they wanted to make a change they wouldn't want to change the titles.

Your vocal work was so important to the success of the Popeye cartoons.

"Well, maybe, they didn't think so. I suppose they figured the character itself and King Features was more important than the voice work.

Everyone who watches the Popeye cartoons loves your ad libs.

Everyone questions the fact why they were discontinued. You see, when we were doing the sound along with the picture, you could see these ideas would come as the picture ran. It just seemed like a natural thing to ad lib as you were watching the action. But then when it was pre-recorded, it was a different situation. I would try to select little lines here and there that would serve as an ad lib thought, and the ad lib is supposed to be thinking to yourself. And then they insisted on having the mouth action along with these ad libs which sort of spoiled that situation, don't you see?

I always thought it was funnier if you didn't see the mouth moving, and they use that in some of the cartoons now as a side remark, and you just see the character standing. They used that now in the modern films. I don't know if they got that idea from the old Popeyes or not.

There's a difference in the thought of the line when it looks like it's just stuck in rather than actually having been written in.

Who performed Bluto's voice?

The first one I worked with was Gus Wickie, and he was a bass singer. And then we had several others coming and going, and I've forgotten them as they were coming and going! And we wound up with Jackson Beck doing Bluto more than anyone else did. I did some Blutos every once in a while, but it was too much. A conversation between Popeye and Bluto is pretty rough trying to switch back and forth.

Did you ever become hoarse? Your natural voice isn't as deep as Popeye's.

As a matter of fact, it's deeper now than it used to be. I used to talk up here more [in a near falsetto voice] you see, but now I've got it down here.

[Virginia Mercer: "He always hated his voice."]

You know, it would always embarrass me when we would be recording, and after doing a Popeye I would ask for instructions, or how do you want this line read, and when I would hear myself back, it would scare the hell out of me! Because the voice would come back like this: [exaggerated falsetto] I'd say "Jesus, is that me?!" [laughter] So I've been trying to get it down lower all the time. As I get older it gets lower. Now when I have to do a high voice, I have to struggle.

Besides you, Mae Questel and whoever was Bluto, were there other people doing voices?

Once in a while, we'd have a larger cast, but most of the time there were just the main characters and the rest of us would pile in and do anything that came along. Someone would say, "You try this character, and you try this one."

And we each one would try out for it, and then they'd say, "You do this one. You take that one." And we get varied tonal qualities. So we didn't have too many people on a cartoon.

Could you describe a story session at Fleischer's?

What would happen would be if there was one story man or two story men, they would get together and try to get an idea for the character that was assigned to them. Everybody got the chance to do various characters. All just didn't have one character to work with, like Popeye. He [the writer] would try to get a synopsis, write that down, and send it to be accepted by the directors who were going to direct the picture. Lots of times they'd all get together and decide if they wanted to do the story or not.

If they didn't like it, you'd try to get another angle, and as soon as they accepted one, then you'd go back, and "gag" the synopsis. Then you'd have to draw it up in storyboards. You'd have meetings with the director, and sometimes the animators would come in, and we'd all discuss the material; if it's funny or not, if it was too long, all sorts of problems.

Then, after it was accepted, as far as we were concerned it would leave the room, and we would try to get another angle on another character.

Also, we were asked to try to create characters. Now, with the Fleischer's, they seemed to be interested in characters with some various capabilities; capabilities different than usual characters. For instance, a ghost that could walk through things rather than a character like, you know, like the Flintstones.

Did you like any favorite directors or animators?

No, we took them as they came! [laughter] Next! Whoever came in, we'd be interested in developing the story for them, and hoping we could sell the ideas to the directors.

Did you ever think of the violence as being bad in the Popeye cartoons?

It never struck anyone as being bad. It was supposed to be humorous. It always wound up in a funny situation even if Popeye was beating on somebody's head or something, it was funny. Bluto always wound up in a predicament that was humorous, humiliating, we thought.

I remember we heard one time that out on the coast they had pictures where the characters would be hit on the head with something, and they'd crack up like a plate, but they'd immediately come together again and be all right and run off. We tried to get some gags like that in our pictures like that, but the Fleischers said we'd better not pull any of that stuff because people are starting to complain.

Did you ever become bored with performing Popeye's voice?

Not really. Every cartoon was different. if you were doing a dramatic show on Broadway, and every night you were doing the same thing I imagine it would get boring after a while. But when you have different stories to do there a constant creating there. We did have other characters to work with. It was a challenge. it was never boring.

I have a little pride in being Popeye's voice.

The actor who was playing Popeye in a "Be Kind to Aminals" in 1935 was Floyd Buckley who played Popeye in the second of two-radio series in the mid-1930s. That was his only appearance in the animated cartoons.

Questel also supplied a Popeye voice for a Famous short when Mercer was not available, a fact that Beck confirmed to me.

Because of the lack of credit there were people who claimed to be the voice of Popeye for their own personal advancement. Perhaps the most prominent was Harry Foster Welch, who did perform the voice once on screen when Mercer was serving in the miliary in WWII. Welch was profiled by Popular Science magazine in 1941where he claimed to "often" perform Olive Oyl, Wimpy, and Bluto as well as being the voice of Popeye. He asserted to have taken over the role from Costello in 1934.

He also said he was the Big Bad Wolf in Disney's acclaimed "Three Little Pigs" short, which is a lie. It has been long documented that actor Billy Bletcher supplied that voice.

Basically, Welch lied throughout the story about what he had done in the film industry.

At no point in the article is it evident that anyone from the Fleischer Studio mentioned. The writer obviously made no effort to double check the hokum being sold by Welch.

It was not uncommon that people would lie about a show business to reporters who had little background to double check the claims. For instance. Mayo Kaan, a bodybuilder and health club owner, started telling reporters in 1997 that he was the model for Superman. The estates of Joe Shuster and Jerry Seigel denied the claim, as did numerous comic book historians.

Carmen Nigro made a whole host of claims about appearing in a gorilla suit in various Hollywood productions. He told reporters he was playing Kong in the sequence in which the giant ape climbed the Empire State Building.

That assertion is patently false and the other films in which he said he appeared in an ape suit involved other performers, not him.

Three stories, though, by a sympathetic reporter in the late 1960s helped make his claim seem legitimate. They were not.

Today, it is far more difficult for people to make such claims.

In this photo/news page Max is seen in an atmospheric shot promoting his 3-D process.

To put the importance of Popeye to Paramount in perspective here are three examples of how Popeye was used to sell Paramount feature films.

The first is a photo of Paramount contract plater Dorothy Lamour taken with a life-size Popeye figure made by Paramount to publicize a world-wide sales campaign, the figure was used in a variety of photos with Paramount stars and officials each holding the country of a foreign country.

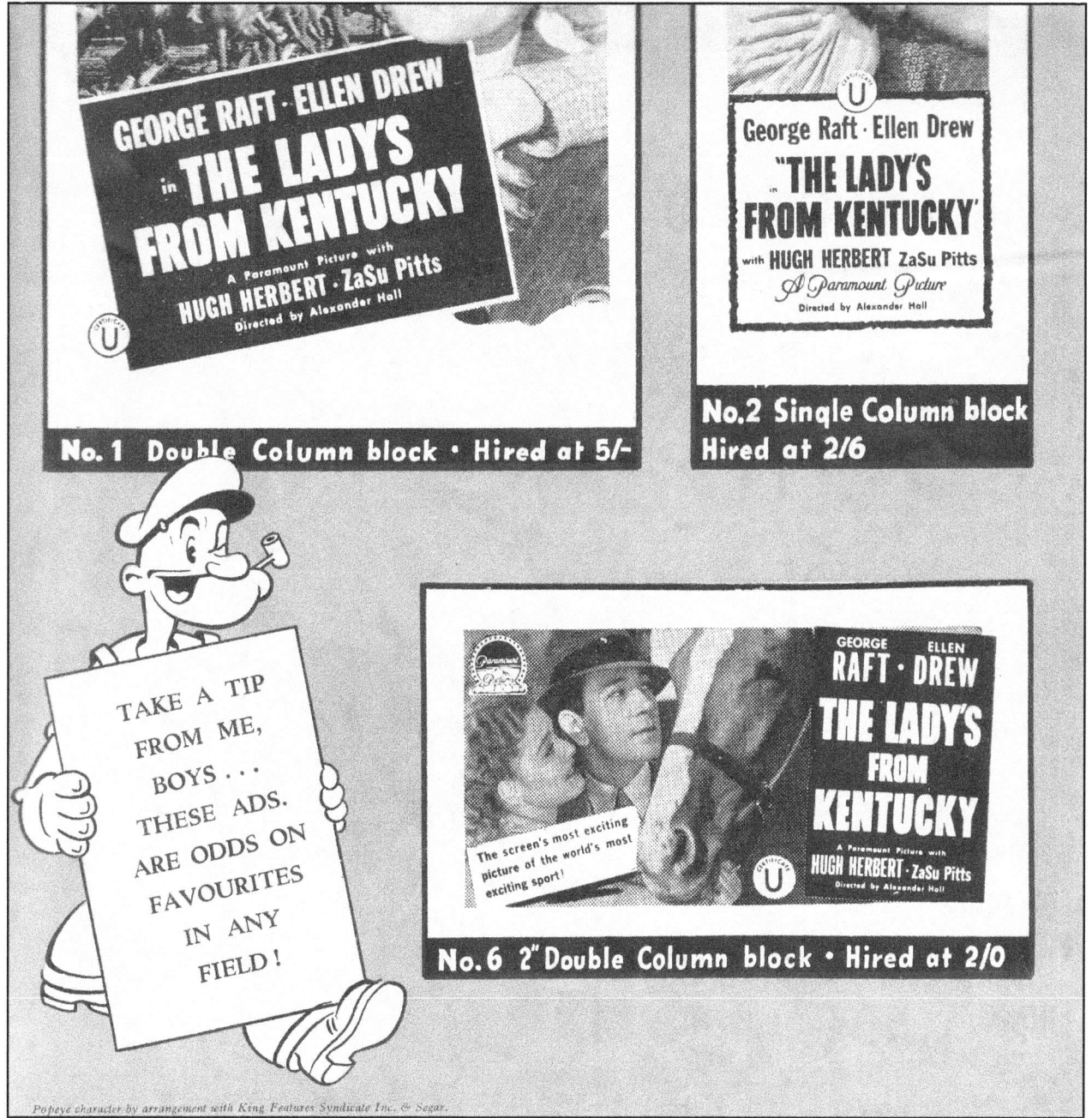

This detail is from the British press book for the film "The Lady's from Kentucky" and Popeye is used to urge theater owners to book it.

This 1938 trade ad shows an off-model Popeye touting a lengthy line-up of Paramount features.

In this era in which the primary technique used to market is through digital means, it may be difficult to understand tools used to sell a movie from the 1920s through the 1990s. These pages were from the press book sent to theater owners to help them market the first Popeye special. It suggested stunts and material for newspaper articles as well as to show the materials theater owners could buy or rent to display in the lobby. By this time Paramount had urged theater owners to form Popeye fan clubs, whose members could be used to help publicize the new two-reeler.

POPEYE MAKES DEBUT IN COLOR!

"Popeye Comes to Town—in COLOR!" And because of that, you're all set for the most colorful, most exciting, most profitable city-wide celebration you've ever dreamed of, on America's favorite comic cartoon character! You've got a made-to-order selling appeal on "Popeye the Sailor Meets Sindbad the Sailor"—to every Popeye fan—to every reader of a newspaper carrying the King Features syndicated cartoon—to everyone who has ever read the fable of Sindbad—and to everyone in town who can hear the news you're shouting about the new three-dimensional color cartoons!

Sell "Sindbad the Sailor" as a FIRST! It's the FIRST colored Popeye! It's the FIRST three-dimensional Popeye! It's the FIRST two-reel cartoon ever made! And when you put all these FIRSTS together—you've got ABSOLUTE TOPS in entertainment value and exploitation possibilities! The suggestions listed below, to get your city-wide "Welcome Popeye" celebration off to a flying start, are tried-and-true ideas. Not one of 'em is theoretical—every stunt on the list has already been tried by experienced, successful, hard-working showmen—and THEY'VE CLICKED! These promotions are easy to do—and they're fun to do because they all mean real hard cash in the boxoffice!

FIND A POPEYE "DOUBLE"

Work with the local newspaper running the Popeye cartoon strip to locate the local citizen most closely resembling Popeye. Illustrate the stories announcing this contest with art taken from the Publicity Section of this Press Book, and have contestants submit photos of themselves in Popeye clothes and Popeye attitudes. As first prize, you might offer a paid engagement to the winner, to act as Popeye during the entire period of the city-wide "Welcome Popeye" celebration which you are promoting.

A local radio station can be tied in on a "Popeye double" contest by promoting a "Popeye Voice" contest over the air. This can be handled either as a sustaining spot or as a gag comedy interlude on a sponsored program already on the air, with the audience voting, by letters and telephone calls, for the best imitation. In addition to whatever prize you are offering, you should be able to promote additional merchandise prizes from the cooperating sponsor of the radio program.

POPEYE CLUBS JOIN WELCOME

Get your Popeye Club Band and Popeye Club Police out to welcome Popeye at the edge of town, to escort the open car in which he is riding to the spot at which he will be greeted officially by the Mayor or whichever other civic official is in charge of the welcome. Line the route taken by Popeye with members of the Popeye Police, designated with Popeye armbands, and have the Popeye Band march ahead of the procession, playing the Popeye Song.

CITY OFFICIALS GREET POPEYE

There's a real human-interest angle in a comic-strip character "coming to life" to present himself, in person, at the Mayor's office, to receive the "freedom of the city," and you should be able to get a newspaper break on this. Try to arrange for reporters and photographers to be present at the City Hall, to get pictures and stories of the official welcome to Popeye.

TIEUP STORES FOR ADS, DISPLAYS

Promote cooperative displays and decorations from stores along the route of the "Welcome Popeye" parade. Furnish colored stills, Popeye pennants, one-sheets and window cards, to dress up their windows and entrances, and tie them into the city-wide celebration. Work closely with the Advertising Manager of the cooperating newspaper to try to promote a special section or a special page of cooperative "Welcome Popeye" advertising. Suggest the Popeye Balloons, illustrated on the inside back cover of this Press Book, as ideal giveaways for all cooperating merchants during "Welcome Popeye" celebration. They are available imprinted with the advertisement of the cooperating store. String these from the theatre marquee, too.

Page 1

"POPEYE THE SAILOR MEETS SINDBAD THE SAILOR"

GET YOUR POPEYE CLUB MEMBERS BEHIND THIS BIG CARTOON FEATURE

IF your theatre is one of the hundreds that have built steady profits on Popeye Clubs, the showing of "Popeye the Sailor Meets Sindbad the Sailor" will give your Club the biggest boost it's ever had! Every stunt, every idea, every giveaway, every gadget described in this Press Book will focus attention on Popeye—your "Popeye the Sailor Meets Sindbad the Sailor" campaign will rouse interest in America's favorite comic cartoon character to top-pitch!

Shrewd showmen in every part of the country know that as their surest bet to keep Popeye Club members at the proper peak of enthusiasm, they must give 'em variety, pep, novelties! "Sindbad the Sailor" offers an unequalled opportunity to go to town with Popeye. In every promotion, stress the fact that the Popeye Club is consistently giving its members all the humor, the entertainment and the fun they can ask for! Promote every exploitation idea in the name of the Popeye Club of your theatre.

POPEYE PIPES
Use This Clever Accessory for Club Meetings and in "Sindbad" Campaign

CHECK with members of your Popeye Club, well in advance of "Sindbad the Sailor" celebration, to make sure that every member is equipped with his Popeye Pipe. The Popeye Pipe, one of the greatest novelties for kids ever offered, is the one indispensable accessory in the activities of the Popeye Club. Made to resemble the pipe which Popeye himself smokes, it is also a "gazoo," that musical instrument dear to the heart of uproarious kids. Every youngster needs a Popeye Pipe to sing the Club song, "I'm Popeye the Sailor Man," and all the other songs which an up-and-coming Popeye Club will sing during the "Popeye the Sailor Meets Sindbad the Sailor" celebration!

Order Popeye Pipes from your Paramount Exchange. Prices are as follows: 1 to 12, each on card, ten cents each; 13 to 143, $1 per card of 12; 1 gross to 9 gross, on cards, $9 per gross; 10 gross or more, on cards, $8 per gross; in bulk, in lots of 3 gross to 9 gross, $8.50 per gross; in bulk, in lots of 10 gross or more, $7.50 per gross.

Every member of your Popeye Club wants an official membership card. This official card, illustrated left, is available on mat at your Paramount Exchange, with space at the top, above the words "Popeye Club," for insertion of your theatre name. Number the cards in printing them, and note on each application (which, of course, you will retain in your files) the number of the membership card which has been issued to each member. In this way, you will have a complete and permanent record of each member.

Print the "Popeye Creed," which is the creed of all Popeye Club members, on the reverse of membership cards, and on all Popeye Club literature, of any nature whatsoever. This "Creed" appears left.

I yam what I yam 'cause I yam a good citizen of my country, my state and my city.

I yam a person who obeys parents and teachers.

I yam always ready to lend a hand to old and young whenever they needs help.

I yam always truthful, even when it hurts.

I YAM A MEMBER OF THE POPEYE CLUB OF THE.........THEATRE.

PROFIT WITH POPEYE CLUB

FORMATION of "Popeye Clubs" has meant tremendously increased business for hundreds of theatres throughout the country. If your theatre is not already the sponsor of such a club, your showing of "Popeye the Sailor Meets Sindbad the Sailor" offers you a swell peg on which to hang the organization of such a group.

A copy of the Popeye Club Manual, which describes in detail how to organize and conduct a Popeye Club, may be secured at your Paramount Exchange. This manual contains full information on how theatres actually formed and profited on Popeye Clubs. No theory—but cold, hard facts, tested by practical showmen! Get your copy today!

Popeye Club Membership Card Available on Mat 2EC—.30

Page 4

"POPEYE THE SAILOR MEETS SINDBAD THE SAILOR"

CARTOON ART TO FIT YOUR EVERY NEED— ADS, PUBLICITY, TIEUPS AND PROGRAMS!

The cartoon illustrations on this page are designed to furnish you with art to meet every need—newspaper publicity, newspaper advertising, heralds, throwaways, etc. The individual drawings on the mats can be used in a score of different ways. Drop one drawing into each ad on a cooperative newspaper page. Use the individual slugs for corner spots on every bit of printed matter you issue. Use them to illustrate publicity stories, in your regular house ads and programs to call attention to "Sindbad the Sailor."

Above—MAT 2EA

ORDER MATS BY NUMBER

Mat 2EA—.30; same art, with figures facing opposite direction, Mat 2EB—30.

Mat 3EA—.45; same art, with figures facing opposite direction, Mat 3EB—.45.

Mat 4EA—.60; same art, with figures facing opposite direction, Mat 4EB—.60.

Above—MAT 3EA

Below—MAT 4EA

page 5

"POPEYE THE SAILOR MEETS SINDBAD THE SAILOR"

(SECOND DAY STORY)

The Fight's On! Color This Picture Of Popeye Battling Sindbad! Prizes!

The big fight's on—between our friend Popeye the Sailor, and that mean old Sindbad! And when all the fireworks are over, (twelve) lucky people will collect the liberal cash and ticket prizes which are being handed out in the (Newspaper's) new laugh contest, which is inspired by the opening of the new full-color Popeye adventure, "Popeye the Sailor Meets Sindbad the Sailor," next........at the........Theatre.

It's not too late to get into this amusing contest—all you have to do is get a copy of yesterday's paper, with the first in the series of five pictures, and start with that. Clip the five pictures as they appear, and color them as attractively as you can. Let yourself go—your colors can't possibly be too lavish or too brilliant! Run riot through your paint-jars—and you may win a cash prize or a pair of tickets to see Popeye. Read the rules below: they must be followed to qualify your entry for one of the prizes.

(PICK UP RULES)

(THIRD DAY STORY)

Battling Sailors Are Mixing It Up! Mix Your Colors—And Collect Prize

Sock! And they're half over! Both of them!

We mean both Sindbad's fight with Popeye the Sailor, and the exciting new coloring contest inspired by the opening of Popeye's new full-color cartoon feature, "Popeye the Sailor Meets Sindbad the Sailor," next........at the ......Theatre!

And that means that the liberal cash and ticket prizes which this coloring contest offers are halfway into the pockets of the winners right now!

Clip the three pictures, including today's, which have already appeared, and the two more which will appear tomorrow and the day after. When you have all five, color them fully—the figures and background, in the way you think is most attractive. Use any coloring material which you please—pencil, crayon, ink or paints—and let your imagination run riot!

Here's the list of prizes and the rules:

(PICK UP RULES)

(FOURTH DAY STORY)

Popeye Needs Spinach—And Color! Here's Fourth Scene in New Contest

Looks bad for Popeye—doesn't it? But don't worry—so long as he's got his faithful spinach to make him strong again, he'll get his revenge on nasty old Sindbad, who's been kicking him around!

And it looks pretty fine for those (twelve) lucky (Newspaper) readers who are going to collect their cash and ticket prizes in this entertaining new coloring contest, inspired by the opening of Popeye's new full-color feature, "Popeye the Sailor Meets Sindbad the Sailor," next......at the........Theatre.

Today's is the fourth in the five-day series of sketches which you are to color as lavishly and as attractively as you can.

Watch for the last picture, tomorrow, and get your entries in! Here are the prizes and rules:

(PICK UP RULES)

(FIFTH DAY STORY)

Popeye Coloring Contest Concludes! Prizes for Twelve Lucky Winners!

It's all over but the shouting! Our pal Popeye has polished off his "emeny," mean old Sindbad—and the (twelve) liberal cash and ticket prizes which have been set aside as awards in this fascinating new coloring contest, inspired by "Popeye the Sailor Meets Sindbad the Sailor," Popeye's new full-color feature, which opens next ......at the........Theatre, are awaiting the winners, right now!

Today's "Sindbad the Sailor" picture is the fifth and last in the series of actual scene illustrations which have appeared in the (Newspaper's) contest. All contestants know what to do—clip today's picture, just as you have the other four which have already appeared, and fill them in with color.

Check over the rules below, before sending in your entry. Entries must conform to the rules, in every respect, to be eligible for prizes.

(PICK UP RULES)

Page 7

PUBLICITY

Here Are Stories Suited For Every Section of the Paper — News, Dramatic, Feature, Science and Woman's Pages Can Be Spotted With Them

Popeye Slams Foes Into Third Dimension Through Fleischer's Camera Wizardry

Complex Invention Gives Illusion of Depth to Super-Short

(Advance Feature)

For the first time, Popeye the Sailor swaggers and fights his way through a three-dimensional world of color in the two-reel animated cartoon, "Popeye the Sailor Meets Sindbad the Sailor," coming ...... to the screen of the .... Theatre.

The film, longest cartoon picture yet released by any company, was made for Paramount by Max Fleischer, pioneer film cartoonist who is himself the inventor of the complex technique through which Popeye's screen world is given the illusion of depth.

To bring Fleischer's method to realization, a mass of technical problems were solved. Special lenses and special machinery were developed and involved formulae to figure angles of perspective were drawn up. Yet the idea itself seems simple.

Uses Miniature Sets

Two-dimensional animated cartoons have been made, in the past, by photographing the animated characters, drawn on sheets of celluloid, against backgrounds drawn on white paper. The new system substitutes a miniature "set" for the flat background.

It's as easy as that, in principle. But the technical problems solved to make it possible were not so simple. An examination of the machinery used indicates a few of them.

Sindbad's Island, in the new Popeye, was constructed in pie-slice sections on a huge turn-table, twelve feet in diameter, which is mounted in front of the movie camera.

Between camera and turntable is a specially designed frame, into which transparent "cels" bearing the individual colored drawings of the characters are slipped, one at a time.

Camera Combines

Picture by picture, the camera snaps a scene which combines the figure and the background. As Popeye walks, the set behind the frame is rotated, so that scenery moves past him. At times other "props" are placed in front of the frame, so that Popeye disappears momentarily behind trees, or boulders in the Sindbad cave.

The turntable is the real secret of the "depth" feeling; always in motion, it duplicates a phenomenon of vision in nature that has been observed by every autoist driving in the open country. To the motorist, nearby things pass swiftly, while distant objects move by his machine at a slower pace. If he looks at the horizon, objects in the foreground seem to be rotating about a point just beyond the horizon-line.

Gives Same Illusion

Fleischer's turntable duplicates that imaginary wheel. Things on its rim, nearest the camera, move rapidly by. Things nearer the center pass slowly.

Fleischer developed a camera lens constructed for a "six-foot infinity," since the axis of his turntable represented a horizon vanishing point. He found formulae to regulate the comparative sizes of objects on the turntable, and the askew lines of larger background objects. On the turntable, they seem grotesquely misshapen. On film, they assume squareness.

A problem of major proportions grew up around the placing of the animated figures on the celluloid sheets. They had to be arranged so that they seemed to walk on the "ground" of the set behind, and so that they increased and diminished in proper proportion as they moved to background or foreground.

Other Improvements

Additional refinements included putting the turntable on a geared shaft so that it can be raised or lowered at will; the camera can seem to rise into the third-dimension sky or sink to the level of the foreground.

Fleischer chose "Popeye" to make his first two-reel, full-color, three-dimension film because the spinach-eating sailor is the most popular of his cartoon characters. His newspaper friends gained by King Features Syndicate are counted in the millions; his film friends, growing daily, run into figures just as impressive.

Details of the means by which Popeye gets a three-dimensional world in "Popeye the Sailor Meets Sindbad the Sailor," now at the .... Theatre, are shown above. Inset is the man who first brought Popeye to film, and who invented the technique permitting "depth photography" of animated cartoons.

Mat 2PB—.30

TWO HUNDRED COLORS USED IN 'SINDBAD'

More than 200 different colors were used by the Max Fleischer Studio, New York, in filming the two-reel, full-color cartoon, "Popeye the Sailor Meets Sindbad the Sailor," scheduled to open ...... as a part of the bill at the ...... Theatre. The first two-reel film cartoon ever produced, "Sindbad" was made with the Fleischer third-dimension photographic technique.

The large number of colors required for "Sindbad" and similar productions results from the method used in making animated cartoons. There must be several shades for each color and each tint.

Drawings for the cartoons are made on celluloid sheets, as nearly transparent as they can be made. Sometimes four and five sheets are used in a single drawing; usually there are three.

Because the sheets are not entirely transparent, each artist must be supplied with separate shades of every color used. So that the red on a top sheet of celluloid will match the red on a sheet below it, the lower red must be brighter by a slight degree. The red on a third sheet must be a degree brighter yet, and still more color must be used on a fourth sheet.

Some of the range of the colors used can be seen in one sequence of the new Popeye super-short. In a spot where Popeye is being throttled by Sindbad, the star's face shades slowly to red, then to a deeper and deeper red, tinged with purple. To make this progression, each of the five tints of the various hues available was called into play.

New Two-Reel Popeye Has Depth and Color

"The two greatest sailors in history" will appear on the screen of the .... Theatre beginning ......, when Max Fleischer's first two-reel animated cartoon, "Popeye the Sailor Meets Sindbad the Sailor," will be a part of the bill. The cartoon is the first of Popeye's to be made in full color under the Fleischer third-dimensional process.

Longest 'Short' Coming

"Popeye the Sailor Meets Sindbad the Sailor," first two-reel animated cartoon ever filmed and the first Popeye in full color and three dimensions, will be a part of the bill beginning......at the...... Theatre.

Page 13

"POPEYE THE SAILOR MEETS SINDBAD THE SAILOR"

POPEYE'S FILM CREATOR AN EARLY FAN OF SAILOR

(Special Advance)

E. C. Segar, famed cartoonist, is the father of Popeye the Sailor, "two-fisked" screen hero who appears in his first full-color, three-dimensional film, "Popeye the Sailor Meets Sindbad the Sailor," coming .... to the .... Theatre. Yet Max Fleischer, producer who brought Popeye to the screen, might easily be dubbed the sailor's godfather.

Fleischer always has been a Popeye fan; his own liking for the character, plus his realization of Popeye's popularity, made him choose this particular hero for the first two-reel screen cartoon he has produced, "Sindbad."

Fleischer followed the Segar-King Features strip "Popeye" religiously before he first conceived the notion of screening the hero. He gives credit for the idea to one of the sailor's earth-shaking comic strip battles.

"I was admiring the tremendous feeling of power Segar had put into the famous 'twisker punch' Popeye gave his adversary," he explains. "I saw that despite the limitations of the cartoon, Segar had achieved real motion in the swing. Then I began thinking of the potentialities of that motion on the screen."

"Popeye's fights always have been sensational. But they really deserved being freed from the limits of cartoon 'boxes,' and they deserved being wired for sound. With 'Sindbad,' Popeye gains another freedom; he can knock his opponents into a three-dimensional lot!"

Local Popeye Club Members To Celebrate

(Club Notice)

Members of the .... Theatre Popeye Club will turn out in full force .... for a special matinee meeting, when the club will celebrate the biggest event in the screen life of their movie idol; his appearance in "Popeye the Sailor Meets Sindbad the Sailor."

The film is the first Popeye to appear in full color, the first Popeye to appear in three-dimensional cartoons, and the longest screen cartoon short ever made, a full two reels.

"Popeye the Sailor Meets Sindbad the Sailor" was made in the Max Fleischer Studio, New York, by the man who first brought third-dimension to movie cartoons, Fleischer.

The theatre has announced that the meeting .... will be a "Popeye Jubilee Meeting," and has urged every member to be on hand.

Has 40,000 Drawings

More than 20,000 drawings, half of them in full color, went into the making of each reel of the two-reel, full color, three-dimension "Popeye the Sailor Meets Sindbad the Sailor," now at the ......Theatre. The cartoon is the first colored Popeye and the first in three dimension photography.

Page 14

Popeye's Pop

Mat 1PO—15

It was a proud day for E. C. Segar, cartoonist, when Max Fleischer completed the full-color, three-dimension, two-reel film cartoon starring his brainchild, "Popeye the Sailor Meets Sindbad the Sailor," now at the ....Theatre.

MIRRORS

Artists Who Animate Popeye Use Them in Work

(Current Feature)

Those queer contortions which Popeye the Sailor goes through in his history-making battle with Sindbad the Sailor actually are "done with the aid of mirrors."

In the Max Fleischer Studio, New York, where the new two-reel, full-color and third dimension Popeye film, "Popeye the Sailor Meets Sindbad the Sailor," now showing at the .... Theatre, was made, a group of thirty-five artists are in charge of animating the Fleischer films.

Near each artist's desk is a large mirror. A visitor watching the group at work soon learns why.

One of the "animators" will be called on to depict Popeye's "windup" for his famous five-ton "Twisker Punch". Now and again he will rise from his board, step in front of the mirror, and try a few poses. Then he'll return to the drawing and translate his own stance and swing into the exaggerated contortions of the picture's star.

For motion and expression the mirrors are indispensable. An artist who would have no difficulty in forming a mental picture of the beginning or end of a facial or bodily motion often is baffled by the "half-way steps" of the same motion.

Wimpy Has a Weapon In Super-Popeye Film

J. Wellington Wimpy, somnolent-eyed hamburger eater who has proven one of the most popular of "character actors" in the comic sheet and movie appearances of Popeye the Sailor, carries heavy armor in the new two-reel, full-color, three dimension "Popeye the Sailor Meets Sindbad the Sailor," coming ....to the........Theatre.

J. W. Wimpy

Wimpy wears a meat-grinder strapped to his waist, for use in making incidental hamburgers while traveling. The new super-short is the longest cartoon film ever made, and the first Popeye in full color and three dimensions. (Cut on Mat 3EB)

HEAVY QUANTITY OF WORK REQUIRED FOR NEW 'POPEYE'

There are between fifteen and twenty minutes of laughs in the new super-Popeye feature in third dimension and full color, "Popeye the Sailor Meets Sindbad the Sailor," opening .... at the .... Theatre. But the work which went into its production almost staggers the imagination.

There are 800 feet of film to each of the two "Sindbad" reels. Each foot of each reel consists of sixteen separate pictures. The making of each picture requires a rough sketch on paper, a tracing on celluloid, inking in of the black lines on the celluloid, and coloring of each part of each figure.

The background of every scene is a miniature set, made up and colored in such detail that every part will be perfect on the screen. What this means can be realized by remembering that objects in the set are but an inch or so high; on the screen they will be magnified to several feet.

The Max Fleischer Studio in New York, maker of the animated Popeye and Betty Boop cartoons and originator of the third-dimension cartoon, employs more than two hundred people, of whom more than a hundred and fifty are artists. It produces thirty-six pictures a year, ranging from the comparatively simple one-reel, black and white, to the record-breaking Popeye in two reels, full color and three dimensions.

Cartoon Has Depth

Popeye the Sailor steps into a new world of three dimensions, brightened by full color, in Max Fleischer's "Popeye the Sailor Meets Sindbad the Sailor," to appear beginning..........on the bill of the......Theatre.

CARTOONIST ONCE WORKED PROJECTOR

(Special Advance)

Popeye the Sailor, favorite screen and comic page character who stars in the first third-dimension, full-color, two-reel movie short ever made, "Popeye the Sailor Meets Sindbad the Sailor," coming .... to the .... Theatre, has a certain odd link with his creator, E. C. Segar.

"Popeye the Sailor Meets Sindbad the Sailor" is the crowning movie achievement of the cartoon figure invented and still drawn today by Segar, one of the nation's leading cartoonists. And Segar, before he became a cartoonist, was a motion picture projectionist.

A native of Chester, Ill., Segar went through several metamorphoses before he took up his pen to make 75,000,000 readers laugh. He was a house painter, sign painter, paper hanger, trap drummer, photographer, window dresser and projectionist.

Today he lives in a big house in California which contains a billiard room having two tables. He says that if his "two-fisked" hero ever goes back on him, he'll open a billiard hall.

'ROKH'

Fleischer Finds Many Variants For Name of Bird

(Current Story)

Every person who has read the story of "Sindbad the Sailor" knows the proper pronunciation both for "Sindbad" and for the giant bird which appears in the story, the "rokh." Yet when Max Fleischer came to the job of animating the picture of "Popeye the Sailor Meets Sindbad the Sailor," now at the .... Theatre, he found many a typographical snag.

Research showed him there are almost as many ways of spelling "rokh" as there are stories in "The Thousand and One Nights." He found it spelled "roch," "ruch," "roc," "ruk," "rook," "rark," and "roork." "Sindbad" appeared with and without the "D." Fleischer chose "Sindbad" and "rokh."

Other spellings for the bird's name, he thought, were either too hard to pronounce or too much like the slang term "rook."

The rokh is but one of the fantastic creations Fleischer has worked into the story of the first full-color, two-reel, three-dimensional "Popeye." Other stars include "Boola," the two-headed giant; sundry dragons, snakes and lions, and odd creatures who protect Sindbad's island.

The Popeye film is the longest animated cartoon ever made, and the first Popeye done in Fleischer's three dimension technique, which is in process of being patented.

"POPEYE THE SAILOR MEETS SINDBAD THE SAILOR"

Popeye, Cartoon Star, Started as an 'Extra'

(Special Advance)

Popeye the Sailor is admittedly one of the world's most forceful, attention-compelling cartoon personalities. He has elbowed and slammed his way into a newspaper following of more than 75,000,000 readers and a screen audience of similar proportions. Yet the first man he had to take by storm was his own creator, E. C. Segar.

Popeye reaches a new climax to his screen career as hero of the first two-reel movie cartoon ever made, the full-color, third-dimension "Popeye the Sailor Meets Sindbad the Sailor," coming..... to the .... Theatre, a product of the Max Fleischer Studio, New York. It crowns a career which began almost accidentally in 1919.

Segar—he signs his cartoons just that way, with a smoldering cigar butt worked into the signature—was drawing a cartoon strip entitled "Thimble Theatre" for the newspapers at that time. Chief characters were Olive Oyl and her brother, Castor Oyl. There was no Popeye.

Olive and Castor were planning a voyage; they bought a ship and were ready to sail when they discovered they needed a deck hand. They spied a sailor on the dock.

"Hey, are you a sailor?" Castor shouted.

"Ja think I was a cowboy?" commented Popeye, as he walked onto the strip for the first time.

Once discovered, Popeye quickly became a favorite of Thimble Theatre readers. Segar couldn't let him go. Gradually the "bit player" took over the strip and became its central figure. By the might of his pile-driver "fisks" and the strength of his "I yam what I yam" philosophy, he climbed to the peak of newspaper, then screen fame.

Today, certain Sunday papers which use his strip label their front pages "40 pages of comics, including Popeye," and put the "Popeye" in huge type. And his screen popularity is so great that Max Fleischer, inventor of the new third-dimension system of cartoon photography, chose him for the hero of the first two-reeler produced.

Super-Popeye Booked By Local Movie House

(Advance Routine)

Max Fleischer's new and greater "Popeye," the full-color, third dimensional, two-reel cartoon "Popeye the Sailor Meets Sindbad the Sailor," will be a feature of the .... Theatre's bill beginning ...., it has been announced.

Longest cartoon film ever made, and the first Popeye in color and three dimensions, the picture has been proclaimed a milestone in movie history. The Fleischer process of placing his cartoon characters in miniature "sets," to add a feeling of reality and depth, has been given its most advanced application in the new Popeye.

Popeye's song is augmented in the two-reeler by a new song, written for Bluto as Sindbad.

"Lovely Day!"

NEW TRIUMPHS

Popeye the Sailor, "two-fisked" hero of cartoon strip and screen, reached an important milestone in his movie career with the production of his first full-color, three-dimension film, "Popeye the Sailor Meets Sindbad the Sailor," the first two-reel cartoon ever made. The film is booked to appear beginning .... on the bill of the .... Theatre. A product of the Max Fleischer Studio, New York, for Paramount, it was filmed in Fleischer's new third-dimension system for animated cartoons.

Wimpy rides in style to Sindbad's Island, in the full-color, three-dimension, double-length "Popeye the Sailor Meets Sindbad the Sailor," now at the..... Theatre.

GIRL IS ONLY MEMBER OF SEX TO BE ANIMATOR

(Special Feature)

Only one woman has ever been able to make the grade in one of the most specialized of artistic jobs in the motion picture industry, that of "animator" for movie cartoons.

She is Lillian Friedman, 22, quiet New York girl who has been employed for three years in the Max Fleischer Studio, New York, where the amazing three-dimensional, full-color super-short, "Popeye the Sailor Meets Sindbad the Sailor," was made. The picture opens .... at the .... Theatre. Miss Friedman is responsible for much of the creative work that went into "Sindbad." Her hand made Popeye wind up to give Sindbad his famous "Twisker" punch, and her pen animated sketches of the two-headed giant, "Boola."

Nobody knows just why, but women generally are not successful as cartoon animators. Artists at the Fleischer studio number more than 200; they are divided into the classifications of animators, "inbetweeners," "inkers" and "opaquers." Many women hold jobs as inbetweeners, inkers and opaquers; only Miss Friedman has attained the top spot of animator. She works in an office with 29 male artists, all of them specially skilled.

The animator actually creates the movement which Popeye and other cartoon characters go through; he draws one out of ten of the pictures. "Inbetweeners" fill in with the other nine drawings; inkers transfer the sketches to celluloid in ink, and opaquers add the color or black, depending on whether the film is in color or black and white.

"Ahoy, Sailor!"

Popeye spies the world's second greatest sailor, Sindbad, in Max Fleischer's three-dimension, full-color two-reeler, "Popeye the Sailor Meets Sindbad the Sailor," now at the........Theatre.

New Popeye Given Sound In Two Ways

(Current Story)

Two distinct techniques are used in "dubbing in" the voices in an animated cartoon for the movies. Both of them were used in the course of the super-short, "Popeye the Sailor Meets Sindbad the Sailor," Max Fleischer's three-dimensional, full-color film now at the .... Theatre. It is the first cartoon to run two reels in length.

The usual method is to complete the film from a script, run it through several times for a rehearsal of the people who are going to contribute voices, and then run it again, recording the voices with their proper timing. This was done throughout most of "Sindbad."

The second, used when special dialogue is called for, is to record the voice first, then animate from it. This was done for the sequences in which "Boola," two-headed giant in "Sindbad," mutters and talks to himself.

The second technique is more difficult, in that animators must have their drawings correspond exactly in the timing of lip movements and gestures with a pre-arranged voice. In "Sindbad," it was made necessary because the dialogue was furnished by a specially-obtained comedian who could not visit the studio.

Popeye Knocks Bluto Into Third Dimension

For the first time in film history, Popeye the Sailor knocks his arch-enemy, Bluto, into a third-dimensional background in the two-reel, full-color animated cartoon, "Popeye the Sailor Meets Sindbad the Sailor." The picture, made by Max Fleischer under his newly-perfected system of three-dimension cartoon photography, is booked as a part of the .... Theatre bill beginning .... morning.

Bluto Is Sindbad

"Bluto," the arch-enemy of Popeye in many and many a past animated cartoon, becomes "Sindbad" in the two-reel, three-dimension, full-color Popeye film, "Popeye the Sailor Meets Sindbad the Sailor," to appear on the bill of the .... Theatre beginning .... night. The film is the first two-reel cartoon ever released, and is the first Popeye in color as well as the first to be produced by Max Fleischer's third-dimension cartoon process.

Longest Short

"Popeye the Sailor Meets Sindbad the Sailor," Max Fleischer's three-dimension, full-color animated cartoon now at the..... Theatre, is the longest cartoon short ever made, a full two reels. It is the first Popeye to boast depth and color.

"POPEYE THE SAILOR MEETS SINDBAD THE SAILOR"

DEPTH EFFECT REQUIRES NEW CAMERA LENS

(Special Advance)

Special camera lenses, with their focal lengths set for a six-foot "infinity," are used by Max Fleischer in filming his third-dimension movie cartoons, latest and most ambitious of which is the two-reel "Popeye the Sailor Meets Sindbad the Sailor," coming ...... to the .... Theatre.

Popeye's new film, the longest cartoon short ever made by Fleischer, was photographed through the new Fleischer system which utilizes miniature "sets" to create an illusion of third dimension. It was photographed in full color.

The Fleischer system, for which patents are now pending, is more than just one using sets, however. The sets are specially designed on a pie-shaped turntable, twelve feet in diameter, which turns constantly, a fraction of an inch at a time, while the characters, drawn on celluloid, and the sets themselves are being combined in photographs. This motion, which calls the eye's attention to the fact that the foreground on the rim of the table moves faster than the background, near the axis, causes much of the depth illusion.

Lines of the buildings and objects in the set are distorted to pre-arranged formulae, so that all lines running from foreground to background simulate the natural diminishing seen by the human eye in looking toward a horizon.

'Sindbad' Gives Cartoon Lovers Newest Thrill

(Current Story)

A new thrill for followers of Popeye the Sailor, and for lovers of animated film cartoons in general, is on the screen of the ...... Theatre this week, where Max Fleischer's phenomenal double-length, third-dimensional, full-color "Popeye the Sailor Meets Sindbad the Sailor" is a part of the bill.

The picture, longest cartoon short ever made, is the first Popeye made in third dimension and the first Popeye filmed in full color. It was produced by the newly-developed Fleischer system which adds depth to screen cartoons by filming them against a background of moving miniature "sets," rotated on a large turntable.

"Bluto," Popeye's arch-enemy of the screen, appears as Sindbad, ruler of an island guarded by grotesque monsters and wild animals. Popeye's terrific "twisker punch" always has had dramatic force; when it hurls Bluto into a third-dimensional lot it is a new thrill.

The technique for three-dimension filming of animated cartoons was developed by Fleischer and is now in process of being patented. Though the fundamentals of the scheme have been published, certain phases remain secret.

Page 16

"Put Up Yer Fisks!"

Mat 2PA—.30

The world's two greatest sailors come to blows—and what blows—in "Popeye the Sailor Meets Sindbad the Sailor," Max Fleischer's first full-color, three-dimension, two reel Popeye cartoon, now at the .... Theatre.

'INBETWEEN' ARTIST IS VITAL TO MOVIE POPEYE

(Special Feature)

"INBETWEEN DEPARTMENT."

One of the first doors to confront the visitor to the Max Fleischer Studios in New York bears this cryptic inscription. It sounds like a bit of whimsey out of Alice in Wonderland, but it is not. It is simply one of the many things which mark the unique nature of the most modern of entertainment fields.

Max Fleischer's studio makes the three-dimensional cartoon movies which have so recently marked the coming of a new era to short-subject entertainment in the films. It turned out the amazing three-dimensional, two-reel color film "Popeye the Sailor Meets Sindbad the Sailor," which opens .... at the .... Theatre.

Fleischer controls the secret process by which Popeye was made to walk through a three-dimensional island and sail his good ship across a three-dimensional ocean. The general nature of his invention has been made public, but technical details of basic importance are withheld.

The studio makes both two and three dimension cartoons. They are turned out at an average rate of one every ten days, by a staff of more than 300 artists working full time. Thirty-five of those artists make up the "Inbetween Department" mentioned above.

The Fleischer studio is a unit as completely organized as any major moving picture production company. It has a script department, where plays for Popeye, Betty Boop and others are written; a music department, directors, technicians—all the usual aides. And in addition it has its huge staff of trained artists.

These artists fall into four classifications. Behind the door with the esoteric nameplate are the "Inbetweeners." Behind another door are thirty "Animators." On another floor are several score of "Opaquers," and elsewhere is a staff of "Inkers."

Once explained, the meaning of the classifications is simple. The "Animators" are the most skilled artists of all; they work from the script and draw the chief motions through which Popeye goes in all of his actions in "Sindbad." Thus, they draw one picture for the moment when Popeye begins his famous "twisker" punch and label it H-45." Then they draw another for the moment that the "twisker" lands and label it "H-55."

These two pictures go to the Inbetweeners, who draw ten figures of the hero and his fist to go between the start and the finish of the punch, filling out the flow of the motion.

From here, both sets of films go to a room of tracers, who transfer all the pictures onto celluloid sheets ("cels") to the trade) and send them up to the "Opaquers." Here the color is put onto the celluloid.

When all pictures are completed, they go to photographers upstairs for the final shooting. Then, if the movie is to be third dimension, they are photographed in front of miniature sets, mounted on a moving turntable. If the movie is to be two-dimensional, they are photographed in front of flat scenes, drawn on ordinary paper.

SUPER-POPEYE IS FIRST MADE AS TWO-REELER

(Prepared Review)

The film cartoon of the future gets a preview this week at the .... Theatre, where Max Fleischer's full-color, third-dimension two-reeler, "Popeye the Sailor Meets Sindbad the Sailor," is a part of the bill which opened yesterday.

The super-short is the longest animated cartoon ever made for the screen by Fleischer, Popeye's animator. It is the first colored Popeye, as well, and the first to be photographed in Fleischer's new "cartoon depth photography," utilizing miniature sets instead of flat backgrounds.

The story, of course, is one built for Popeye; it tells of the meeting of the two greatest sailors in the world, and their ultimate earth-shaking battle. Settings were chosen to give full play to the advantages of the full-color and third-dimension features.

Max Fleischer Patents Many Movie Devices

(Special Advance)

Artist and inventor are about equally balanced in the makeup of Max Fleischer, originator of the third-dimension movie cartoon technique through which the sensational two-reel picture "Popeye the Sailor Meets Sindbad the Sailor" was made.

The film, longest cartoon ever produced by Fleischer, is photographed in full color. It is scheduled to appear beginning ...... on the bill of the ...... Theatre.

A native of Austria, Fleischer was brought to the United States at the age of four. He studied in the New York public schools, then studied art at the Art Student's League and other New York academies. He first worked as a cartoonist on the Brooklyn, N. Y., Daily Eagle, later becoming art editor of Popular Science Magazine.

During the War, Fleischer was connected with the General Staff of the U. S. Army, and devoted himself to the production of educational films for the soldiers. Later he became a pioneer among producers of animated film cartoons, creating the "Out of the Ink Well" series which amazed and tickled early movie-goers. Its hero was "Ko-Ko the Clown."

At the same time, Fleischer has contrived and patented a number of movie devices, all of them now in common use. Patents on the processes involved in his third-dimension technique are pending at present; the idea and the machines which make it possible are to be fully protected.

The new Popeye film is double the length of the ordinary animated cartoon, approaching the nature of a second feature.

Chapter Six

The world in which the studio was operating was changing and by 1937 an era was about to end.

In May 1937, a strike started involving in-betweeners. The story department nor the animators participated in the work action that demanded better working conditions as well as pay increases.

Many of the people with whom I spoke described a family atmosphere at the studio. The company newsletter certainly seems to confirm that as well as photos taken at Christmas parties, bachelor events, etc.

In his 1939 autobiographical essay one gets a look at his attitude towards his employees. He wrote, "I had a colored man in New York who was with me for about 10 years. He was a bright chap. At that time, I didn't have enough stenographers, so I had a portable typewriter near my desk. Every time a stenographer wasn't handy, I knocked the work off with the two-finger system, then set the machine down on the floor. One day I noticed the typewriter missing. I called the porter and asked him to make a search. but he couldn't find it.

"A short time after the detective bureau called and asked whether we had a colored fellow by the name of so and so working for us. I said, 'Yes we have.' He told me the machine was located and pawned by this man. He said if I sent $5 up to the man he would release it, which I did.

"I called the porter and asked him how he happened to steal the typewriter. He said he really didn't steal it. He was in need of money. His wife was in the hospital, and it was his intention to return it as soon as he got his pay.

"I asked him if he ever had any trouble before borrowing money. 'Rather than do a thing like that why didn't you ask me for the money? Did I ever refuse you a loan? It's easy for me to say 'get out of here and don't come back.'

'I ask you: What would you do with you? I leave it to you and be honest about it.' He said, 'I would fire me.' I said, 'I don't want to make things any worse for you. First of all, I'm going to tell the detective bureau I'm not going to press any charges, because I think you needed the money and didn't know how to get it. How much do you need to get straightened out?' 'About $25.' 'Well, I'll show you the difference between you and me. You would fire yourself and I'm going to try to remake you.'

"I called my secretary and had her make out a check for $23 and gave it to him. From that time on he would get up on the ceiling to dust; he polished corners. etc.

"He used to drink, and I warned him never to enter the studio with an indication of drink.

"One day he did, I told him I never fired a man in this organization, and I never will.

'But I told him, 'If you get drunk, I don't want you and I don't want to fire you. You'll have to fire yourself.'

'He said, "Yes if I ever come to work drunk, I will.' And one day while I was away, he walked into the manager's office drunk and said, 'Max said any time I came in drunk I should fire myself and I'm firing myself now.'"

There is no conclusion of the story – did Max rehire this employee? – and the tone is certainly paternalistic.

The death of an artist named Dan Glass was often used by the strikers as a reason to improve their working conditions. The crowded working conditions as well as the pressures of the job were thought by many as the reason for his illness.

Glass was an inbetweener from Arkansas who worked at the studio for two years and left because of contracting tuberculosis. In the January 1935 edition of the studio newsletter, Max wrote about the creation of employee relief fund funded through sales of the monthly newsletter. Max noted Glass received $30 from the fund as well as train fare back to his home – where he would succumb to his illness. His fellow employees also took up a collection for Glass.

Glass' death proved to be an on-going rallying call for many people at the studio. In the studio's newsletter dated April 1935, there was a front cover message from Max.

"Many of you may have read the pamphlet issued by the so-called Animated Motion Pictures Workers Union and undoubtedly you have certain reactions to its contents,

"It appears than a number of our members were incensed by the personal attack upon me and several of them have expressed their resentment of such tactics.

"[Animator] Tom Johnson, who happened to know the circumstances relating to Dan Glass was particularly aggravated by the statements issued by the Union regarding my lack of interest in the welfare of our employees, and particularly Dan Glass.

"Tom Johnson found it impossible to resist revealing his own viewpoint and reactions and accordingly made it his business to write a letter expressing his opinion to the so-called Union.

"Tom called my attention to a copy of the letter he had sent the correspondence on the following pages should prove interesting.

"I wish to make it clear that Tom's letter or my letter is not to be considered in as an argument for or against unions.

Max concluded, "The correspondence that follows is merely presented to your attention as an indication of the resentment of many of the members of our organization to unfair and misleading tactics."

Johnson's letter to the Animated Motion Pictures Workers Union dated March 20, 1935, spoke about Glass.

Johnson wrote, "Who said Dan made $12? His weekly check showed $22.

"Why didn't you state than Dan besides inbetweening, carried a very heavy night school program while at Fleischers? He himself complained of the strain and gave up this outside activity. Two years of night school averaging three nights a week? Could that have hurt him?

"And didn't you 'forget' that Max urged Dan to take a week's rest at a Jersey resort which Dan did as Max's guest?

"And didn't you 'forget' that Max urged Dan to return home long before he did and at that time offered to send him?

"I have a letter from Dan's mother. I knew her and she wrote to me after his death. A quotation shows her attitude, 'Mr. Glass and myself will always feel deeply grateful to Mr. Fleischer and all of Dan's friends in New York who helped him in his recent illness.' Dan and his family, it is obvious, had no complaint. I have a hunch they would be deeply hurt in knowing that you used Dan as a 'spearhead' in an attack on Max Fleischer who really did all he could do to help Dan. And with your logic and deductions you ask me to sign up with you?"

As noted in the New York Times edition of May 7, 1937, about 100 employees voted to strike the previous night. This action was taken after Max had refused to "grant union recognition, improved working conditions, higher wages and vacations with pay."

According to the time about 170 people were employed at the studio and "the animators who have separate contrasts have agreed not to cross the picket line."

As noted by several people with whom I spoke, Max was very paternalistic, but not everyone, especially those who supported the labor union moment, appreciated that approach. The Great Depression brought many people to focus on the great divide between what workers and owners were making. Seeking the representation and protection of a union made sense to many workers although that point of view was not necessarily shared by owners and management.

In his 1939 autobiography Max wrote, "Everyone in this organization can come right into my office and air their grievances and their troubles and speak directly to me. Everyone in this organization call me 'Max.' Not merely as a convenience but I feel I have actually earned this salutation."

Nowhere in this document is any mention of the strike. It clearly was clearly a painful time in Max's life however one could draw a conclusion that Max was still seeing himself as that paternalistic head of the company.

On May 8, 1937, The New York Times reported that 14 pickets were arrested in a fight on Broadway.

Strikers defied a police order and a riot broke out with 14 arrested. Fists and placards were swung, but no injuries were reported, A crowd of 2,000 gathered to watch. Police tried to remove the strikers as they had monopolized the sidewalk.

"Placards read: 'I make millions laugh, but the real joke is my salary.' And 'We can't get much spinach on salaries as low as $15.'"

Max "issued a statement early in the evening expressing surprise at low salary – inexperienced employees receiving the lowest salaries are advanced after a short time to $40, $50 and some as $90 and $200.

"The strike was called when allegedly 15 workers were fired for by union activities.

"The strike line started at 6:30 with trouble beginning as non-striking workers tried to get through the picket line to go to work."

How the police behaved that night drew a formal complaint from the president of the Commercial Artist' and Designers Union (CADU) to the mayor of New York City.

On May 23, 1937, The Times noted, strikers picketed the Paramount and Roxy movie theaters for showing Popeye cartoons. Sixty marchers picketed the Paramount for twenty-five minutes then the Roxy for a short time."

On May 27, the protesters blocked the entrance of the Paramount Theater and sang "I'm Popeye the Union Man."

On July 2, 1937, nine strikers were arrested at the studio and police were investigating the throwing of a "stink bomb" at Dave's house.

In early August, the National Labor Relations Board ordered the studio to conduct an election within fifteen days. Eligible voters are all personnel as of April 30, excluding all supervisors, musicians, cameramen, clerks, and maintenance workers.

On August 5,1937, The Times reported the strikers had rigged a balloon sign to rise up alongside 1600 Broadway to "encourage to threaten loyal employees to vote for the union." The sign carried by the balloon read, "Don't be a scab, you'll never live it down."

The election for the union was Aug. 16, 1937. At that point seventy-two employees had been on strike for three months. Max protested the vote by refusing to provide poll watchers and a list of employees on his payroll.

By mid-September, the National Labor Relations Board had named CADU as the official bargaining agent. Of the one hundred and twenty-nine eligible employees, seventy-four cast votes were cast "and sixty votes counted; it was sixty votes for the union and none against," the Times reported. Max announced he would contest the vote through the courts.

The strike concluded according to The Times on Oct. 1 with an oral agreement between CADU and Max to the signing and ratification of the formal contract, which defined wages, hours and working conditions.

On Oct. 13 the agreement was signed by the union president and Max. The contract gave the union members a 40-hour week, sick leave, vacations with pay and overtime.

Alden Getz was an inbetweener at the studio and was involved in the negotiations. He met with me in 1978 about the conditions at the studio at 1600 Broadway.

He said he worked on "everything:" Popeye, Betty Boop and Color Classics. He also worked on "Gulliver's Travels."

Speaking of the level of creativity in-betweeners had, "There wasn't much you could do [to improve or change a production]," he explained. "Much of the picture was written and once storyboards and exposure sheets were set, everything was set by the animators."

He said he could see the personality of the animators in how they animated the character.

He continued, "George Germanetti's Popeyes looked like George Germanetti."

"It was like piecework. Everyone jealously guarded their position," he said. Getz started to write and said the writers didn't want him in the same office. He sat in the vestibule with a typewriter. "All the stories came from the same five guys," he said. None of his stories got produced.

"The whole thing was a young person's business," Getz said. The supervisors were in their thirties.

About contact with Max and Dave, Getz said he would see them in the elevator. Dave would walk through the inbetweening area and some artists thought they were being observed.

Getz made contributions to the studio newsletter and noted, "There was a camaraderie was sorts but not with the highest levels," he said. "There were cliques. Couldn't walk to up to the table of the inner clique."

Getz believed that Max could not have known everyone.

"I don't think anyone really cared if Max and Dave weren't friendly…didn't expect them to be palsy-walsy," he said.

Sam Buchwald, the general manager, not Max, was the guy people saw with problems, he noted.

"Desks were on top of one another. I was sitting under a coat rack. Some desks were in a darkened room. People would be in that room working day and night," he said.

Following an early attempt that failed to bring a union in, Getz, said, "Took another year and two before there was an attempt. I was asked to come to a meeting by Leon Jasin of Jasin Art. I went to the meeting and learned something about unions. From an idealistic point of view, it seemed like a good thing. Certainly, the conditions in the studio were quite strict … if you went to the bathroom too many times you were observed."

He continued, "If you were late or sick, no such thing as sick pay. You were just docked. You got no vacation. These things are unthinkable today, but they were par for the course."

He added there was a 9 a.m. to 6 p.m. schedule with lunch and that people were fired for minor reasons.

"As union became more of a fact and after they had approached Max Fleischer … tension began to grow inside studio. Your desk was searched. People were advanced according to their sympathies," he said.

He recalled, "We're being forced into showdown… called to union hall on Friday night [when working late] and came back with picket signs." Getz participated in the strike picketing and wound up in jail until 2 a.m. when the union's lawyer was able to free the protesters.

Getz admitted, "There were some pretty rabid people, one or two were probably Communist."

The American Federation of Labor Unions (AFL) would not help so the strikers turned to the rival Congress of Industrial Organizations, the CIO. Other unions representing musicians and projectionist were in support of the work action.

Once the strike was settled, Getz and other union members were offered employment at the new Miami studio.

"Everyone was invited," he said. He explained the non-union people went first and received assistance finding housing. Union employees were housed in a hotel, "but now the polarization was enforced."

While Getz spoke of advantages of the new studio he added "There was a low-key terror that existed."

Getz entered the army. He later worked in advertising and apparently did well as his Park Avenue apartment would indicate. Looking back, he said, "Strangely enough, the union failed, it really succeeded because that was the beginning of a series of union activities at Disney, Schlesinger's… the whole animation industry became unionized."

It's interesting to note the swift sequence of events that followed. At the time of the strike the Christmas special "Popeye Meets Ali Baba" was about to be released. Variety reported on Feb. 23, 1938 that Paramount had decided to go into the field of a feature-length animated movie.

The move to Miami was also underway. Variety noted on March 2, 1938, "under the deal with Fleischer who makes Betty Boop and Popeye cartoons for Paramount, both will be jointly interested in the project. Paramount has already made the first advance to cover partial cost of production. The budget is not known probably being dependent on the story to be chosen. Paramount has two stories in mind but is keeping the identity a secret for reasons."

The story continued, "Fleischer will start the feature cartoon in New York and finish it in Miami, which will be ready for operation about Aug. 15. Consequent upon the decision to go for full length cartoons, Fleischer is altering the original plans for the Miami plant, increasing the space on which he will build to nearly 32,000 square feet. Or about four city blocks … construction starts this week."

On Aug. 3, 1938, Variety reported that Max entered in new negotiations with Local 60 of the United American Artists of the United Office and Professional Workers of America, a CIO affiliate. The contract agreed upon 1937 was going to run out in November. A following story on Sept. 21, 1938, showed the contract was still in negotiations.

In his book, Richard Fleischer wrote of Max's feeling of being betrayed by those employees. "Max was truly shocked by the intensity of the strikers' emotions. He was both angry and dismayed that so many of his people weren't totally loyal to him and the studio. He couldn't understand the violence." Richard noted there was irony in that both Dave and Lou were members of the American Federation of Musicians, which was supporting the strike.

Required Viewing

The whole point of this book is to encourage people to seek out and watch these classic cartoons. To encourage that goal, here is a number of key cartoons and where you can find them.

For Chapters One and Two, the following productions can be seen on YouTube®:

- Fishing
- Modeling
- A Trip to Mars
- Ko-Ko Trains 'Em
- Ko-Ko's Earth Control
- Koko in 1999
- The Cartoon Factory
- Ko-Ko Explores
- Ko-Ko's Catch
- Ko-Ko's Haunted House
- Ko-Ko's Queen
- Toys will be Toys

The documentary features:
Theory of Relativity
Evolution

An essential collection of early animation, "Cartoon Roots," has been assembled by archivist and historian Tom Stathes and can found both on Amazon, Oldies.com and at www.cartoonsonfilm.com for purchase. Also, from Thunderbean Animation, the Blu-ray collection "Fleischer Rarities," from https://www.thunderbeanshop.com.

Subscribe to the Max Fleischer Cartoons channel on YouTube.

If you're on Facebook, ask to join The REAL Fleischer Studios group

Chapter Three

The following productions can be seen on YouTube®:

- Musical Justice (live action with Mae Questel)
- Bamboo Isle
- The Old Man of the Mountain
- Snow White
- Minnie the Moocher
- Hollywood on Parade 11 (Bonnie Poe as Betty Boop)
- Betty Boop's Hollywood Mystery
- Betty Boop's Rise to Fame
- Ha! Ha! Ha!

Purchase the four volumes of Betty Boop cartoons that have been released through Olive Films. Available through several on-line services.

Chapter Four

To review the Color Classic series yourself, purchase the set produced by Jerry Beck "Somewhere in Dreamland" from www.vcientertainment.com. Oldies.com also offers a volume of Hunky and Spunky shorts, which got their start in the Color Classics series.

Undoubtedly, because of the music rights, a collection as of this writing of the Screen Songs have not been formally collected.

On YouTube®:

- I Ain't Got Nobody with the Mills Brothers
- Dinah with the Mills Brothers
- When Yuba Plays the Rumba with the Mills Brothers
- Kitty from Kansas City with Rudy Vallee
- Snoopnocracy with Stoopnagle and Budd
- Time on My Hands with Ethel Merman

– Romantic Melodies with Arthur Tracy

– The Peanut Vendor with Armida

– Boilesk on archive.org

Chapter Five

The Warner Bros. release of the Popeye cartoons is still available through outlets such as Oldies.com.

Other books:
Tom Sito's "Drawing the Line: The Untold Story of American Unions from Bosko to Bart Simpson" is an excellent overview of the labor union movement in animation.

"He Am What He Am! Jack Mercer the Voice of Popeye" by Fred M. Grandinetti

With some reservations, I also recommend "Out of the Inkwell: Max Fleischer and the Animation Revolution" by Richard Fleischer and "Talking Animals and Other People" by Shamus Culhane.

To experience the genius of E.C. Segar, seek out the Fantagraphics six-volume set of Segar's collected comic strips

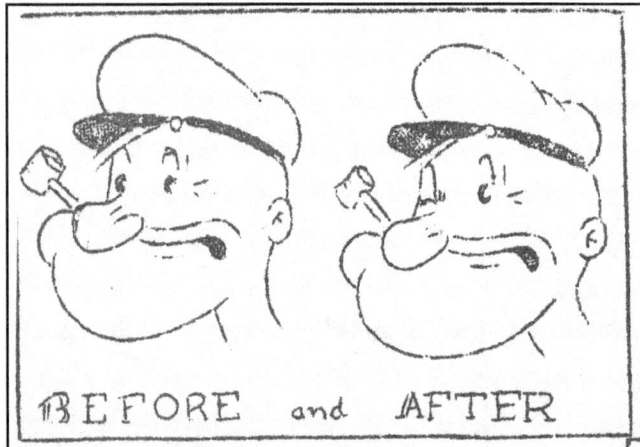

Encyclopedias of History
Tell of men that live and die,
But there remains one mystery –
How did Popeye lose his eye?

He might've been clipped by Bluto,
Or perhaps, some other guy.
Or then, some overactive grape-fruito
Might have popped that other eye.

Now, a bedpost, door, or clothespole
Could have been the reason why.
Again, maybe the keyhole
Caused that havoc to his eye.

What e'er it was, dear grand-children,
You know no more than I.
So you can tell your children's children
The mystery of Popeye's pop-eye.

Fleischer artist Alden Getz speculated about Popeye's missing eye in a cartoon that ran in the studio newsletter.

Afterword

I am now preparing the second volume of the project which will follow the studio through its relocation to Miami, FL, the production of its two features, the Superman cartoons and then the end of the organization, restructured by Paramount and moved back to New York City.

I hope you have found this book interesting and a worthy introduction to the work by an extremely talented group of artists.

The goal is to reinforce the work of other scholars in trying to place the work of the Fleischer Studios into the proper historical context.

I'm happy to hear comments and can be reached at gmdobbs@comcast.net.

G. Michael Dobbs

www.ingramcontent.com/pod-product-compliance
Lightning Source LLC
Chambersburg PA
CBHW081159070526
44583CB00021B/2914